365 MEDITATIONS for Grandmothers

Gloria Gaither

Margaret Anne Huffman

Betty Steele Everett

Marilyn Brown Oden

Nell Mohney

DIMENSIONS
FOR LIVING

NASHVILLE

365 MEDITATIONS FOR GRANDMOTHERS

97 98 99 00 01 02 03 — 10 9 8 7 6 5 4

This book is printed on acid-free, recycled paper.

Library of Congress Catloging–in–Publication Data

365 meditations for grandmothers / Gloria Gaither . . . [et al.].
    p.   cm
    ISBN 0–687–41893–3 (alk. paper)
    1. Grandmothers—Prayer–books and devotions.   I. Gaither, Gloria.
  II. Title: Three hundred sixty–five meditations for grandmothers.
  BV4845.A16 1994
  242'.645—dc20   94–11026
                                                      CIP

The scripture quotation noted NIV on page 12 is taken from the Holy Bible: New International Version. Copyright © 1973, 1978, 1984 by the International Bible Society. Used by permission of Zondervan Bible Publishers.

The scripture quotation noted KJV on page 25 is from the King James Version of the Bible.

The scripture quotation noted RSV on page 348 is from the Revised Standard Version of the Bible, copyright © 1946, 1952, 1971, by the Division of Christian Education of the National Council of Churches of Christ in the USA. Used by permission.

Scripture quotations unless otherwise labeled are from the New Revised Standard Version Bible, copyright © 1989 by the Division of Christian Education of the National Council of the Churches of Christ in the USA. Used by permission.

Meditations for the month of January copyright © 1994 by Gloria Gaither. All rights reserved.

The poem on page 309, "A Piece of Clay," the author is unknown.

MANUFACTURED IN THE UNITED STATES OF AMERICA

365 MEDITATIONS for Grandmothers

Grammy
Happy Mother's Day!
all our love
Dave, Chris + David

About the Writers

Gloria Gaither (January) has won two Grammy Awards and numerous Dove Awards for her songwriting and singing with the Bill Gaither Trio, with whom she has recorded some forty albums. Gloria has co-authored close to five hundred songs and ten major musicals. She is also the author or co-author of eleven books, and the editor of *What My Parents Did Right*. Gloria and her husband, Bill, live in their hometown of Alexandria, Indiana. They have three children—Suzanne, Amy, and Benjy—and one grandson, Will, age two.

Margaret Anne Huffman (February - April), former family editor and reporter for *The Shelbyville* (Indiana) *News*, is the author of *Second Wind: Meditations and Prayers for Women* and *Everyday Prayers for Grandmothers;* and a contributor to *365 Meditations for Mothers of Young Children*. In addition to freelance writing, Margaret Anne devotes her time to community speaking and community and church service. She is an ordained elder in her church in Shelbyville, Indiana, where her husband serves as pastor. They have three children and two grandchildren: Aaron, age eleven; and Kali James, age two.

Betty Steele Everett (May - June) is a freelance writer whose work appears regularly in numerous Christian publications. She is the author of six books, including *I Want to Be Like You, Lord; I'm Still Learning, Lord;* and *I Love Grandparenting, but....*

Betty lives in Defiance, Ohio, with her husband, Horace. Their favorite pastimes include camping in national parks across the country and spending time with their four grandchildren: Sheila, age ten; Lincoln, age eight; Molly, age seven; and Suzanne, age five.

Marilyn Brown Oden (July - September) is the author of numerous articles for Christian publications and professional journals and several books, including *Land of Sickles and Crosses* which was inspired by her church work in Russia. She has been an elementary school counselor, has taught writing to university students, and has been a keynote speaker and retreat leader for various events. Marilyn and her husband, Bill, reside in Baton Rouge, Louisiana. They have four children and three grandchildren: Chelsea, age four, Sarah, age two, and Nathan Bowen, age one.

Nell Mohney (October - December) is a writer and lecturer who leads seminars for business and professional groups, spiritual life retreats, and family life enrichment seminars nationwide. She is the author of *Don't Put a Period Where God Put a Comma* and writes a weekly feature for two regional newspapers. Nell and her husband, Ralph, live in Chattanooga, Tennessee. They have two grandchildren: Ellen, age twelve and Wesley, age nine.

Contents

Foreword

— 9 —

January
Letters for a Grandchild
Gloria Gaither

— 11 —

February
The Promise of New Life
Margaret Anne Huffman

— 50 —

March
Wondrously Made
Margaret Anne Huffman

— 74 —

April
A Season of Rebirth
Margaret Anne Huffman

— 101 —

May
A Grandmother's Love
Betty Steele Everett

— 127 —

June
Grandmother Days
Betty Steele Everett

—— 156 ——

July
Our Beloved Grandchildren
Marilyn Brown Oden

—— 183 ——

August
A Grandmother's Vocation
Marilyn Brown Oden

—— 213 ——

September
For Everything a Season
Marilyn Brown Oden

—— 242 ——

October
New Beginnings
Nell Mohney

—— 269 ——

November
Thanks-Living
Nell Mohney

—— 300 ——

December
The Gift of Love
Nell Mohney

—— 330 ——

Foreword

This unique collection of daily meditations is written especially for you: a grandmother. Whether you have one grandchild or many and whether they be infants or young adults, you will find words of inspiration and spiritual insights that speak to your experiences as a grandmother and a woman of faith.

Five Christian women who also are grandmothers share a variety of experiences and perspectives to illustrate how being a grandmother enriches a woman's daily life and spiritual journey. As you make your way through the year with these women of faith, you will explore common themes of grandmothering and gain new appreciation for the ways in which being a grandmother has affected your sense of God's presence in your life, your understanding of God's plan for your life, your relationships with your own child or children and others, your attitudes toward creation and life, your feelings about Christian and family heritage and tradition, and more.

Each meditation begins with a suggested Scripture reading and ends with a brief prayer. Feel free to pray these prayers as they are written or to shape them into your very own. Regardless of the place and time you choose for reading these meditations, it is our hope that the discipline of daily meditation and the thoughts that will be triggered by these pages will make every day more meaningful for you.

JANUARY

Letters for a Grandchild

Gloria Gaither

🍂 January 1

Dear Little Will,

Because I so firmly believe that God planned for you "before the foundations of the earth," that he was there watching you and was present with you while in your mother's womb you were being "formed in utter seclusion," it seemed natural—sometimes even necessary—to write to you as soon as we were sure you were a possibility.

These epistles cover much of your incubation period and the first fifteen months of your life. During that time and to this moment I am overwhelmed with the wonder of you, as I was with the wonder of your mother when I held her in my arms for the first time. I am still amazed when I look at her and see God's plan unfolding in the life it was once my privilege to carry and nurture in my own body and then teach and embrace as a growing human being.

Even more amazing may be the overwhelming experience of seeing my child's child—to hold her in my heart as my precious little girl, yet at the same time hold you in my arms and watch you reach across the years into my very soul.

When your mother was skipping across the same hill-sides on which you now play, your grandpa and I wrote a song she used to sing:

I am a promise—
I am a possibility—
I am a promise
With a capital "P"
I am a great big bundle of potentiality!
I am learning to hear God's voice
And I am trying to make the right choices—
I am a promise to be . . .
Anything God wants me to be.

As God keeps the promise he made with the life of your mother, he has breathed a new promise with the birth of you. With my very life I pledge to do everything in my power to help you keep that promise. As the days pass and seasons change, I dedicate myself anew to be a constant in both your and your parents' lives.

May it be true in our family what the Psalmist David predicted so long ago:

All the ends of the earth will remember and turn to the Lord, and all the families of the nations will bow down before him, for dominion belongs to the Lord and he rules over the nations. . . . Posterity will serve him; future generations will be told about the Lord. They will proclaim his righteousness to a people yet unborn—for he has done it. (Ps. 22:27-28, 30-31 NIV)

Thus, I proclaim to you, my child, the righteousness of the Lord, for you are a promise!

God, thank you for the miracle of birth and the promise of new life.

Read Psalm 139:13-15.

You are now in your fourth month of life in your mother's womb, and I'm afraid we have not given you the attention you have deserved because we have been so concerned about your mother. Please don't misunderstand this and conclude that we have not been excited about you. How we have wanted you, needed you, prayed for you!

It's been nearly three years since your grandpa and I were given a highchair—my one Christmas request—so that if and when you came, there would already be a place for you saved at Grandma and Grandpa's table. Then last year I asked for a cradle, and your uncle made one! I lined it with clean little sheets and a soft comforter and put it right in the dining room.

Your daddy and mother wanted you, too, and were so afraid you would never be.

So, you see, we're very excited about the whole possibility of you. Your mother, however, has had such a time! She had what turned out to be major surgery to correct endometriosis —a very advanced case. Little did we know—and the doctor could not believe—that you were already making your pilgrimage into your mother's womb and firmly, very firmly, implanting yourself there. You hung on for dear life during the surgery. What a marvel you are! We already know this about you: You're tenacious and persistent, and you love life. You will have a fierce will to survive.

Now that your mother is beginning to get her strength, we are all thinking about you more and more. We find ourselves looking at baby beds and "fish" wallpaper and tiny soft clothing. Your mother makes frequent trips to see and hold her cousin's new baby, Lauren, and I know she's trying to imagine you. It will be fun having you and Lauren so near the same age. Maybe you will play together as your mother and Lauren's mother did, and maybe you will be great friends. You will come to know how important cousins are and how fortunate you are to be close to each other.

God, protect this child growing in my daughter's womb. You are there in that dark and life-giving place. Even there your hands will guide, your strength support. I must —I do trust your hand.

🍒 January 3

Read 2 Timothy 3: 14-15.

Today I am thinking about birthdays in our family. Your great-grandmother Gaither will celebrate her seventy-eighth birthday in a few weeks, and then five days later your great-grandmother Sickal will celebrate her eighty-third. How we hope that they will both be here to know you and hold you and impress their personhood on your virgin memory. How rich is your heritage—"good, strong stock," we like to say. Honest, true, hardworking, resilient, God-fearing people preceded you, and they are a part of you and what you will be.

Even before these who will live to touch you and see you are those whom you will never see, those members of our family who came before you. They, too, are contributors to the reality and fiber of you. English, Irish, German, Native American, and Italian—farmers, poets, lovers, well-diggers, pioneers, homesteaders, dreamers, and doubters —all march in a procession past your cradle, gently passing their precious bundles of contribution to you.

History, too, shapes you, because it has and is shaping the world in which you will take your first breath, hear your first sounds, see your first view of your surroundings, and take your first step. You will be born into a world where you can travel by jet, hear music on digital recording reproduced by laser beam, and see events happening on the other side of the world on television via satellite. The record of your birth will be kept on a computer disk and faxed across the country to your relatives.

As you are being formed in your mother's womb, our country is discussing and debating proposed solutions to the problems we face: air pollution, unemployment, skyrocketing costs of a decent education, housing shortages for the disenfranchised, and an economy reeling from poor management and indebtedness. Sadly, government has become so convoluted that it seems to matter little who is our chosen leader. Yet, you are coming into a country where there is still the possibility that ordinary people can choose to change the system; our Constitution gives us the power to try.

Today, little one, your grandmother is flying from Portland, Oregon, where I spoke at a retreat, to Kansas City, Kansas, where I will join your grandfather for a concert. This is a strange life, and it, too, will affect you. For one thing, you will be surrounded with music, and you will know from the beginning that life itself is a song. I can't wait to see what songs you will inspire. One thing is for sure: Your parents and grandparents will all sing a little more because of you.

So many things and people will shape this little life, Lord. Some—a few—I can control, but most I cannot. Protect this baby from harmful, injuring influences and multiply the life-affirming influences. Save this child for your Kingdom.

❦ January 4

Read Psalm 90:4-5.

As I write, this is the year of my fiftieth birthday. How appropriate that you are being formed in your mother's womb as your grandmother is beginning another half century. We once thought it wild to imagine the year 2000, but it will be a reality for you; and this anniversary will be celebrated in your eighth year of life. If Jesus has not

15

returned for his family by then, you will be told, as I was and as your parents were, that Jesus is coming soon.

Soon is a relative term, as you will "soon" learn. When you are tired from a long trip, you will say, "When will we get there, Daddy?" and your daddy will answer, "Soon." When you are toddling about the house, someone who loves you will be sure to say, "That baby will be in kindergarten before we know it—all too soon." And at some family reunion, one of the more mature relatives is sure to say to your mother, "You better enjoy that child while you can. Pretty soon she/he will be pulling out to head for college."

It will seem strange to you that all these far-off things will be considered "soon." But you must trust what a very short lifetime and a little wisdom has taught: Kindergarten comes in the time of a day; trips with someone you love are all too short; childhood whizzes by; babies leave for college before you know it; and Jesus is coming soon—in the twinkling of an eye.

Lord, just my short lifespan has taught me that time is so fleeting; I have learned that a day is truly like a mist, a fog, that disappears the instant the sun shines. If such a few years have given me this perspective, remind me that when you say "soon" and I think "soon" will never come, in reality your coming is just a blink away. Help me to be patient as I wait for your eternity to envelop us all.

🌱 January 5

Read Psalm 8.

My watch says that here on this tiny island it is 1:30 P.M., and that seems to be the time for afternoon rain. It rains here while the sun shines. A cloud just passes overhead and rain comes out of it, but all around the one gray cloud there are blue skies and sunshine and white fluffy clouds that don't look anything like rain clouds. Often there is a rainbow because of the sunshine and rain coming together.

Grandpa and I have come here just to rest, love each other, and be together. We have seldom done that—just the two of us—because we've always taken the whole family on vacation and often we've taken whole or parts of other families. But this time it's just us two.

I am on the porch of our room watching the warm rain, listening to the Caribbean music down by the pool, smelling the hamburgers grilling, and thinking about vacations we all will take someday with you. If you were here now, I would show you the tiny lizards that skitter up the trunks of the palm trees and scurry through the warm rocks in the gardens that line the walkways. We would pick the blossoms of hibiscus bushes and watch for bees and hummingbirds that love these blossoms so much and get nectar from them. We could play in the sand along the shore, and look for minnows and the long "needle fish," as your mother used to call them. You would love to watch the pelican that has been fishing down there all day long, tirelessly plunging into the waves for some fish only he can see from that great height.

There are so many wonders waiting for you. We eagerly await you, for you will teach us to see them again. What joy it will bring us to watch you discover all those new things. We need you to bring back a sense of delight to our lives.

Lord, thank you for this new little person you are bringing into our lives. As I show this baby the wonders of your world, let me learn wonder again from this child. May I see everything all over again with childlike delight!

🍒 January 6

Read Psalm 91; 1 John 4:13.

Last week your parents moved into their new house. Already it is beginning to look like their own home. This week I will help them hang pictures and get things tucked away. We will make a corner for your crib in your parents' bright, happy bedroom, and that will be your place for a while—until you're big enough to be upstairs.

"A place to be" is very important to us all. You will take for granted—as all children should be able to do—that you have a place to belong. You will have a place in this house. You will have a place at the table, and every morning it will be empty until you bound down the stairs and slip into your chair for breakfast. You will have a place to be in the car. At first it will be a special car seat for infants, then a bigger one for toddlers—a seat made to government specifications to protect you.

You will have a place in the circle of your family. Even now there is a change taking place in your parents' relationship. They are holding tightly to each other while at the same time hollowing out a safe place in the circle of their love for you. As you gradually slip into that place—a process that already has begun—that circle will widen yet grow deeper and stronger. It will be your coming that will teach them that giving love away only makes it multiply and expand.

There will be a place for you in the extended family. Your Grandma Jennings is already putting away little things for you, planning where you will sleep when you come to visit her and thinking about how she can make more trips to see you. And your place at our house is ready and waiting for you. There are sheets and a soft comforter on your cradle; your high chair sits near the kitchen table; and I've been thinking of ordering a baby seat for the swing set that has sat empty all too long.

Your great-grandparents have a place for you, too. How I hope you will know them! I want you to remember watching the ducks and geese, birds and squirrels out of your Great-grandmother Sickal's big window and hear her tell you stories of the wondrous ways of God's creatures. I want you to remember the warmth of Grandma and Grandpa Gaither's farmhouse, smell the meat loaf and green beans on the stove, watch Grandma's hands cutting egg noodles and beating the batter for a German chocolate cake. I hope you will get to go with Grandpa to feed the calves or horses, pick fresh tomatoes from the garden, and ride the mower around the pine trees in the yard.

And there is special space for you at the homes of your aunts and uncles and great aunts and great uncles.

There also will be a place to belong in the arms of the family of God. This is the most important of all places to belong, because this circle embraces all the other family circles and outlasts them all. Your mother is already planning the day when, with your daddy, she will bring you to the altar to be dedicated to the Lord. On that day and in the company of a body of believers, they will make public the commitment they have already made to God to "bring you up in the nurture and admonition of the Lord." And that body of believers will make a public statement of their commitment and responsibility to teach, encourage, protect, and lead you in the "paths of righteousness for his name's sake."

Finally, you have a place to belong in the very heart of God, for he planned for you "from before the foundations of the earth" and is watching as you are even now being formed in your mother's womb. You are precious to him and have been marked and singled out for a purpose unique to you alone. At great price God has made provision for you to be the companion of his heart, and he has plans to walk and talk with you, to "commune with you in the cool of the day." No matter what voices call for your attention, no matter what forces conspire to detract you, you will always be restless, you will never be content, until you settle into the most important of all places to belong—the center of the very heart of God.

Lord, may the security of our family and the tranquility of the home we want so much to provide for this child be only a path leading to the place you have prepared for this child—the security of your arms and the place of peace in the center of your own heart.

19

Read Isaiah 58:8-11.

As I am writing this, today is May Day, little one. This day is related in my memory to your mother's childhood, for it is a day she celebrated on her own. When she was very small, she began making May baskets. I don't remember giving her the idea; perhaps she made one at school. But faithfully, each year she made them. Then early in the morning before anyone else was up, I would hear stirrings in the house. I would pretend to be asleep until the doorbell rang. Sleepily, I'd go to the door; and there, hanging on the doorknob, would be a construction-paper basket full of fresh-picked flowers from my bulb garden. I would act very surprised and ask loudly, "Where could this have come from? That's strange. No one around, but the doorbell rang! And look! Here is this beautiful basket of fresh daffodils and tulips. Wherever could they have come from?"

Then from behind the bushes I'd hear a small giggle, and a cheery voice would shout, "May Day!"

Out she'd bound, and I'd enfold her in a hug, proclaiming how surprised and delighted I was to have such a wonderful beginning for May.

Last week your mother planted flowers around the porch step of your new home. Your daddy bought an apple tree, a cherry tree, and a dogwood tree; and we planted them in the yard. And I have saved a box of daffodil bulbs for your mother to plant this fall.

I wonder if some early Sunday morning on the first day of May, she will hear stirrings in the house and presently be pulled from her bed by the sound of the doorbell. Will you be the nymph who has left a magical surprise hanging on the doorknob to celebrate the birth of summer?

Joy, Lord. This child reminds me that you delight in us, and you invite us to find delight in you. Surprise me with joy. Take away the shadows of winter and make my heart to know that where you dwell there is springtime and May Day and joy.

🍒 January 8

Read Isaiah 54:13.

Your daddy bought a new tractor to mow your lawn this spring. Great-grandpa George said to him when it arrived, "I'll bet you won't want to go to work tomorrow." He just knew that even though it's a long time until spring, it would be hard to keep one's mind on office work when there was a new piece of machinery in the garage!

Well, this tractor had to be partially assembled. The instructions on the box said "Easy assembly," but, of course, it was anything but easy! Finally, though, the tractor was in working order, and your parents were talking about spring and how they will care for the big yard where you will play one day.

They were planning the gardens they would plant and the fence they will build to confine you from the busy road and keep you safe. They talked about the little puppy they want you to have, and the swing set they want to construct. They talked about picking cherries and apples with you from the trees that are barely larger than twigs now.

When you are old enough, your dad will talk to you about nature, let you sit on his lap when the tractor is not moving, and teach you to hold the steering wheel so that one day you will know how to take control of machinery and safely guide the vehicle where it needs to go.

In dozens of other ways, they will teach you to take control of power and be responsible. They will teach you to think and reason, question and learn. You will learn to read the written thoughts of others and write your own ideas clearly. You will learn to speak articulately and assimilate information to make deductions from it.

They will teach you to be aware of others in your life, for

at first you will only be aware of your own needs—and of your mother because she can supply them. But gradually you will begin to be sad when others are sad, to laugh when others are laughing, and to look through your toys to find just the right thing to share to bring someone else pleasure.

They will teach you to be responsible, because what you do will affect someone else—that leaving toys on the floor makes your mother or daddy work extra hard, or that leaving your tricycle in the driveway is inconsiderate if someone else has to move it to get the car out of the garage.

Little by little they will put your little hands on the steering wheel of your own life, and they will show you that the instructions are not just to prove a point but to help you operate the equipment you've been given safely, efficiently, and for the good of life on this planet.

Lord Jesus, as we all teach this child the skills needed for safety, community, and relationships, may we remember to teach best those things that will last . . . forever.

🐚 January 9

Read Ephesians 1:3-14.

Our favorite beach—many of your mother's important memories were shaped here. When she was only seven, she first walked this beach and jumped these dunes. This place with its glorious sunsets always was the setting for our vacation farewell ceremony. The Petersons would bring their biggest station wagon cab and haul all of us and the groceries out to this place for a picnic or clambake. The children would help carry the supplies to a cove sheltered from the wind; then they would scatter to wade in the shallows, dig sand crabs, or feed hot dog buns to the gulls. Before long, though, they would all be jumping the dunes. With arms outstretched, little bodies would sail through the sea wind to the warm soft sand below, and each fall would be accompanied by squeals of laughter and shouts of "Let's do it again!"

Over the years the jumping bodies grew, from sturdy nursery and elementary school children to the strong athletic bodies of teenagers. Now I watch your mother struggle up the dunes, not to jump but to find a sheltered place from the winds to sit and rest; for her body is heavy with the weight of you growing inside her. She doesn't bend beside the tide to dig sand crabs—she can barely bend at all. And today your daddy does not race her down the beach to tumble with her in the warm sand behind the screen of marsh grass. Instead, he walks patiently beside her, giving her a hand where the banks are too steep, then spreading a blanket for her to rest on from the task of carrying you.

She chatters cheerfully with her sister, Amy, about other nights on this beach and the many combinations of families and their children that have come with us here. They recall the campfires and the times when their brother, Benjy, played guitar so we could sing—and the night our group was so diverse that the only songs we all knew really well were "Kum Ba Yah" and "Twist and Shout." That was the night when a promise was made by the teenagers around the fire to follow God and keep his promise to the world to impact it with their lives.

One day you will run and play here, perhaps, and you will be part of the pledge your mother has kept. Maybe those who follow your little footprints down the beach will be part of that promise, too. For you, too, will be a promise God will make to the world, and all of us are going to help God keep that promise by helping you become all you can be by his grace. Places like this will help you do that.

Father, set your seal upon this child. More than any other dream or hope for this life, I pray that you will make this child a holy man or woman of God. I give myself at any cost to this end.

Read Isaiah 40:31.

This morning when I awoke in Ketchikan, Alaska, and saw the eagles soaring outside my window, I thought of something a man said in his prayer at your Uncle Ben's college graduation a few days ago. He prayed that these graduates would "fly on dove wings." I remember thinking at the time that wasn't quite what I would wish for my son . . . or for you. Doves are wonderful, peaceful, gentle creatures, but they are not famous for their ability to soar, to rise high and disappear into the heavens. They have wonderful qualities, many of which I might wish for you—serenity, faithfulness, affection, contentment—but I would not wish you dove wings.

I thought, as I heard that prayer, about other wings—the wings of long-distance flyers such as geese and ducks—that will persevere against the elements and fly into the winds of time. These flyers will fly in formation because they understand the advantage of working together to conquer their deficiencies—cutting the wind with their corporate V, trusting the sense of direction of the strongest, wisest among them. I would wish you the wings of endurance—the wings of a long-distance flyer.

I thought of the wings of strength—the wings of the herons and storks, the wings of the swans and the gulls—wings that can lift the weight of their own bodies, span great distances, and lift great burdens at a moment's notice to flee danger or to flog and threaten a predator or an enemy of their young fledglings. I would wish you strong wings, protecting wings, wings to lift burdens.

Finally, though, my mind considered the wings of the eagle, for the eagle can fly long distances without tiring. The eagle can fly alone, even when no one will follow or when there is no one trustworthy to follow. The eagle has wings of strength, enabling it to lift burdens. It can seize the enemy with its feet and turn that threat into sustenance to nurture its young; it turns death into life. The span of its wings is an awesome thing—wide and strong and sure. But beyond all this, the eagle's wings enable it to mount high into the sky—higher than the earth, beyond the forest, above the mountains, deep into the mystery of the clouds, and beyond the clouds into the crystal of the sky. Above its enemies, beyond limitations, higher than its own nest on the peaks and the tips of the giant pines, the eagle rises—and rises above it all on wide, strong, secure, long-distance, protective wings.

Yes, I would wish you the wings of an eagle. So for now you must wait, but in waiting you will grow wings.

Lord, your Word promises that "they that wait upon the Lord shall renew their strength; they shall mount up with wings as eagles; they shall run, and not be weary; and they shall walk, and not faint" (Isaiah 40:31 KJV). Teach us. Teach us, Lord, to wait; for in waiting, walking, and running we are growing wings . . . the wings of an eagle.

🍓 January 11

Read Ephesians 3:14-19.

Your daddy left this morning to go see his brother, your Uncle Tim, because this will be his last chance to see him before you are born; and he wants to stay close to your mother for the rest of her time. She will come in to town to stay with us while he is gone.

It is a glorious morning. Grandpa and I are having coffee on our new front porch thinking about you running down the hillside and playing on the swing. We hope you will love this place as much as your mother has, and will be excited to come here.

The remodeling we've been doing is finally finished, and the house is all put back together. We had hoped it would be done before your mother needed our full attention—and it is! Our new spacious bedroom and new bath sparkle like a freshly polished gem, and the new porches look over twenty-five years of tree planting and beautiful memories. You will add to that treasure, for your very presence in our lives will be a walking testimony to the grace of God.

Some people wonder why we didn't just sell this old house when our needs changed and buy another, why we didn't move to other cities more advantageous to career or opportunity. We stayed here because things are planted here—trees, grass, flowers, shrubs. We stayed because foundations were poured here on strong footings—the house, the garages (where your mother's tiny handprints are still in the cement), the playhouse, the swing set. We stayed because things have been built here—walls of protection, roofs, rooms, gazebos, the duck shelter, and dog houses. We stayed because we've made adjustments and adaptations here—built on, torn out, restructured, rearranged to meet the growing and changing needs of the various stages of our lives.

Yes, we've stayed because there are roots, foundations, constructions, adjustments, adaptations, and growth here. I hope you'll love wandering between the growing things, the groves of trees, the orchards. I hope you love this meandering old house with its additions and corrections; love its rooms with their varied and strong "reasons for being" and their histories. And I hope you will be enfolded in this place and your being will bring new changes and you will leave a few of your feathers in this nest after you have flown.

Lord, in this world of shifting values, fogged viewpoints, and goal-less journeys, may we help this child to see clearly, walk with purpose, and know where to go. May this child's roots go down deep into the soil of your marvelous love.

Read Ephesians 5:33; Romans 8:22.

Still no sign of you, except the swollen, weary body your mother carries with great effort. You've grown in this last week so much that even the doctor was amazed; she says you will likely be a very large baby. Still there are no delivery signs. But that could change overnight.

Your mother was discouraged with the news that there was no sign of labor beginning. She has tried so hard to keep a positive outlook and a good sense of humor through all the changes in her body.

And your daddy has been so good. For their anniversary he gave your mother some beautiful perfume, cologne, body cream, and powder; took her to dinner; and left her several beautiful cards and romantic notes around the house. They spent the night at the cabin where they spent their wedding night. Your mother had a beautiful picture and poem matted and framed for your daddy. Some day she may show it to you and explain it.

You are so fortunate to have parents who love each other and are eager to enfold you in their warm embrace.

God, it hurts me to see my child so miserable. Yet I know this is the process for a miracle, and it reminds me that all creation is in labor, waiting for the return of the Son of God. Help me on both counts to trust you and be patient.

❧ **January 13**

Read Matthew 11:25.

Well, Will Garrison, you have a name, an identity, and a personality. You are alert, bright, and interested, but you are also contented and secure. You love to be snuggled and touched. You nursed for the first time at 6 A.M. and were amazing (even though your mother had to have you positioned upside down over her shoulder, for she has a very sore tummy and must lie flat on her back until noon). It was an incredible experience for both of you, as anyone could plainly see. Your mother was filled with the wonder of you, the miracle of you, the beauty of you.

She stroked your little cheeks and head, picked out features that belong to your relatives, and was very grateful for the gift of you. She says you have your daddy's hands and lips and feet. I say you have your mother's eyes and nose. Your body is a long tube, just like your Uncle Benjy and Grandpa Sickal. In you there are equal portions of Jennings and Gaither, Smith and Sickal, and a host of others including the Hartwells, the Mahoneys, the Bosters, and the Woodalls.

Your mother and daddy are taking much delight in you. There is nothing sweeter than to watch your mother rise in the night to hold you close and nurse you at her swollen breasts—her silhouette and yours in the dim light like a sacred painting of Madonna and child. There is in you both the fulfillment of promise and the seed of the divine. Like Mary, your mother has been chosen to deliver the promise of God in you to this earth, to protect and nurture it no matter the cost in pain or glory. And, like Joseph, your father stands quiet and strong in his obedience to the mandate of the Holy One—to be wary and wise and to listen to the warnings of the angels along his path, so that no harm will come to you two. Already you and your father have a quiet understanding, and it is he who stills your troubled spirit in the night.

Lord, suddenly I know that this baby is the teacher and we are the students. We will get a refresher course in what life is about, in the wonder of it all, from this child. Those "mysteries" that you have held from the wise and prudent and revealed to the babes—let me glimpse them through this child.

Read Psalm 139:1-18.

This is your one week birthday. You are getting accustomed to this world, to the faces of those near you and the sights around your house. And you are making us get used to your preferences. You have let us know how much you like the warm breezes and the bright sunlight. You love the sounds of the cicadas and the birds.

Last night at supper you lay in the new stroller your Great-grandma Sickal gave you, close to the table where you could hear familiar voices, and you were so pleased to be a part of things.

You are nursing about every two hours during the day and sleeping for five-hour stretches at night, which is almost too good to be true. When you are awake during the day, you love to be carried and talked to. You like the visitors you're having as long as there aren't too many at a time, and, of course, you love being rocked by Great-grandma Gaither and walked around by Great-grandpa George. You love Grandpa Bill's low voice and Benjy's warm body lying close to you while we're watching T.V. Your daddy's so good to change you and hold you; he loves to talk to you and rub your belly. Aunt Amy and Uncle Andrew were so thankful to be here and be a part of your whole birth process, and Grandma Jennings treasured every moment with you.

When any of us look at you we see a marvel. You are so perfect and beautiful that it's almost more than we can hold—the joy you bring, the confirmation of life!

People ask me, "So, how does it feel to be a grandmother?" I can only answer, "Grateful!"

Lord, I rest in the promise that you scheduled each day of this child's life. Whatever happens, I know you are sovereign and will finish what you have started in this little life. Finish what you've started in me, too.

❦ January 15

Read Proverbs 22:1.

Will. They named you Will—after all the Williams and Wilfreds and Wilfords who have preceded you. I think of them and now of you, so small, so bright, so full of potential. I think a name is very important, and I think of all the serious consideration your parents gave your name. They wanted the poetry of the sound to have music—Will Garrison. Will Jennings. Will Garrison Jennings. They wanted your name to fit your look and nature. They wanted a name accessible and gentle, yet strong and wise. *Garrison* stands for strength—a protection, a fortification, a place where others can find endless supply and safety. *Will,* likewise, means "protector." Will you be responsible for the safety and survival of many?

I think "Will." What will he be? Where will he go? What will he believe? How will he think? Whom will he admire? Will he be patient? Will he be kind? Will he be gregarious? Will he be pensive? Will he have a sense of humor? What will Will teach us? Where will he push us—into what new territory—by his interests, dreams, and drives?

One thing's for sure: No one around here will ever be the same because of Will—Will Garrison Jennings.

God, fulfill the promise you've made to the world with the birth of our grandchild as you are fulfilling the promise you made through the life of our own child. Long ago we gave our child to you; now our child has a child. Protect the marriage and the home that produced this child.

❦ January 16

Read Ephesians 5:1-2.

Yesterday you were two months old. You spent the day traveling home from Virginia where you visited your other grandmother and your aunt and uncle. Your parents say you loved traveling and never cried a bit on all the long plane rides and car trips. Somehow, that doesn't surprise me.

When you got home, your mother brought you to our house, where I'd made a pot of hot vegetable soup and a big pan of stewed apples and cinnamon. Your daddy came home from a half-day of trying to catch up at the office and ate while you, your mother, and I took soup and apples to Grandpa, who was editing at the studio. Uncle Benjy held you, too, and we stopped by to see your great-grandmother, who is recovering from back surgery. It seemed to be a shot of vitamins to her just to see and hold you.

How important family is, and how very much we need one another: You need your mother and daddy for love, communication, and sustenance. Your daddy and mother need each other in this awesome task of raising and protecting you. You need the joy and approval and adoration of your grandparents, great-grandparents, aunts, and uncles. We all need you to renew the wonder, awe, and utter joy in being alive. We all need one another for identity, support, confirmation, history, and encouragement.

God made no mistake when he made "family" the natural habitat for human beings. Yes. I'm sure of it.

God, there are so many fragmented families today. Bless all the children who need nurture and a place to belong. Use our family to be "extended family" for someone outside our circle.

🍂 January 17

Read Psalm 67.

As I am writing, this is the season of thanksgiving. Little pilgrim, you have landed on a strange and alien shore, climbed from the ship that brought you here, and found in the light of dawn a brand new land. Now you explore what you believe to be a virgin forest, a place of promise, a territory for the taking where you can stake your claim. The foliage is lush; the soil is rich. The generous, warm sea of life laps around your eager feet and coughs up fat oysters and scallops for you to taste.

The delight that dances in your eyes tells how glad you are you've come. New friends dance around you, too, and share their planting secrets of corn and roots and herbs. They lay the venison at your fire and run with you naked through the trees.

But winter is coming to define for you what thankful is. When frozen seas and barren trees turn their chilling back on games and feasts, when roaring winds strip solace from the glen and teach you to seek shelter, you will need to turn to a source older than the trees for knowledge, for sustenance, and for help.

When the hope of spring planting and the hot toil of summer pass and you have learned the treasure of the harvest, you will again sing—this time a better song of praise, a wiser hymn of gratitude. And you will trade the dance of innocence for the better, grander festival of joyful thanksgiving—the thanksgiving of one forgiven.

Lord, we are all "strangers and pilgrims" here. During every season may our family keep our eyes set on the land to which we are going in glad thanksgiving for your bountiful provision in Christ Jesus.

🍎 January 18

Read Isaiah 64:8-9.

Will, how can I say what your coming has meant? Already you have a certain personality and very definite opinions. Your pleasant, happy nature blends with a sense of justice, right and wrong, and what "should be." May you always be a happy, winsome child who will bring much joy and optimism to those around you, but may you not compromise your convictions for peace and comfort. May you always try to find peaceful solutions when you can, but be able finally to confront injustice or behavior that violates principle.

Your parents are learning—from you—how to parent you. It's a strange thing to say, but each child must teach his or her parents how to parent, because each child has an individual set of needs. There will be little need for harshness with you; you want to please. But if there is a wrong on your part, you will have to be convinced, not coerced, because you will have a strong sense of right and wrong. May we all learn from you how best to shape the best in you.

God, as you shape us like clay in the potter's hands, teach us to shape the impressionable personality of this tiny child. Put your hands around ours so that the impressions we make are, in fact, the impressions of your own hands.

January 19

Read Psalm 127.

I just phoned to check on you, Will, because your daddy slipped on the ice with you last night. He held you so tightly to protect you that he landed on his back, hip, and elbow, but you weren't hurt. I hope he is all right.

Your mother said you were "playing the piano" at a family gathering and began singing as you played. They moved you higher on the bench to take a picture, and as you moved up the keyboard your voice pitch went higher, too. It was so funny to see a five-month-old baby singing and playing that they all cracked up laughing. I have a feeling your parents need to get used to you doing inventive things that involve music. This is probably just the beginning.

You are growing so fast; you're reaching for everything, trying to crawl, and eating three meals a day of "first food." Some weeks you just can't eat enough to keep up with your growing. You love to laugh and play little games, and you are totally fascinated with your hands and what they can do. You reach for faces and play with your own feet, and you love to drink out of a cup. Your walker is one of your favorite things just now. It gives you freedom and lets you bounce, which you love to do so much that it's hard to hold you. To us, everything you do is a wonder.

You make me so glad that one day I fell in love with your grandpa and that our love over all these years has produced your mother, Aunt Amy, and Uncle Benjy. I'm so thankful that your parents found each other and that their love produced you. This is how love is supposed to be.

Lord, this baby is like a slender arrow we shoot into the future—where we cannot go. Thank you for the love that produced this child. And now we trust your love to protect this child in the unknown territory to be traveled—we know your love has no bounds. For this marvelous assurance, we sing this day our anthem of praise.

January 20

Read 2 Peter 3:18.

It was one year ago today that I first began writing to you, Will. Then you had no name, and we didn't even know you were a boy. Now I can't imagine life without you. Your sunny little disposition warms the room when you're there and brightens the darkest days. Today you are half a year old and have definite opinions, preferences, and desires. You like being where everybody is—rooms full of talking and joy and love. You love weather—all kinds of weather—and being outdoors in it. When we take you for walks in the park, you are mesmerized by the birds, the trees, the sky, the breeze against your face, and the sounds of children, traffic, and nature.

34

You are beginning now to reach for your mother when there is too much noise or too many unfamiliar faces; you lift your arms to be taken. You get very excited when your daddy comes home, and you love for him to play with you on the floor. He holds his big hand against your feet when you're lying on your stomach, and you push yourself to get toys just out of reach. Soon you will figure out how to get traction with your knees, and you'll be off!

You love to be read to and you "read along" whenever your mother starts a book, leaping in excitement at each new colorful page. And you love mechanical things—the phone, the remote control, the radio buttons. I found you a toy remote control that has different sounds and blinking lights. Your parents got you a play phone that talks back. You may be very useful to this family if you grow up and learn how to fix things.

Your parents are a marvel! What a miracle to see a baby born and come to be. But maybe a greater miracle is to see two people who already "are" turn into parents who care and nurture and teach. That is indeed a wonder to behold. I am very sure that family was God's idea—and one of his better ones, at that! No wonder the Enemy tries so hard to break it: when the family is broken, the world is broken.

Lord, just as this child is eager to learn everything we are able to teach, help me to remain eager to learn everything you have to teach me. Help me today to "grow in the grace and knowledge of our Lord and Savior Jesus Christ."

January 21

Read Isaiah 1:18.

Will, here I am in Syracuse, New York, and so far thirty-eight inches of snow have fallen since yesterday morning! Wouldn't you know I'd be speaking at a retreat in the very spot where all this snow is falling!

All the airports are closed, and now I am at the home of some kind people who have taken me in until I can find a way to go home.

I wish you could see this snowscape. As far as you can see—which isn't far—everything is white. Nowhere is there dirt or trash or junked cars or ugly holes. Everywhere there are trackless white waves of snow. The winds have made peaks and points like meringue on a lemon pie. All the lines against the white sky are curved, graceful, artistic, soft lines. Everything is still—silent. What a beautiful silence! The only motion is that of the blowing snow and an occasional flicker of a red wing in a bare black tree or a gray squirrel on a branch.

I can't help thinking of the beautiful verse from Isaiah that says: "Though your sins are like scarlet, they shall be like snow" (Isa. 1:18). Truly, there is no white whiter than snow. It is so dazzling that I can barely stand to look at it. It is a "clean" that is almost "glory." And snow covers any flaw, any dirt, any ugliness, any mistakes. When there is deep, white snow, everything is suddenly perfect and beautiful.

Will, I can hardly believe it, thinking of you now, but someday you may do something you're ashamed of. You may make some mistakes. You may make some wrong choices. There may be some nights when you go to bed and cry into your pillow in shame and disappointment in yourself. It is then that I want you to remember this great snow. Remember that your grandmother saw it for herself and described it to you to let you know this: God's love, grace, redemption, and forgiveness can come down from heaven and gently, silently cover all your sins, and cover them so deep that no sharp edges or ugly protrusions will show through. The covering—that's what "atonement" means—of God is so deep that only beauty and graceful lines will remain. And unlike this deep snow, God's grace never melts!

O Lord, build a wall of protection around this child. I claim this child for your Kingdom and pray that the "covering" of the blood of your Son be applied to his life.

🍎 January 22

Read John 12:24-25.

As I am writing this, death and resurrection dance together today, not only in the death and resurrection of our Lord, but also in spring's final battle with winter. Today, Will, I sit by the bedside of your great-grandmother, my dear mother. Alphas and omegas, beginnings and endings. They whirl and clash in such a blinding confusion that it is hard to tell them apart. It is obvious there is struggle in both dying and birthing—and although we tend to think something has to be born to die, the truth is, says the Word of the Lord, that something has to die to be born. "Unless a grain of wheat falls into the earth and dies, it remains just a single grain; but if it dies, it bears much fruit" (John 12:24).

This time last year, Will, we were helping your mother with some very hard days. Pain of the process and glory in the promise of you were dancing in her, and we all felt the conflict. Out of the pain and the struggle that upset the systems of your mother's digestion and our too-well-formed schedules, finally came the fresh newness of you.

This year we struggle with winter as the spirit that would be born fresh and new battles with the pull of earth and decay. It is a hard fight with much pain. Earth does not give up easily, and winter sometimes rages its final gasping storms very violently. But winter is doomed, nonetheless, and spring *will* win.

Not long ago, it seems, we sat on the front porch and watched the flowers bud. We planted summer seedlings and strained together toward the promise of summer and you.

Now we wait long hours in a hospital room and struggle with death. Over and over death has reared its head and shaken its fist at life, but life doesn't give in easily. Yet this process will be completed because life—perfect life—will win, even over the love of human life. Death will be swallowed up in victory. And the ultimate irony is that in losing life—even as well as she's loved it—Grandma Sickal will be taken over by a life even better. The process—this alpha-omega dance—may flash and rage and look threatening, but death—though it will have its ugly moment—will itself die. Our Lord's resurrection is our proof and our promise.

There is Easter in our bones!

O Lord of life, O Master of rebirth, pull away the stones that block my escape into life. May the birth of a grandchild and the death of a loved one teach me that there is eternity in each moment and that alphas and omegas are one in you.

🍂 January 23

Read James 4:14.

Your great-grandmother is struggling with a disease called cancer. You went again today to visit her as you have every day. Your precious mother took you there because she so wants you to remember. You ate your cereal and one of Grandma's graham crackers in the hospital room. You crawled up on her bed beside her and grinned the way you do, then laid your little cheek over on hers. How she loves you!

The other night when you were alone with Great-grandma and your mother, Great-grandma said, "Aw, Will, I'm afraid you won't even remember who I was. I just hope something I did or said will make an impression on your little mind." We know you will remember. There will be so many wonderful stories about her life and her humor—and she is a part of you.

Today, Will, you also cut your first tooth! Your mother was excited about it. I felt your lower gums and, sure enough, there were tiny jagged edges of your first tooth! You looked so proud when we all cheered this milestone.

How thankful I am for God's balance in things—that the hope and promise and adventure of your first tooth can remind me how good life is on this day when my precious mother is letting go of these things to grasp a life of which the one you are beginning is only a shadow.

Lord, life is such a wonderful, fragile gift. May we use the days we are given to "store up treasures" that outlive this world. Thank you for the lives of my grandchild and mother. They both help me remember what is really important.

January 24

Read Romans 3:23-26.

As I am writing this, today is the day that payments to the government are due from every citizen of this country: tax day. You don't seem to be concerned about this day one bit, but are content to let your parents worry about such things. They take care of all the debts and expenses of your life for you. Your food, your clothes, your house, your transportation, your health care—anything at all is taken care of by them, so that you can live debt free. They pay it all.

One day you will come to the "age of accountability," and you will have to assume responsibility for your own debts—and even the debts of others.

There is another way in which you are covered now and free from any accountability. Your innocence is your protection from the debt of sin that has been adding up, charged to the human race. Even though you will do some wrong things, you will not be held accountable until you reach the "age of accountability." That age is different for each person, but you will know it as surely as Adam and Eve knew when they ate of the tree of the knowledge of good and evil.

But this accountability will be different from the debts of taxes and living expenses. When you get to the age when you are aware of the debts of sin that you are beginning to stack up to your personal account, I want you to know that your Heavenly Father has done an amazing thing. Although you will have laid up many charges to your account—charges you could never pay—and will be responsible for your debts, God has found a way to pay everything in full for you. If you acknowledge his plan and accept this provision, you can go on living in freedom and joy—debt free!

Now you live your life in innocence—unaware of any mistakes and unaware of how debts are paid. But then you will live not in innocence but in faith—knowing and choosing to accept and deposit in your account a payment you never had to make. It's like finding out that someone who loves you has written a check to cover your taxes for the rest of your life!

God, just as a child doesn't yet know the price that is being paid for his or her needs, I once was ignorant of your sacrifices for me. Now that I know, help me to live in gratitude, always aware that it is your love that paid it all and that, like a good parent, you don't even keep track of what I have cost you.

🍃 January 25

Read Isaiah 11:1-10.

This has been a week of celebration. You attended your first big party of the summer down at the creek where your mother grew up celebrating summer. This party was in honor of Aunt Amy's and Lisa's birthdays, Amy and Andrew's anniversary, and the Fourth of July—which isn't for another week, but we threw that in because Benjy will be playing with his band on the Fourth.

We had a beautiful day. A big yellow-and-white tent fluttered in the afternoon breeze, and music floated on the air. A table in the tent was full of presents, two cakes, and a red, white, and blue dessert in a crystal bowl.

Seventy friends and family members ate barbecued chicken, corn on the cob, cole slaw, potatoes, fresh vegetables, and fruit. Kids and grown-ups, alike, played volleyball and watched the spectacular fireworks show that Uncle Benjy planned and executed.

You, Will, were a delight—floating from person to person, eating strawberries, and being adored. It seemed so natural for you not to be afraid of new people. You have never known betrayal or fear or desertion. You have only known love and security and confirmation.

I kept wondering what a person would be like who could reach adulthood fearless, confirmed, and loved. I think there will be persons in heaven who went there as children, never knowing pain. And the rest of us will be restored to that undamaged state, yet we will have knowledge and wisdom. Just that alone—and the presence of Jesus—would be heaven.

What a party you, Oh Lord, have made of life! We bask in the joy of relationships. We are as adored children, content in the security of being loved. Today I throw my hat in the air and blow the horns of celebration for abundant life in the family of God!

♥ January 26

Read Mark 10:13-16; Hebrews 4:16.

I've been watching you, Will, and I'm excited to learn from you. Jesus said that little children would teach us how to be Kingdom people, so I want a refresher course from you in all the ways of the Kingdom.

Teach me to pray. You are not embarrassed at all or even humble when you ask your parents or grandparents for something you need. In fact, you have pure audacity and unspoiled expectation. You've never run into anything they can't supply, and you have no doubt they love you and want to give you what you need. There is a simple awe in you in the knowing that these parenting figures can actually do things, fix things, provide things. They can soothe, smooth, comfort, and assure; and you believe that you can go to sleep or go to play, confident that they are there, should any new threat or problem arise. I would be so with my Heavenly Parent—confident, secure, audacious, in awe, and joyfully at ease. Teach me to pray.

Teach me to copy. I watch you watching your family. You have so much to learn: walking, talking, singing, reaching, reasoning. So you copy. You shape your mouth like our mouths and push sounds out through your lips. You hear us singing and hold tones as long as you can. You stare intently and point at the bright pictures in books, connecting the words you hear us say—such as kitty, puppy, chicken, cow, and fish—with the pictures we point to. You see us keeping time to music and showing excitement by clapping our hands, and you clap your hands together excitedly. You watch us moving from one place to another by standing and taking steps, and you pull yourself upright and try to move along by standing and putting one foot ahead of the other. Teach me to mirror the behavior of my Heavenly Father—moving, speaking, touching, reaching, making music, embracing, forgiving, delighting.

Teach me to rest. I watch you sleep in your mother's arms. There are no wrinkles on your brow. Your breathing is even and peaceful, with no irregularity or tension. You do not toss or twitch or fret. You are totally at rest. Despite all the urgency of your learning and growing, when it is time to rest, you are easily and totally at rest. Teach me to rest.

Teach me to be generous. Without a thought of counting the cost or protecting your turf, you thrust at me the biggest hunk of your cookie, the bottle of juice you love so much, your favorite toy, or your most treasured book. You watch my face, for you have given just for the sheer joy of watching me find pleasure. Teach me to share.

Teach me to forget. I make mistakes. I let you fall by not reaching out to you soon enough. I make a loud noise and scare you. When I go out to get the mail, you awake from your nap and are frightened when you cry out and coo but no one comes. Yet only minutes later you have forgotten. You throw your tiny arms around my neck, lay your head on my shoulder, and pat me lovingly on the back with your little hands. You bring me your ball and books and invite me to play. Teach me to forget the infractions—small or large—that come with relationships. May forgiveness be a way of life, not an isolated incident.

I have lived half a century, Will. By now, adults begin to grow wary and cynical. We lose our childlike wonder. But Jesus said that to be a part of his Kingdom, I must be like you. So teach me today to be a child again. May I not miss the Kingdom. Make me like you.

Jesus, let me sit at the feet of this child today and learn your ways.

January 27

Read Colossians 2:2-3.

Tomorrow you will be one year old. It has been only one year, yet you have woven yourself permanently into the fabric of our days and our lives until it is impossible to imagine life without you. Your happy spirit walks the corridors of my sleep and dances like nymphs across the meadows of my mind. I see your little finger pointing at everything in wonder. I see your nose wrinkled up, imitating a pig snorting or smelling the flowers in the garden. I see your little eyes winking and hear you telling me what

43

the cow or kitty says. I see you toddling toward me with all your energies focused on the marvel of your new solitary journey.

This will not be the last time you will learn to walk alone; no, it is only the beginning. Soon you will have the joy of discovering for yourself that letters make words and words join together to make sentences—and then that those sentences can let others know what's in that spinning little mind of yours. You also will learn that others have ideas, too, and that those ideas are not always ones you can accept. Thus, you will have to exercise your thought processes as you now are strengthening your legs, so that when the time comes you can walk alone on the paths your choices take you.

You will have to walk alone, too, in the unique path God has gifted you to pursue. Some things you will have in common with your parents, your siblings, your cousins, or your friends. But the particular combination of abilities and interests that merge in you will be like no other. We can all encourage you, support you, cheer you on, and, at times, protect you from distraction; but, in the end, your path will be uniquely your own. Yet in all the places and ways you will learn to walk alone, there is only one Other who can walk with you. He will never let you fall and damage yourself if you will always reach for his sturdy hand. Even in the fog or dim light of uncertainty, you need never be the victim of panic, for he will never leave you or desert you.

Tomorrow, before your birthday meal at the cookout your mother has planned, you will fold your little hands, mumble to yourself quietly, and then grin your infectious grin when we say "Amen." Soon you will come to know that this new gesture is different from waving "bye-bye" or winking or wrinkling your nose. This new thing we call prayer is the first baby step to the most amazing and necessary relationship you will ever have. Go ahead! Walk to Jesus! He won't let you fall!

God, help this child come to know the secret of the universe: that when he has Jesus, he has everything. Walk with him always.

January 28

Read Isaiah 12:1-6.

You have just experienced your first trip to the big city. From the excitement of the long hallways in the airport and all the planes to the streets and noise of the big city, your eyes danced and your little mind strained to comprehend. From our room on the twenty-eighth floor and your parents' room on the thirty-first floor, you watched the traffic below snaking its way between the columns of buildings—honking, shouting, whistling, sirening traffic.

You ate in fancy restaurants, rode in elevators, and were pushed in your stroller through the streets; and everywhere you smiled and waved, blew kisses, and wrinkled your nose. Like a tiny saint you blessed the cynical masses, and your blessing transformed people if only for a moment. On the streets people looked at you, at first as if you were an alien from another planet and then, with slow recognition, as if remembering for the first time in a long time that human beings begin life as happy, innocent babies. Suddenly faces that were granite softened. Women who have learned to protect themselves by never speaking or focusing on other human eyes were somehow given permission by your presence to speak and then to talk freely to you and your mother. Men long jaded by the suspicion and competition of the city reached down to touch your cornsilk hair or recite details of their own families.

We took you to a large toy store to see more toys than either your mother or I knew existed. Your eyes danced, and you clapped your little hands with joy to see so many things with steering wheels!

Last night you slept with Grandpa and me while your

parents went to the theater. How small you looked in our king-size bed to be so aware, so full of personality. My heart wanted to spin a cocoon around you to keep you from what the city knows, from the realities that have hardened the hearts of its grown-ups and banished the dancing feet of its children. Knowing I could not spin a cocoon, I wrapped you in prayer and placed you forever in the hands of the Lord Jesus, who makes all things new and calls us all to be transformed into one like you.

Lord, keep us from cynicism. In spite of the harsh experiences of life, keep us trusting, reaching, and loving. May the wonder in our eyes transform the hostile masses. May they dare to look into our faces, and when they do, may they see you smiling back at them.

❦ January 29

Read John 1:1-5.

You shaped your little mouth to make new sounds today, and you have discovered that your tongue has something to do with communication. You flip it back and forth as you remold the vowel sounds you've been saying. Your little eyes dance as you discover that these sounds are words and words are ideas! You clap with joy to give things and people names. You are like a tiny Adam in Eden going about the happy task of giving things their identity, as if by doing so you personally have spoken them into existence.

"Dadoo" is Daddy. "Pawpaw" is both Grandma and Grandpa. "Moo," "arf," "s-s-s-s," "meow," "quack" are words that have connected you to the creatures you love; and "car," "truck," and "bus" have let you give shape and size to the motor-driven vehicles that excite you more than anything.

What joy it brings us all to watch you make friends with words, to sense their power, to learn that they are expressions of those marvelous ideas that have been trapped in that teeming little mind of yours.

As you speak your ideas into existence, I think of the incredible Word that preceded all other words—the Word with the capital "W"; the "Word" that was in the beginning; the Word that was with God and, indeed, was God. May you one day come to know this Word that has such power that when it is uttered into the void, all things come to be—and all that comes to be is alive with his life. How I pray that one day that Word will be spoken into the void that is you; and this incredibly powerful Word will call out all the particulars that are churning in you, and you will be alive with his life who is the living, breathing Word.

May the "big idea" be spoken in you, our tiny word-shaper.

Jesus, speak into the void that is me today and say your omnipotent words "Let it be!" Make me alive with your life. May my life be a living, walking word—the word of life.

January 30

Read Genesis 1:1-31; Psalm 104.

One of the animal sounds you're learning to say, Will, is the sound of the snake. So along with toy ducks and cats and cows and dogs, I found you a very real-looking rubber snake. My friend thought you would be afraid, but, just as I suspected, you grinned your wide grin and said, "s-s-s-s." You held the snake in your little hands and stuck your nose up against its nose.

I knew your reaction was the result of two parents who have never taught you to be afraid but have taught you to recognize snakes as helpful creatures that can be our friends—just as they've taught you that cows give milk, that dogs are great companions, and that ducks swim on the pond. When the time comes, they will teach you to recognize dangerous snakes and unfriendly dogs and raging bulls; but for now you only know that God has made all things bright and beautiful, all creatures great and small.

Thank you for reminding me that the earth is to be cared for and creatures are to be appreciated—and that life is to be protected, for it is sacred. May I look again at all God has created and see that "it is very good."

Forgive me, Lord, for my failure to enjoy nature and delight in the creatures you have made. Remind me that they are a part of the wondrous chain of life and that all creation is intertwined: What hurts nature, hurts me. Teach me again that you look at all you have made and say, "It is very good."

🐛 January 31

Read 2 Corinthians 3:17-18.

I cannot believe it, but I have turned into one of those shameless grandmothers who show pictures of naked (and clothed) grandchildren to everyone who will stop long enough to look and listen. This morning I had coffee with an old friend I haven't seen for a while and—you guessed it!—it wasn't ten minutes before we were both exchanging photograph folders and cute stories of our grandbabies and their amazing development.

As corny as that is, I know the reason grandmothers the world over are so silly is the deep, profound truth that life is such a miracle, such a wonder, that no scientific advances can explain away its glory. And we grandmothers are, of all creatures, most blessed because we now have the time, the perspective, and the experience to pay attention to this amazing wonder.

When we were young mothers, we were so intense and so intent on mothering that sometimes we felt guilty for just meditating, basking in the glory of the wonder. Or, more likely, we were too exhausted. When the time for meditating came, we took a nap for survival! But now I am a grandmother, and without shame I bask in the glory. I think, too, that you remind me of the promise that we will go from glory to glory. So if you are so lately come from God, "trailing clouds of glory," as Wordsworth once said, maybe I am closer to the reality of going back to God, embracing clouds of glory. Thanks to you, I'm getting a head start.

Would anyone like to see some pictures?

Thank you, Lord, for allowing me one of the greatest experiences of human existence—the gift of beholding and holding my child's child. With this child you are leading me from glory to glory, tearing the veil from the illusions of this world. May I, in turn, lead this child in the path of everlasting life.

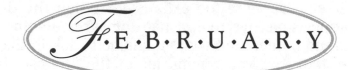

The Promise of New Life

Margaret Anne Huffman

❧

❧ *February 1*

Read Isaiah 46:4.

Standing at the window, boots laced and parka zipped against the snowstorm, I debated going to town.

With snow pelting the windows, it's easy to understand why cheery Valentine's Day comes in February, the month a friend of mine calls "Tuesday of the year." And just as this celebration of the heart is so happily received on cold, cabin-fever days, so, too, is grandmothering, which often comes when "snow" appears on our hair.

For many of us, this month, like middle age, has little of the excitement of first snowfalls nor the giddy relief of the last ones. And then into February comes red-hearted love; into our middling lives come grandchildren, turning snowdrifts into castles, blizzards into adventures, cabin fever into companionship, and middle age into joy.

Energized by anticipation of the grandchildren's weekend visit, I headed for town. Halfway up my lane, I met the mail carrier, who was delivering a package from a friend: paper white bulbs to bloom early. Spring, even in pale February sun.

Like these whispery white, fragrant flowers, grandchildren bloom into our days, reminding us that even in this "Tuesday" month, we can be visited by joy.

Venture with me into this middle-month, middle-age wonderland, inviting God to come with us as we make paper-white angels in the snow, lying side by side with grandchildren come to lead us into spring.

Thank you, God, for grandchildren, who are like flowers in the snow.

🌑 February 2

Read Psalm 139: 5*b*, 13-15.

Journal entry: February 2

My grandbaby just moved, a whispering greeting to her mother on this, the second day of the month of love. And never have I felt more loved than this winter, wrapped up in the promise that, come summer, I am going to be a grandmother. It is an unexpected bonus.

Words from my journal, read today over the shoulder of a little lady who loves to hear tales of her beginnings. And Mammaw is only too happy to oblige, snuggling us in a quilt before the fireplace, Nutmeg Dog and the cats on our feet.

She was not supposed to happen, medically speaking, and yet here she is. She was knit that winter beneath her mother's surprised heart. Her brother, my stepgrandson, was complete when we met, but we enjoy knitting him together in all our hearts in stray strands left from a late introduction.

"Mammaw," she says now, "I want to pick," pointing to the snowy yard empty of any hint of pepper and tomato plants she "harvested" last summer nor roses she picked. "Where are them?"

"Waiting beneath the snow," I explain.

"Sleeping?" she asks.

"Sleeping," I agree.

The flip side of the winter covering my wooded riverbank

garden is the promise of new life—the expected, like roses and peppers; the unexpected, like grandchildren—hidden now, like roots and bulbs, to unfold in new seasons.

Blanket us with your loving hand, Lord, as snow on sleeping gardens.

February 3

Read Jeremiah 29:11.

His grandmother's pantry was a dark, scary cave, my husband recalls, shivering even from a forty-five-year distance. The only good thing about it was the battered tin cookie canister sitting on a shelf. He was, he confesses, always torn about that pantry: hungry for Grandma Nellie's cookies and scared to death at what he feared "guarded" them.

With him treading carefully in her wake as she took a few dark steps to the light chain, they retrieved the cookies together, treats in the darkness.

Pondering that memory and looking around the dark corners of our sprawling house in the shadowy woods, I got tiny flashlights for our grandkids to put beneath pillows when visiting overnight.

There *are* dark valleys of shadows in life where monsters might lurk, waiting beyond the light to pounce. When our grandchildren hesitate, instead of scolding or pushing them, let's slip a flashlight into one small hand—ours in the other—and go with them into the shadows.

In a flashlight beam is a beginning place to understand that when God, like grandmothers, has "special treats" that require our grandchildren to enter "scary" places—places such as new schools and neighborhoods, new families, new jobs—there is Someone there to turn on a light for them.

Dear Lord, thank you for not ridiculing our fears. Help us respect the terrors of children, to whom monsters are as real as those on the front pages of our lives. Be the light guiding us, young and old.

_____

Read Isaiah 43:1*b*.

I am named for both of my Tennessee grandmothers—Margaret and Annie—and, in fine Southern tradition, I use both names, for I am a blend and don't want to waste a drop of either.

One grandmother kept a cane fishing pole and straw hat in the trunk of her Cadillac—just in case fish were biting. She cured country hams in the attic of her elegant home and sent me salt-savory pieces. Her cream candy is legendary, as is her humor, kindness to cats, and irrepressible spunk.

The other grandmother bought shoes that didn't quite fit—not only because she couldn't resist sales, but also because she knew someone needy could use them. She *gave* piano lessons—for if some impoverished but musical child she met riding on a city bus or walking past her house couldn't pay, she swapped small chores for lessons. Some star pupils never paid a cent.

I miss both of them, and I hug their memory about me like an old quilt each time I use my name. I search for shoes to share and a cream candy recipe to replace the one a stroke stole from Granny's memory so that I can pass these, like family names, on to my grandchildren, heirs abundant.

Thank you for whispering our names daily, Lord.

❦ **February 5**
_____

Read Proverbs 12:10 *a*.

I can't read my computer screen; Annie Cat is sitting in front of it. How the grandbaby loves her. "I hug her," she says, doing just that. And Nutmeg Dog is curled on my cold feet. How my fifth-grade grandson loves them, too—his first friends in this step-grand house.

I enjoy sharing my four-legged friends with grandchildren, both as joy *and* responsibility. So I had not a leg to stand on when I discovered the grandbaby stirring dry dog food into the dog's water and feeding it to the bemused dog. Her dripping whiskers indicated she'd taken the damp food in the spirit it was offered. "I feeding her, Mammaw," she explained so proudly, so damply. I patted both of them on the head and mopped up the leftovers.

In a world where life is less and less connected to earth and critters, a big, fat, tortoise-shell cat on my computer and a damp dog on my cold feet help me teach of things past, of bonds and tending animals which, some say, were the first to say "Nowell" on that long-ago stable day.

Pets are blessings any day, especially one as winter-dreary and cold as today. As I told the grandkids on our way to a good read on the couch, it's going to be a "three-dog night."

Reconnect us to our earthy side, Lord; for it is good, as are all your critters.

February 6

Read 1 John 3:16.

At 11:00 A.M. I got the call; by 1:10 P.M. I was airborne, mentally checking off all that was left undone behind me and wondering what I'd packed.

"Have to do" items shrank behind me along with familiar hometown scenes as I flew north, skimming the clouds at 35,000 feet, to take care of an ailing grandbaby and her equally bronchial mom.

What a joy to be needed, to have something as substantial to offer as dishwashing hands, a storytelling lap, and my sure-to-cure chicken wild rice soup. My longing to live closer increased with each mile we covered; how I wished that helping out need not be a pilgrimage.

Yet soon there I was . . . but she was not. "Too sick," her dad explained, shuttling me home in a hurry. Mother-and-daughter coughs welcomed me. Tossing coat and suitcase aside, I happily jumped into sickroom chaos, as cheery as only a long-distance Mammaw come to help could be. I was needed.

I'd forgotten just how short nights with a croupy toddler can be, for they are short. Groggy from dozes between her coughing spasms and soggy from vaporizer mist, I lullabied her about grandmas flying on rainbow-strung clouds to bring chicken soup and hugs to make it all better.

Being needed: the perfect benediction for any day.

What joy it is, Lord, to give of myself for my grandchildren.

February 7

Read Isaiah 66:13 a.

"Fixing once, fixing twice, fixing chicken soup and rice," I sang to myself in a raspy croak, borrowing a line from the book I'd been reading to the still-coughing granddaughter, who now had an ear infection.

Same song, but second verse, for now I, too, was sick. In a feverish haze, I drove to the doctor, sat up nights coughing in duet with the grandbaby, and fixed all of us comfort foods that had soothed her mother and grandmother at her age. Cinnamon toast was an instant hit—heredity perhaps? And she shared some crusts with her ailing mom and grandma.

Bathing fevers away—three generations worth—connected me like dot-to-dot pictures to sleepless nights of long ago when I paced a worrying path around sick children.

We were mending, though, avoiding serious complications—unless you count the fact that Mammaw couldn't seem to master all the words to the "Baby Songs" tape, their melodies swarming in my throbbing head like moppet mosquitoes. I played, read, and rocked the baby, marveling at my patience and humor, which were in shorter supply when I was child-tending full time.

Have I improved with age? Possibly. It is more likely, however, that I found energy simply from knowing I was just a "temp."

Help us mend, Lord, as we help one another.

🌱 *February 8*

Read Psalm 127:1a; 133:1.

What house is large enough to hold two families? It was a question to ponder as bronchitis, croup, ear infections, sleepless nights, and, in my case, the mother-in-law lingered beyond anyone's first estimate.

Even though I cherish antiques, I don't know if I would've been a good "antique" woman. Many old ways might not suit me—particularly generations sharing homes, as do nearby Amish. "Grandparent" houses are cozily and thriftily connected to the main farmhouses. I've always admired their sprawling homesteads.

Throughout history, many families have shared homes. Yet most families have lopped off these connections, leaving us woefully out of practice at community.

Community is a skill quickly mastered, however. So we drifted into a satisfactory routine of sharing chores, television "zapper" (remote), and baby. Roles remained clear; joy in sharing them, strong. My "reward" was a compliment from my son-in-law, who teased that I was "not too bad to have around."

Sharing adult children's lives is joy *and* education. I admired both daughter and son-in-law all over again as I observed them working, relating, laughing.

What house is large enough to hold two families? One in which, in God's design, people make themselves fit, like a hand in a glove, each finger in its own space; together, creating a warm, handclasping welcome.

Lord, we are grateful to know you anew in community.

❦ **February 9**
_____

Read Philippians 4:13.

Fax machines might have been devised by working grandmothers who are away from home tending grand-babies and needing to meet long-distance deadlines. If somebody else hadn't thought of it, I would have, for even as I, a journalist, was ladling medicines and simmering soups, I was also writing articles with deadlines. My notes were at home, ditto my office; my heart, however, was here, with a Fax machine connecting me and my work.

Long-distance speaks not only about miles but also about styles of living: We are a fragmented people. As I parcelled myself out in pieces of time for the grandbaby—time to nap, time to tend my own bronchitis, and time to write—I became even more impressed by how today's young parents mentally and emotionally juggle more than one important task at a time.

Taking a cue from what they do so well, I became more intentional about what to do *during* my time segments, so that when I was *with* the grandbaby, I was *truly with her.* Too often we are not present for one another; instead, we are mentally and emotionally already on the next task.

The smell of menthol will forever remind me to retrieve my scattered thoughts and reassemble them into an attentive, listening heart, giving steady, eye-to-eye sharing. Too soon grandbabies seek long distances on their own, and there is no way to fax a hug.

Give us strength, Lord, to prioritize, focus, and accomplish the important things before us. With you at our side, all things are possible.

February 10

Read Matthew 7:7-8; 1 Corinthians 7:7*b*.

Throw pillows make great wheels, turning 'round and 'round on trains, cars, bulldozers, or even candy-making machines. I hadn't thought of that in years, until my recovering granddaughter "drove" me to the doctor. She played all the parts, and I dutifully "took" the medicine she invented. As she bustled about, I was reminded of her Uncle Rob's long-ago candy-making machines that used every pillow, chair, and pan we owned plus the vacuum cleaner hose. Thank goodness I didn't overly fret at the mess.

Child's play, or essential building blocks in the mysterious realm of creativity? Of invention?

Without room to expand their imaginations, children remain dwarfed in spaces as narrow as our neat lives and imaginations—grown stiff and arthritic from disuse, not age.

Our world needs so much, and each new generation carries the promise of being the source of solutions. May we lovingly tend the children, happily sipping their "medicines" and sampling "candy." The child/doctor who concocts healing potions of raindrops, dandelion fluff, and imagination may be onto something, for that child is tuned in and turned on to possibilities.

How grateful I am to be a child's first patient, first customer, first passenger.

From your gift of imagination, Lord, inventions can come bringing abundance, healing, and sustenance for our world. Bless the playful process.

February 11

Read Philippians 1:3-4.

She cried, "Mammaw, Mammaw," and I leaped from my bed to hurry to her, not realizing until my feet hit the cold floor that I was dreaming. She may have been crying "Mammaw," but I couldn't hear her: I was back home, snug in my own bed—with a broken heart.

Yet even if we lived in the same town, I couldn't be her primary caregiver, for grandparents are one place removed from that parental place of honor. Parents and children learn as they go; too much grandmothering interrupts, as a stick in bike spokes.

It is, I confess, a luxury to again sleep through nights, uninterrupted by a little one's leftover cough; it is a luxury to finish reading a book, writing an article, and taking a bath or nap without little soft hands leading me back into her agenda for me.

Loneliness is a luxury, too, for I know even as I mope through these first days back in my own routine that, like February bronchitis, it is only temporary: She and her family are coming next week. I chuckle as I snuggle back in my own Bappaw-warm bed. You'd better rest, Mammaw.

Lord, we thank you for the chance to help, the time to come home, and the anticipation of the next time.

February 12

Read Isaiah 11:6*b*.

Lulled by routine and vague melancholy as I approached my middling years, I concluded I was pretty well a "done deal." I had had my chances; taken my best shots; and collected memories, plaques on the wall, and stories to tell. Passion for daily tasks, joy in the doing and being, was faded and slow, like tapes played at the wrong speed.

I couldn't even work myself up to a midlife crisis, for it felt more like a midlife bore—rather like this month, stuck between the excitement of first snows and the exuberance of spring.

In the smile of a small blond grandson and the grasp of an infant granddaughter's finger, however, I have been galvanized into movement and light; and I haven't stopped since—changing, changing, changing. And not just diapers, either. For, like the abundant life promised, I am rediscovering a world I'd grown sluggish about; it is reflected back to me in the joy these grandchildren bring with them.

Grandchildren are blessings for middle age, like the doves that visited Noah, telling him to keep on sailing. And so shall I, realizing that there are so many new shores to visit, so many new tales to tell, so many new directions in which to dance.

Lord, if you hadn't sent grandchildren, then there would've been doves of another form. You are so fond of sending children to lead us into the dance of light and life. Thank you.

February 13

Read Ezekiel 11:19a.

As I perspire my way through this current life change, my moods are not much better than my two-year-old granddaughter's. Neither of us is who we once were, or who we are yet to be. And judging from the stubborn jut of our jaws, neither of us is going forward without a struggle. We are at such difficult ages!

In a "flash" of insight, I see myself in her perplexed eyes, for we both are struggling with independence. It is grief-producing and scary, leaving us contrary—but not just to cause trouble, as some mistakenly criticize.

To go forward is to leave warm nests behind. We do, but we don't want to. While we are curious about the next stage, we cling to this one and its familiar blankies, diapers, breasts, childbearing, vigor, firsts.

Yet we want to be on our own, even as we fear it. Watch, for today I am like a two-year-old. She ventures down our long halls and scattered rooms only to keep coming back to see that Mom and Dad are within calling distance. Watch as I, a changing "middler," keep going back to check that my husband, children, and youth are nearby.

Give us a new heart and a new spirit, Lord, as we look eagerly and fearfully forward.

February 14

Read 1 Corinthians 13.

What *is* love? Today is the day to ponder this question.

I have a "love letter" from my granddaughter affixed by a gazillion star stickers to my desk and a clever story written by my grandson on the refrigerator. They both work: I feel loved.

There are as many different ways of loving as there are lovers and lovees. I can barely see love's faint outline beneath today's snow around the blue ash tree outside my windows. It is a flower bed that was designed and dug last fall by my husband and me, who are poles-apart "landscapers" and lovers.

Beginning on opposite sides of the big tree, he brought a level, tape measure, and string to lay out a precise circular bed; I brought a hoe to hack out weeds in an approximate oval, mulch to dump, and spring bulbs to poke in random pattern. Our intentions were the same: a beautiful spring flower bed. Our methods couldn't have been more different.

61

Love is about respecting, negotiating, and even designing flower beds. Love is as simple as grandchildren live it with stickers and stories; it is as complex as their grandparents' marriage.

The joyful reaping will soon be evident in early crocuses peeping up in our lopsided flower bed, planted there last fall by both our loving hands.

Help us, Lord, love one another as open-handedly and accepting as do our grandchildren; love is a sticker-studded delight.

🍃 *February 15*

Read Proverbs 6:20-22; Psalm 144:12.

Doctor, meteorologist, mommy, daddy, zookeeper, preacher—I hosted them all this weekend as the grandchildren played "pretend" at being grown-up. Another time, one was a baseball player; the other, a lady going to work, complete with baby to tell, "Bye, Mommy will be back."

I am accumulating props for their play with a hat and tie here, a cast-off stethoscope and lensless glasses there. As their experiments widen along with their horizons, so, too, will the clutter in my closet.

A grandmother's closet is a treasure trove of possibilities, a safe place where children may try on many different "hats" as they experiment with roles, ideas, relationships, and careers—some of which probably are not going to work out. I, for instance, once had a wannabe lion tamer at my house.

Parents are sometimes a little uneasy that kids' dress-up choices will be life-binding, but we grandmothers can recall these parents' own childhoods—when to dream is to be, to pretend is to prepare and rehearse. Even today, as I gently remind, it is good to keep your options open, for you never know when there will be a great need for lion tamers.

Lord, bless this cluttered closet of possibilities children can draw from, like life-giving water from a well. Flexibility and hope are suitable accessories for any future role.

February 16

Read John 10:10*b*.

This year I'm not giving up anything for Lent, the forty-day period of preparation for the Resurrection Event of Easter. Instead, as my grandkids show me in their generosity, I will be adding as many new and creative experiences to my life as I can.

This is the season—the season of Lent and the season of grandmothering—for expanding, not shrinking; for adding onto and taking in more, not doing without and passing by. I am not speaking in materialistic terms but, rather, in *spiritual* terms. Shouldn't we prepare ourselves and, by example, our grandchildren for more joy, not less? Isn't this the way our life has become since the story of Easter, since the advent of grandchildren: more joy, not less?

I've changed my mind. I *am* giving up something for Lent: the thought that God wants me to have less—not less materialistically, but less spiritually. If that were so, why would I have been given these heirs to expand my seasons—especially this season of renewed hope—into abundance and overflowing cups? From this abundance may I draw the strength to grow creatively in God's love.

Help us, Lord, to know Lent as a season of abundance.

February 17

Read John 16:24*b*.

"Is it okay, Grandma?" she asks before eating a leftover Valentine candy heart. "Yes," I answer, "thank you for asking."

The question is one we applaud each time the little lady asks it before doing something questionable or perhaps unsafe. We have to teach little ones to take care of themselves, body and soul.

At first I worried that we were making her indecisive; now, however, I think she is simply gathering more information for the running of her own life. She seeks opinion, not permission.

The most important information she's picked up from her questioning is the knowledge that asking her family is okay; she is learning that we are approachable. Therefore, we must ration our disapprovals, keeping the "not okays" for important things such as putting pencils in electrical outlets, tasting someone else's medicine, and chasing balls into the street.

After years spent with kids of all ages, I finally understand how important it is to keep them not only safe but also inquisitive and willing to share the decision-making process with us. Only then can we show them how we pray in Jesus' name, asking for guidance. If we grandmas aren't approachable, then how can we expect grandkids to believe God is?

When our grandchildren come to you, Lord, with their questions, grant them an active conscience for governing their own choices.

February 18

Read 1 John 4:19.

I had the honor of being a "borrowed" grandmum for a Scottish lassie during our recent vacation to Scotland. She was the daughter of our landlady and landlord on the Isle of Arran, the same age as our grandson, and a wonderful companion in our lives. I have a letter ready to mail to her today.

I was honored at her informal assumption that I was a kind of "Mammaw" for her, too. Her natural grandparents live a long distance away, and I happily filled that small gap in her island life; I know what it is to have miles between generations.

We played games, babysat together, and swapped Scottish for American words, such as *brolly* for umbrella and *jumper* for sweater. We had a great time, and I discovered that I am not only a Mammaw to my own brood, but also a generic grandmother who fits into the four corners of the world.

There is a universal love of a grandmother that gives her the ability to play checkers and games all afternoon without letting on that she is falling over from jet lag. There is a universal appeal of grandchildren the world over with their open minds and outreaching hands. There is a universal connection that draws both together over language, culture, and distance barriers. We borrowed "grands" recognize one another by our ready smiles and unconditional love on both sides of any sea.

Thank you for being the bridge that connects all of us, Lord. Keep our hands always reaching to one another.

February 19

Read 2 Corinthians 5:17; Philippians 4:13.

My grandson and I made a beeline for seats in front of the airplane wing. Fortunately, we were ahead of the Sunday evening pack who were hot on our heels because, thanks to traveling with a child, I got special treatment—as if the journey itself weren't special treatment enough, I thought as we flung ourselves aloft into the wintry sky, homeward bound. Homeward, at least, for me. He, child of divorce, was like a gypsy between campfires, returning to his mom's from his dad's where I, too, had spent the weekend.

What a privilege to travel life with a grandchild; what a double-dip treat to be extended the invitation to be grandmother by a child who so easily could have decided he already had enough grandparents and didn't need another rather zany one, anyhow. But he does!

Last Christmas, comrades in change, he and I received matching BB guns—for target shooting only! Together we draw a bead on our cardboard targets; together we "guard" the wildlife that live in our woods, as vulnerable and apt to shy away as a small boy once was. Now, though, he is as much at home here in the woods as in the planes that take him here and there.

Thank you, Lord, for your gift of change. Bless our travels between who we used to be and who we can yet become.

February 20

Read Matthew 10:29-31.

"I don't believe in babies!" her grandson shouted, tears splashing down his freckled cheeks. "I don't even want a baby sister," he sobbed.

Ah, such betrayal. He'd wanted a puppy, and they'd brought him a baby sister instead.

Another grandmother friend shared with me a cloudy-day picture that her grandchild had drawn for her. Above a house overflowing with round-faced babies, he'd filled the sky with clouds. "God lives there," he'd explained sadly, "and I want to go be with him. My house is too crowded with sisters."

It is a simple, scary sadness, and one we can reach into our own memories of sibling ambivalence and rivalry to understand. Even as we reason with our grandchildren when introducing a new brother or sister, we can sympathize, for it *is* difficult to love a bunch of people equally.

Can we grandmothers, then, offer extra laps for displaced big brothers and sisters? Sure, for we can be special outings and moments geared for nonbabies only; we can provide nuggets of reassurance, such as cookies in apron pockets for their insecurity. Most of all, we can let them know we understand, for laps are difficult to share.

No matter our age, Lord, we fear we are not special enough to be guaranteed love. Is it any wonder, then, that we vie for your attention, as if pleading "Me first, me first!" Calm our jealousies, Lord, and remind us that you know even the number of hairs on our heads. Your lap, like a grandma's, is ample to cradle us all.

❦ February 21

Read Genesis 21:1-7.

Although we were only a few years apart, I was expecting a grandbaby while she was expecting a baby of her own. This time, she said with her wry, radiant smile, the leap in her heart, the quickening of unexpected joy, mingled with heartburn and tiredness from this surprise middle-age pregnancy.

The impending arrival came complete with a layette of mixed feelings, for the dismantled crib was awaiting grandchildren; likewise, the mother-lap for childbearing days was no more—or so she and her family thought.

Yet she's in good company of many older moms who celebrate later maternity with steadfast, well-prepared joy. I chuckle at the "news" that having later babies makes, for have times really changed? Is this a "new" trend?

Perhaps, instead, we have caught up with our common-sense selves, for not so long ago, babies were born throughout a woman's life, not just in her youth. Once again we are considering all our creative options.

So I celebrate for her and her now-toddler, even as I mourn a little for myself. I know that now is a changing time when I move beyond who I once was, like clearing out a closet to make room for who I am now: a lover of babies and singer of lullabies—this time a beautiful generation removed.

Whenever I see a body blossoming, ever-creating Lord, so does my soul, cradling both memories and promises that come in the seasons of being woman.

🍂 February 22

Read Psalm 121:8.

Something old, something new, something borrowed, something blue.

Bike, tires, helmet, fenders: old, new, borrowed, blue.

A friend gave me her son's outgrown blue bike, which will become an eleventh-year birthday present for a grandson to ride when he comes here. Like passport stamps, he has bikes at all of his houses, for as a child of remarriage, he has several different homes; different childhoods.

I first thought the blue birthday bike was about recycling, and it is. Already he has taken this lesson to heart—even teaching me. But it also is a gift about movement; about mobility; about moving on and away from the confines of this yard, this hillside, this neighborhood, this childhood.

And as he pedals away, my prayer is that he takes with him an everyday faith shown him by a blend of family who love him and send along a piece of themselves each time he leaves our sight on a bright blue bike.

Whirling in the spokes as they go 'round and 'round is my constant prayer: "Be with him, Lord. Be with him, Lord. Be with him, Lord." A recycled faith: the most sensible.

Stay with this special grandson, Lord, for you are our link to him as he travels between spots on the map of his life. Be the highway upon which he moves, the compass points he consults as he ventures beyond our care.

🕊 *February 23*

Read Proverbs 17:17.

No one can convince me that one reason a friend's baby is doing so wonderfully well in neonatal intensive care isn't her grandmother's steadfast vigil. As I chatted with this grandmother today, I wondered where she gets her energy.

Perhaps I, and others who have an easy grandparenting "job," can help her keep it, for surely there are things that we who have nonspecial-needs grandchildren can do for those who don't—besides praying, of course, and offering that first sympathy and support.

How about supper? a friend suggested, recalling a neighbor who traveled each day to the rehabilitation center bedside of her granddaughter to feed her supper in order to lift her own daughter's burden. *Each day.* In the face of such devotion, her friends provided a weekly supper for this special grandmother, so that nourishment was passed all around, even in the simplest form of macaroni and cheese and meat loaf.

We are a unique sisterhood, we grandmothers; and we understand that to help another bear a burden is little burden at all. One shared is not nearly as heavy as one carried alone. May we keep holding hands beneath the weight of our burdens.

Lord, be with those of our sisterhood who are helping their hurting children and grandchildren. Send us along; we can help, too.

🕊 February 24

Read Philippians 4:8-9.

I don't have a solution, so perhaps it isn't fair to complain; but aren't there too many choices for kids these days? The main reason I care? Simple: Will my grandchildren have time for me—without an appointment?

My friend's grandchildren don't, and today, over cups of lemon tea, we have been "worrying the problem" like dogs with a bone. Is family time a luxury only a few can have today?

Yet, which of their wonderful activities would I want the kids to give up? Even though they "run, run, run," like the characters in a first primer, they're usually running to activities that keep them current, smart, and literate—and even to activities that are grounded in faith, for churches, too, pluck kids from home and play.

There is no easy answer to this matter of busyness, and I guess we'll adjust to living with time-pressured grandkids. My biggest worry: Should we? If not, what else can we do? No answer comes quickly to mind.

Lord, help the grandchildren find time to visit us, talk on the telephone, or drop us a note, for we yearn to be much more than a stop-off on their rounds. Help us all slow down, choose wisely, and spend time where it matters. We adults are, after all, the ones from whom the young are learning how to run, run, run.

February 25

Read 1 John 4:7-10.

Bappaw-to-be—although he didn't know he'd be called that—listened to the grandbaby's heartbeat during a doctor's visit with our daughter several years ago. And in the doctor's office, as his ears filled with the drumbeat of promised life, he began bonding with a granddaughter who now calls him long-distance at least once a week after she wakes up early with a need to hug Bappaw (as she explains to her sleepy Mom and Dad).

What joy it is to share grandparenting with a man who can cry as he holds a tiny newborn he's known only through a heartbeat and sawdust dreams; with a man who, like a carpentering father before him, knows about building for children; with a man who before her birth built a changing table from cherry wood harvested from our land; with a man who tonight is creating sawdust again as he builds a child-size table and chairs for a birthday surprise.

I can't watch this carpentering scene without thinking of Jesus' father, who had young children underfoot as he worked. Perhaps, in time, he also had grandchildren to play among the wood shavings and papery wood curls and, in the doorway, as I am now, a grandmother watching with a lump in her throat.

Belonging and bonding are such mysteries, Lord, and we know them in powerfully new ways as grandparents. We are grateful that you are the connecting link in our bonds of love.

February 26

Read Psalm 36:5.

Movie scenes in which folks are running to catch trains bring a tear to my eye along with a chuckle these days, for we did just that to meet a grandbaby who was never supposed to have been.

"We're on our way to the hospital; this is IT!" called our daughter who lives another state away. Having heard this numerous times before, with my heart leaping into my throat until all problems had been avoided, I wasn't sure how to respond. Yet the baby was late; perhaps this *was* it.

"We're going. Can we make the nine o'clock train?" asked the grandpa-to-be, echoing my yearning to bridge the waiting distance.

With workplaces notified and clothes tossed into suitcases, we sped to the train station, saved only by the train's habitual tardiness.

I stood guarding suitcases piled on the sidewalk. "A baby granddaughter!" he shouted as he burst through the doors of the business where he had asked to use the phone.

Within minutes, we were cradling this new little one, railway grit sluiced away in our tears of joy. Those first moments—a family legend now, complete with photos—have forged a bond even distance cannot dislodge.

Thank you, Lord, for being a traveling companion on our journeys to see grandchildren; and thank you for guiding our grandchildren into the waiting arms of a loving family.

🍎 February 27

Read James 4:12.

I chuckled as I listened to a radio announcer speculate about love in the next century. I idly wondered what I will be wearing to grandchildren's weddings. Since one grandchild is a preschooler, another is in elementary school, and others are still dreams in my heart, I admit to a bit of premature fashion planning!

Always one to look ahead in case I can find something to worry about, I began to wonder whom my grandchildren will marry. On the heels of that came a tidal wave of concern: Will they be persons worthy of my grandchildren?

And what will romance, marriage, and family be like by that time? I think of all the societal changes that have taken place just since I became a grandmother, and the pace of change shows no signs of slowing—even though I wish it would.

I fear the hatred that is keeping right in step with these changes—hatred of those who are different. And I wonder what it will take for us to support all families as they love one another, their offspring, and their Creator from unique, even out-of-the-ordinary homes.

The gift I hope to bring to grandchildren's weddings is a

world in which people do not point fingers at love or loved ones they don't like.

Help us, Lord, not to judge those who are different but to love all persons. With you at our side we can graciously and gracefully celebrate in love's future. Be with grandmothers of today's and tomorrow's unique families, for theirs can be a lonely celebration.

❦ February 28

Read Luke 10:30-37.

A friend's granddaughter showed up on her doorstep at Christmas, and she is still there.

The casuality of a messy divorce, the teenager had tried in the ways teens do to get attention; and as those ways so often lead, she went backward. She was in trouble at school, home, and church.

"Do you have any bunny scraps left?" she asked at the front door. "My old one is all worn out." She later told her grandmother that she had held on to the stuffed bunny her grandma had made for her during her little-girl years.

"All worn out." So, too, was the child—never mind that she arrived at grandma's in green hair, black leather, and near-starvation skinniness. Without a word, her grandmother drew her in the door and onto her lap where she sang soothing lullabies until they could figure out the next step.

We grandmothers can be a respite for the troubled young who wander through our lives if we will set aside our preconceptions about things such as green hair—which could mean as little as a passing fad or as much as a "go ahead" green light, urging "Grandma, help me."

Strengthen us, Lord, for the tending of hurting, often hurtful teens in our families. We can be their advocates for change and their companions in the process.

Wondrously Made

Margaret Anne Huffman

❦

❦ *March* 1

Read Romans 7:19; Isaiah 11:6-9.

March has come in like a lamb, but if experience is any teacher, it'll go out like a lion. Each year here in the Midwest, this month reminds us just how difficult it is for lions and lambs to occupy the same place!

It's a month rather like two-year-old grandchildren's moods, I thought this morning as I watched a little lady struggle with wanting to be a lamb and play with her dolly or wanting to be a lion and throw blocks.

As I was pondering this, the dog and cat got a little rough in their play before the fireplace and quit being friends, reverting to natural enemies who spit, hissed, and barked at each other.

So, too, do we all, with our complex dual selves, for it's tough being "both/and." Might it be easier to do away with one or the other? Yet would we really want months, moods, and people blanded into one-note songs? Not healthy, say the pros; a "flat" person is one to worry over.

So, as I told the baby while scooping her into my arms for a wild dance around the squabbling pets, we might as well learn to love our lions and our lambs; together, like this month, they create a delightful combination.

Help us cuddle both the lion and lamb within us so that they may become companions, not enemies; they are us.

🍒 March 2

Read Deuteronomy 28:6.

Our first house, an old rental, had two electrical outlets per room, only one of which worked. So in our new home, we put them everywhere!

We should've thought ahead to grandchildren, for I lugged home a huge sack of receptacle covers last month only to run out when half-finished. There was no time, however, to get more before the young family arrived; so, plotting at a child's height, I first covered the unobvious ones, barricaded unprotected others, and walked right behind our toddler granddaughter's every curious step, ready at a moment's notice to run interference.

I got them all covered this week only to discover I've short-circuited myself, breaking fingernails from prying one off just to vacuum!

A ten-finger set of broken nails would be worth it if I could stay at the grandchildren's heels, popping covers over all the dangers within range. Instead, however, I must teach them first about plugs, then streets, strangers, and all the other "uncovered" possibilities for injury, so that they can learn how to protect themselves.

There are, alas, not enough plastic covers in the world to keep them as safe as I yearn. Knowledge and a close-behind-you grandma is as good as I can do. May it be enough.

Go with grandchildren everywhere, Lord, into the awesome possibilities for trouble. Help them develop street smarts, but not cynicism and fear; knowledge, but not firsthand experience. Keep them safe.

❧ March 3

Read 1 Corinthians 13:13.

With a tilt of my head, I get a multiview of the world through my red-rimmed spectacles. Aim my vision a few feet to the right or left or too far away, and the world is blurry, for I am looking through the wrong spot on the lens.

Grandmothering—with all its accompanying limitations such as trifocal vision and stiff knees—also brings with it an absolutely clear picture of children and childhood: past, present, and future all in one.

I never saw it or believed it to be so when the children were young—and I was peering at them on the same level: daily family life. But having experienced it firsthand and now having the vantage point of a grandmother, I can see what parents cannot: The future arrives and the present becomes the past.

And it is good, very good.

We grandmothers can actually see the transitions and milestones that are, to parents, now merely anticipations, even dread. And we are living proof that there is life after children; that romance and noontime pleasures are real, attainable—yet another tilt to the lens.

We *know,* while parents, preoccupied with training wheels or learner's permits, are still struggling to *believe* that children do grow up and drive away and that we, still parents, are part of this revolving—from generation to generation.

Help us, Lord, grease the wheels for our grandchildren's journeys with faith, hope, and, most of all, love.

❧ March 4

Read 1 Corinthians 6:15.

I wish I had been there. Today my granddaughter, standing at the front of the sanctuary where her minister

76

father was leading the children's moment, suddenly stood up and announced, "I need to potty!" The sermon was parenthetical to that moment. Church members are still chuckling!

On the basis of this, I can see the handwriting on the wall for our upcoming family vacation. Care to guess how many potty seats Mammaw will be visiting at the beck and call of a small girl?

Yet I am glad to be present even at this very primitive transition, for we are nothing if not constantly changing, moving from one stage to another. First smiles, first words, first steps, first songs, first days as a "dry" big girl. In constant rebirths, our old passes away, yielding to new beginnings.

In addition to the simplification of life that her new status will bring, her unselfconsciousness about it pleases me more; and I am so relieved that she feels no shame. In a world where bodies are used to sell cars and good times, she is not likely to think hers is a commodity.

Lord, keep our sense of humor buffed and ready for such moments our grandchildren create. May we never inflict shame upon their innocent endeavors to grow up.

🍓 March 5

Read James 3:16.

I still don't know who will get to grandchild-sit this weekend for a friend's child who is caught in the crossfire of dueling grandparents.

There's nothing like a grandchild to make outlaws of some in-laws. Vying for "favorite," they talk about, put down, compete with, and keep tallies to outdo and undo one another with verbal slingshots.

And so this wise but sad young woman is rehearsing a way to say to both sides that a *loving* grandmother will help a grandchild best by finding something good in the other grandparents, not widening differences. If that doesn't work, I've promised to hold her hand when, heaven forbid, she will draw boundaries around her child to guarantee emotional safety from both opponents—a tally resulting in everyone losing.

This has been a good secondhand lesson for me. When a green-eyed monster taps *my* shoulder, I can shoo it away, knowing that a grandchild adored by *all* relatives is truly blessed.

Lord, help us respect others' rights to love and remind us that we'll get our turn.

March 6

Read Matthew 12:35a.

The centerpiece on my kitchen table is a bird feeder made by the hands of a proud, fledgling carpenter; we will hang it from the maple tree so I can see it as I write.

I prefer to "decorate" our part-log home with living things: plants, bags of birdseed in the hall, pawprints on the hearth, hand-thrown clay vases overflowing with last fall's leaves, yarn-entwined cans holding my pencils. I am rich with all the stuff—the treasures—grandchildren bestow.

Such "wealth" reminds me of two women. One, a former neighbor, had a white couch, white carpet, and pristine refrigerator. Her grandchildren weren't allowed to . . . well. . . do much of anything. The other is my grandmother, who kept drawings, stories, and creations made by me and her other grandchildren. I found them after her death and was warmed by the honor she gave my efforts, transforming them into treasures.

It is not surprising, then, that one of my most valued possessions is a trio of babies' teeth marks on an old wagon seat used as a table. It's just the right height for toddlers as they pull up, stand, and walk away. And so quickly they do, which is why I spotlight my refrigerator door art gallery and this bird feeder catching its light from just outside the window. These grandchildren's artifacts in my life are without price.

Lord, bless the fingerprinted spots of my life where grand-children are leaving traces of their love scribbled around my heart.

🍂 March 7

Read Matthew 5:9.

I am so tired; I can barely count out two scoops of sugar for my tea, much less balance the checkbook. It reminds me of mothering. This time, however, I've only had pneumonia, not kids.

I used to call this condition "mush brain." No doubt the name came from the bottomless bowls of oatmeal I fixed during those years.

Yet women get "mush brain" not only from cooking oatmeal but also from raising kids alone and being away from interesting people, uplifting conversation, and challenges greater than getting oatmeal out of a baby's hair and camouflaging vegetables. It is the first symptom of burnout for the fortunate, because time cures it; for some, however, it is the first step toward child abuse.

I'm especially aware of this because a young acquaintance is so "mushed out" that she is just about to hit her children; she already spanks too hard and too often, she confesses. I need to intervene, but how?

Can we, the mothers, mothers-in-law, grandmothers, and friends, do anything to help these pre-abusers not feel so isolated and so vulnerable to avalanches of oatmeal and hopelessness?

We can volunteer for a "Mom's Day Out" program or a prenatal clinic; we can babysit. Whatever it takes. Caring is the best prevention. With all of us helping, child abuse can be wiped out in our lifetime.

Make us instruments of your family peace, Lord.

❦ March 8

Read John 20:1.

Easter is approaching, and I've just returned from giving a church program focusing on stones; for to consider Easter is to decide what to do about stones rolled in front of the openings of our lives.

Midway through my talking I had to pause and laugh, explaining that as my hand reached in my jacket pocket, I encountered small stones left from the grandbaby's latest visit. She had cooked up a stew of driveway stones in an old kettle, and, of course, Mammaw dined on many helpings! I told them that I wish those were the only stones ahead for any grandchild, who sometime will not be chosen for the play, the team, or the guest list.

Our grandchildren will be picked on, teased, and taunted. They will, along the way, gather a pocketful of stones of rejection. This is where we, in our already-tried-and-tested lives, come in. We can help them deal with the pain of rejection, for a grandmother's solace is okay for even a wounded grown-up grandchild.

Let us send them back into the fray with a small pebble from our yards or driveways to carry as a reminder of the obstacles that can be rolled away—like a big stone once was.

Put your shoulder to the rock, Lord, and help us roll stones from the grandchildren's paths so they can move freely where you lead.

🍂 March 9

Read Proverbs 22:6; Matthew 7:20.

A three-way-mirror image of one another—grandchild, child, and mother—locked stares over the "great nap debate" today. Looking at the three of us deadlocked in hopeless debate, I collapsed in laughter.

The contest was lost before it was ever begun, for, as the saying goes, "The fruit doesn't fall far from the tree." If ever there were three stubborn women, each intent upon having the afternoon go her way, we were they.

Turning back the clock, I saw my child, now a mother, sitting on the bottom stairstep, so sleepy that she was tipsy yet assuring me she wasn't tired. Today, here is her sleepy girl using the same logic, the same stubborn eyes.

The "nap stalls" her mother used made the perfect nap time story. And, after negotiations, the littlest one and I curled in a quilt nest to "rest" (as I renamed it): a successful ploy I used years ago, too. Both baby and I got a nap, barely making it to the end of the story about her mother versus naps.

One thing today proved: parents can't teach their growing-up children everything—including the wisdom of afternoon naps. Some things have to wait. But they can do their best. One day the fruit of their labor will be seen!

Memory is such fun, Lord, especially the sharing of it with grandchildren who, like relay runners, are here to pick up their part of our family story. Help us include lots of laughter in the story as we participate in the rearing of these precious gifts.

🍂 March 10

Read Psalm 139:14.

Bappaw fixed French toast this morning. Our entire clan sat around the table, buttering and devouring. A son is a master cook; son-in-law, ditto. Both daughters know enough about cars, locks, drains, and tools to get by; and I can wield a sturdy hammer.

Doesn't "girl-guy" self-security begin in youth? Yes, with a yellow dump truck my granddaughter is driving; with meals a friend's grandson concocts; with sports and singing and tears and toughness for both.

Why are we so afraid when kids wander across gender borders we put in their way? Do we prefer stereotypes? Are *we* stereotypes?

Despite the psalmist's observation that we are all wonderfully made, we try to steer children and grandchildren into lopping off some parts of themselves. Security, however, comes not from limiting a child's development but from expanding it.

Yet mixed messages are sent, toys are withheld, subtle values are set. Girls, be nurses, and boys, be doctors; girls, rock dolls, and boys, build with blocks—as if some of the finest nurses aren't men and the finest doctors, women; as if some of the most nurturing parents aren't fathers and the most creative architects, women.

So at Grandma's house, let's stockpile blocks and baby dolls, kitchens and scrap lumber. Let's sew tool belts and aprons, letting the grandkids try on first one and then the other to discover their wholeness as holiness.

Help us not to live in stereotyped fear, Lord, and forgive us when we use limiting words.

🌿 **March 11**

Read 2 Corinthians 9:7.

"Wanna come with us?" she asks. "Want a chizbrgr? Frfries?"

Generosity is found, strangely and paradoxically, in the heart of a two-year-old, the most self-absorbed creature on earth—at least until adolescence. I am jolted by her sharing heart.

She wants us, invites us, to have what she has. She offers with open hands and "fixes" favorite foods for us; shares her books; lets us hold her Scotty Bear, Barney, and Big Girl Baby; and even invites us to rest on her quilt . . . until she no longer wants to. And with the quicksilver mind-change of a two-year-old, she erupts into a tearful declaration: "It's MINE!" As I look into her furious face, I see my reflection, for like her, I am both/and.

We all are both generous *and* stingy; sharing *and* snatching. Like her, we give with one hand and take back with the other. Unlike her, however, we are more civilized and faith-filled, at least in theory, and can swallow those "MINE" declarations—most of the time.

Lord, may we be as gentle with ourselves when we don't want to share as we are with these little learning ones, for it is hard to share. Keep us practicing, for like two-year-olds, we can, in time, do better. Right now, forgive our tightfisted reluctance to share.

March 12

Read Psalm 34:19-22.

One day you're visiting grandma; the next day you could be a full-time stand-in mother and father. At last count, there are more than three million children being raised by grandparents for various reasons.

If that is not tragic enough, a double whammy hit an acquaintance: Her daughter was murdered by an abusive husband. I'm looking at my assumptions through new eyes, for danger stalks along familiar, familial hallways.

In the aftermath of this event, I pray that my friend will find strength, for I don't know how women our age can find energy, wisdom, and time to do child rearing again.

And I weep in sympathy, for this time it will be so different. Tending little ones is done now with a broken heart. And what of those other grandparents, whose son pulled the trigger? Will they ever snuggle their grandchildren again?

Tragically, this family is not alone: Thousands of mommies are killed annually by daddies, leaving grandparents to pick up the pieces not only of their own lives but also of the little ones left behind.

You know who they are, Lord—the families who fight behind closed doors. Equip the grandmothers with vigilance and diligence. When that is not enough, support them as they are left with grief and grandchildren. Remind them that they may find refuge in you.

March 13

Read Psalm 139:14.

"It smells good," the grandbaby proclaimed, deeply sniffing the fragrance of a fire in our fireplace. Buried somewhere in her heart is that fragrance, along with the aroma of Bappaw's French toast and the green peppers she picked last fall and the sound of ice creaking on our river.

What smells and sounds remind you of your grandmother? For me, there is the perfume of fruitcake spices, magnolias, and mimosa in her yard; the pantry with its sewing machine oil, slightly damp mop, onions, and potatoes; the sound of her summer-hot roof pinging and her piano pupils practicing, inspiring me to practice; her voice reading scripture and saying a grace for fried chicken, fine weather, and forgiveness.

Our grandchildren, in their generous way, have given us back those childhood moments, reconnecting us to our senses. On the heels of that thought comes another: What will our grandchildren take from us to keep in a treasure chest of sensory moments? As the psalmist reminds us, we are "wonderfully made" by a generous God who intends that we live from an overflowing cup of senses. There is no finer place to do this than at Grandma's house—the one remembered or our very own.

Thank you, Lord, for memories stored in ears, hearts, fingers, and noses; we are relearning how to use them alongside the best smellers, listeners, and touchers in the world.

🍂 **March 14**

Read Psalm 65:5.

The shortest distance between me and the grandchildren is a straight line. The shortest span between their needs and my response is instant. No detours.

It has taken me years of mothering performed by the "just-a-minute" method to learn this intricate dance step between the needs of children versus mine. Now I don't make the grandchildren—or anyone—wait "just a minute" unless it is essential; now I quickly fulfill bargains struck or promises made. Now, I am more dependable.

Is it because now I also have more time? Is it because now I am more aware, more available? This is partly so, but mostly it is because I now understand those "waited minutes" tally up to a lot of time I wasn't really present for my children; a lot of minutes I was preoccupied and distracted. And I wish I had them back—not to always jump at every little "Mommy, come here," but to acknowledge the need instantly, negotiate for time to do whatever needs to be done, and then follow up with my presence when I agreed I would, not in "just a minute."

Unlike detours on country roads, the lives of kids and adults don't run in parallel lines. We may not arrive at the same destination if we don't travel together, avoiding detours wherever possible.

It takes just a minute, Lord, to answer a child who only needs acknowledgment. Help us respond quickly and with full attention, as you do.

❦ March 15

Read Luke 12:22-31.

The young mother, a friend's daughter, collapsed today beside her car, the engine still running after one of her daily car-pooling trips with the children—made *after* she gets home from a full-time job. Now Grandma has the kids while Mom recuperates from her busy life.

Myths of success abound, heaping upon our daughters, daughters-in-law, and granddaughters many options, many role models, and many things we want for them too.

Almost everyone believes women can have it all today: marriage, family, career, and a perfectly kept home with a perfectly landscaped yard and organic garden. We can even have perfect bodies thanks to gyms at the workplace. But how do we—especially these young mothers we older women raised to set accurate goals of achievement—determine what "all" is? When is it enough?

Perhaps we in the grandmother generation, who helped begin this wonderful tide of progress for women, can finish what we began by creating a more supportive network for the exhausted, overwhelmed, and overloaded. Central to this network needs to be discussion of how to make choices between all the wonderful possibilities we now have. While we were leading and inspiring, perhaps we forgot to mention the costs.

Lord, help us understand that to "have it all" does not necessarily mean to have it all at one time. Teach us patience and balance, reminding us that you will provide for our needs. And insist that we honor one another's choices.

❦ March 16

Read Luke 21:19; Proverbs 17:22.

I just remodeled my kitchen, tearing out a wall to make an eating bar, widening a window to see outdoors better, and putting down an indestructible, cleanable floor. In the process, I also made better arrangements to accommodate grandchildren and their grandmother klutz, for we are not far apart in our abilities to spill, drop, and splatter!

One of the first words the grandbaby learned at my knee was "Whoops!" I take it as part of my responsibility to help the grandchildren learn to be the first to laugh at themselves when they stumble and fall. It seems that my habits are contagious, so they'd best be prepared.

Laughing at ourselves is the first step in redemption, in redoing what we've managed to fumble and foul up. And, as the grandkids are teaching me as they make jokes out of accidental spills and dribbles, it takes imagination to be humorous in the face of your own foibles.

Lord, teach us not to take ourselves so seriously when we stumble and fall. We act as if there is no getting up and starting over. Is that why you send us in the wake of toddlers? To remind us through their giggly second tries to chuckle and go on? Good suggestion; help us to do it.

❦ March 17

Read John 13:34-35; Solomon 5:16b; 1 Corinthians 13.

Forming the base of the intricate creation of family is love between woman and man. Few things, however, can topple this wondrous coupling more quickly than having children. A few sleepless, colicky nights; mountains of laundry and clutter; and the constancy of kids' needs can knock the props out from beneath even the sturdiest union.

That's where we grandmothers come in: through the front door to babysit, bringing treats for grandkids and tickets for disheveled parents to enjoy a play, a ball game, a movie, dinner out, or even the circus in town. We can, with a little delicate balancing of our roles and intentions, shore up their foundations.

Advice, as my father often observed, doesn't hurt you until you take it. So I've always felt free to scatter my suggestions at will. The best bit of advice I offer parents is to go on regular dates—alone; snuggle on the couch; talk, talk, talk—and not always about the children.

Habits are difficult to break. Once a couple gets in the habit of focusing solely on the children, they one day find themselves strangers across the wide chasm left by empty chairs at the family table.

Despite hectic lives and the awesome project of building a stepfamily, I am down-on-my-knees grateful that my mate and I never quit being best friends through the construction; it's a wonderful habit.

Lord, we thank you for our special companions.

❤ **March 18**
_____

Read 1 John 4:11-21.

His favorite sandwiches were egg salad. As he sat in the shade of a plum tree, eating them from a tiny lunch box, he was as tall as the grandfather and uncles who'd taken their lunch boxes to work early that morning. He was one of them; he was included.

In the simple act of cutting a sandwich into triangles small enough to fit in a pint-sized lunch box and a small boy's hands, my husband's grandmother offered him assurance that he was special.

Like "Leap Frog," busy parents often jump over what their children need, not taking time to do little extra things—as little as sandwich triangles—that can make such huge differences. Grandmothers, however, can know in a glance what is needed, what to do, how to draw a small child to his or her fullest, tallest self.

Like a loving grandmother, God "leaps" over others' oversights, meeting us as little children who need to be reminded, "You are special; I care about you."

So I ask myself, What "triangle sandwiches" has God put in your hands? The answers are too numerous to count, but one is evident now: The privilege of having a loaf of bread in one hand, a sandwich-cutting knife in the other, and a tiny lunch box on the kitchen counter before me.

Love, in lunch box tradition, remains fresh when passed on.

Thank you, Lord, for seeking and finding us beneath the trees of childhood; send us into the lives of our grandchildren with love.

❦ March 19

Read Proverbs 2:1-10.

When was the last time you watched cartoons? What has happened to humor since I last did is not funny; it is scary. Violence masquerades as comedy.

Equally opposed to censorship and bad taste, I am caught trying to protect the grandchildren from the entertainment crossfire as both sides of the issue—controlling versus flaunting—aim legal points at each other. My worry is that television is many kids' favorite messenger; they consider the flickering screen reality for how to relate, love, and laugh.

Dare we grandmothers watch alongside our young viewers? And then, dare we talk, especially about sex? It's on all channels, but in a confusing conglomeration of sex-as-sales-gimmick and sexual issues of serious concern.

Banning such programs as "Something About Amelia" or "Roots" because they deal with violent themes (child sexual abuse and racial terrorism, respectively) is to miss the point; kids need information. Wouldn't it be better for us to screen prime time, comedy channels, and commercials and then discuss what we oppose and support? They need to learn *how* to choose, clicking past unhealthy shows when Grandma's not around.

As I reread this, I realize I've done it, too: confused violence with sex, switching subjects mid-paragraph. But as I "channel surf" this evening, I see why it's an easy mistake to make.

What passes as entertainment for our grandkids is no laughing matter, Lord; help us to guide them wisely.

March 20

Read Romans 15:1, 5, 7.

I don't know if I could love what seem to be unlovable strangers as well and as fairly as a friend of mine does her step-grandchildren.

At first glance, they appear to be intruders into an already balanced, perfect roster of in-laws and grandchildren. It *is* stressful, she acknowledges. But she's as straight as an arrow with them and herself, explaining that yes, the grandchildren who arrived first and have been around longer are treated differently: like old friends. And they, she assures, are new friends, who in time will become old ones, too. Differences are about time, not value.

That explanation works for me, and I am humbled by the size of her heart and the scope of her grandmothering arms, patterned as they are after a loving Creator who welcomes us whenever we arrive.

Although she was worried at first, she now sees them as prizes in boxes of Cracker Jack. In that reflection cast back to them, like an image in the mirror of love she holds up, I can see, amazingly, they are becoming just that.

Lord, help us hold up loving mirrors, even for those we do not readily recognize as lovable. If we see them as prizes, perhaps they will be.

March 21

Read Matthew 6:19, 25-31; Psalm 116:11.

It used to be, BG, that I let clothes hang beyond their season in my closet, with tags intact behind plastic garment bags. I was the original packrat, a hoarder of favorite things from soaps to soups to shoes. But now, AG, I open my closet doors and use all within sight.

BG: Before Grandchildren. AG: After Grandchildren. The boundary line is as bright and real as a shaft of sunshine falling across my floor. On one side is sensible, even if a bit unnecessary, saving and stockpiling. On the other side is an understanding that time passes so quickly that clothes and moments become quickly outgrown, outmoded; and that things unused—such as laughter, play, and adventures—grow musty and faded no matter how diligently we try to store them in protective packaging.

Things we use do wear out and need to be patched or replaced, but their blemishes are from use and pleasure, not dry rot.

A grandmother has experience with moths, which can chew a hole in the finest suit despite mothballs in the pockets. We also know that garments—moments, if you will—hung outdoors on a sunny day have the best chance of staying in good condition.

91

Hoarded objects and moments only collect cobwebs and dust, not the fine patina of happy, well-used memory—the best resource for days when they are finally gone.

Make us spendthrifts of our joy, Lord, instead of misers. Throw open our spirit closets to the sunlight of grandchildren and us at play.

❦ March 22

Read 1 John 3:18; 1 Peter 4:10.

Today marks the anniversary of my mother's death, a day on which I can't help contemplating those sad, imponderable "might have beens" with a mother I miss in different ways as my life follows a path she never saw me walk. For now I am a busy grandmother, and I know how much she would have enjoyed sharing in this adventure as great-grandmother.

She, too, enjoyed being a grandmother; likewise a long-distance one. Evidence of the special bond she had with my trio was unearthed when I cleaned out her belongings.

All of the kids were represented: photos, letters, every stick-figured picture colored and mailed, every carefully printed note. Always living far away from her, I worried that we didn't do enough to include her and that she might not have known how the kids felt about her.

Mother's overflowing boxes, however, told a different tale. They comfort me today as I write at my desk beneath her smiling photograph on my office wall. Her mother's photo is beside hers, and *her* mother's photo the next one over. It is a grandmothering lineage I am passing on from a beloved lady who went home too soon.

Help us remember, Lord, that little things do, indeed, mean a lot. They mean it all when sent from the loving heart of a grandchild straight to the heart of a long-distance Grandma.

Read Proverbs 31:15, 18, 21, 27.

What can we older generation do to honor and help our daughters, daughters-in-law, and granddaughters as they mother? Applause comes to mind, for they are doing wonderful jobs, both full-time stay-home moms and those moms who work in and out of the home.

A friend whose daughter stalled an outside career to tend young daughters has come up with an "applause": professional business cards emblazoned with "MOTHER" along with her address and phone number. How clever and right on the mark in times when staying home is an often difficult choice to make. The cards are for her daughter's fun-filled Easter basket, along with bubble bath, matinee tickets, and a gift certificate for professional house cleaning.

Full-time mothering deserves a line of print equal to that of what others do, for it is easy to overlook how out-of-the-loop these young mothers feel. Think back, I've reminded myself, to when I envied my peers who wore classy suits and made policy while I wore jeans and made tapioca pudding—and vice versa when I changed roles. In hindsight, I cherish those days; in hindsight, too, I recall how I wish I'd had a bit of applause.

I've decided to order some business cards for my daughter. And when I order them, I'm considering a set for me: "GRANDMOTHER." I'd be proud to carry them; grandmothering is a full-time love occupation.

Lord, bless all our work.

🍃 **March 24**

Read Ezekiel 34:11-16a.

She wandered to our table at the restaurant and, as I poised a pancake midair, explained that she was lost. A young man—a grandson, I assumed—quickly arrived to return her to her biscuits, gravy, and worrying family. As a daughter-in-law of an Alzheimer's sufferer, I recognized both her frightened stare and his sadness.

Like Little BoPeep, she had lost her grandchildren and didn't know where to find them. They are, knows her frustrated, grieving family and its counterparts the world over, the same place the rest of her has gone: into the vacant crevices of disease.

Explaining Alzheimer's to its sufferers' grandchildren is difficult, and I watch in fear and awe as friends become both caretakers and victims. Yet even young grandchildren can understand parts of this malady, for they know about being lost, needing a hand to hold, being afraid of the dark. They are surprisingly kind.

And they, like this grandson who retrieved his grandmother from the frightening maze of the restaurant, understand more readily than we frightened peers about shepherds coming to find the lost, no matter how stuck in a dark crevice they may be. Let us, in small ways, include the grandchildren in caring for these, perhaps the most lost of all of God's children.

Shepherd God, comfort those grandchildren who lose a grandparent down an Alzheimer's crevice. Retrieve the lost and take them to your fold.

❦ March 25

Read Matthew 19:14.

I was never wiser nor more profound than when chopping nuts, stirring in raisins, and drizzling molasses into brown bread batter. I was equally wise when pulling taffy, cutting out buttermilk biscuits, sealing fruitcakes, and canning watermelon rind pickles.

My grandmother's kitchen was my first forum; her

white enamel table, my first podium; and Mammaw herself, my first applauding audience. It was my first venture into a bigger world beyond my own home.

I always felt welcome and needed; I felt listened to and able to listen.

For into all those foods and fancies we stirred up, we were adding traditions of talking, of sharing feelings and experiences. These were the foundation of communication habits to come, rooted as they were in a deep faith that talking, like praying, was the best way of staying close.

And so now I am Mammaw, listening, smiling, and applauding as a new batch of grandchildren stirs, pours, measures, and talks. We grandmothers are their first experimentations with sharing thoughts and feelings away from the protection of Mom and Dad. What we take from the labor of their stirring hands is not simply fruitcakes, brown bread, and biscuits, but an overflowing batch of trust.

Strengthen us, Lord, when we sigh at the sight of our disheveled kitchens, where grandchildren are flexing their spirits at our aproned knees. May we remember that flour sweeps up; lost opportunities don't.

March 26

Read Matthew 18:6.

I am as sad as can be that their family is not the one it should be and, as we now know, never was. But their family was dangerously not as it should be, so I, sadly, turn a deaf ear to suggestions that they "deserve" to hold their grandchildren.

Holding is what got them into trouble in the first place, because they held their own children down in the dark and sexually abused them. That it remained a secret for years and that the kids are healing and strong now are

95

beside the point. They also are now parents—good parents—who are protecting their young from people who never got the message: Parents protect their young, even from their own rages and urges.

So strict boundaries are drawn, and all contact is avoided. Big people who aren't sorry, who don't get the message about parents protecting their children, can't be around little people—whether they are grandparents or not.

It is a sad situation on the one hand; on the other, however, it is a family triumph, for the now-parents have broken the circle of family violence. How tragic that breaking the family circle was what it finally took to do it; a double tragedy, for the abusers still don't get the point.

O Lord of little children, help parents who were abused by their parents from becoming victims of parental needs once again; the sacrifice would be too great.

❦ March 27

Read Isaiah 2:4; 1 Corinthians 7:15*b*; 1 Thessalonians 5:13*b*.

Sidestepping the sword-brandishing children, I carried the sweet potatoes to the dining table for Palm Sunday dinner. Grandkids and cousins, running circles around me in hot pursuit of one another, were wielding swords they'd made from palm fronds received at church.

War between appetizer and dessert.

The mood at our home was not unlike the historical one we'd celebrated at church, complete with a donkey, a palm-waving crowd, and the triumphant arrival; for quick as a flash, the kids had turned a "Hosanna" celebration into playful attack before the benediction was cold. What an example of our tendency toward violence, even with a peace branch in our hands.

Instead of soap-box shaming these wee warriors, as I was first tempted, we grandmothers can help best by reshaping the swords into palms or sticking them into vases or baskets where they can reclaim their original purpose: to say welcome, hosanna, the Lord of Peace is here!

Lord, take away our love of violence, of creating weapons from peaceable moments. Heal our hurts and fill our hearts with love.

🍎 March 28

Read 1 Corinthians 13:4.

I unashamedly eavesdropped today on a grandmother and two granddaughters who were shopping for spring clothes. The girls, with grandma trailing in their wake, had made their selections—sensible ones of jeans and baggy shirts, sweatshirts, and dresses—when the youngest one spied jewelry. "A necklace, Grandma!" she exclaimed. "And look! It matches my dress perfectly!"

I heard her words from my watching place behind raincoats and identified with the grandmother's small sigh. Even from my distance, I saw what she had; while "perfect," it was also tangled and knotted.

It was the next step that separates mothers—or at least the busy one I was—from grandmothers. Then I didn't have patience or time, and my shopping recollections are littered with "hurry ups" and "not todays." As a grandmother, however, I love to shop with the youngsters, letting myself be educated by their enthusiasms for purple dinosaurs and shirts that glow in the dark.

So I silently cheered on this grandmother—purse at her feet, new clothes draped over her shoulder, and bifocals adjusted—as she untangled a "just right" necklace for a charming, grateful granddaughter at her elbow.

We grandmas can be counted on to try to unsnarl even

the most knotted of problems, especially those of finding enough time.

Thank you, Lord of grandmother time, for a new dimension in which we find ourselves blessed with patience unimagined.

🍎 March 29

Read James 1:22; Matthew 28:20*b*.

Last Christmas I enjoyed helping introduce Jesus to our two-year-old granddaughter; now, however, I am hunting a good explanation of why he lives in a shoe box the rest of the year.

Not the real Jesus, of course, but the tiny one that belongs in the stuffed stable ensemble I sewed for her. She played with all the figures at Christmas, snuggling Jesus on her shoulder along with dolls and raggy bears, until the holidays were over and the decorations put away.

Now, here it is nearly Easter, and we are talking about a Jesus holiday again. "Where is him?" she asked, remembering the tiny figure. In a shoe box?

We got her a new Jesus book, and I am concocting a stuffed Easter Jesus to snuggle in the off season until she understands symbols and spirits.

Even now, though, as we are explaining to her, the real Jesus lives in our hearts and our actions all year long. In time, when she can understand, I will bundle her in the tie-dyed comforter I made for her before she was born, explaining that the spirit of Jesus is like Mammaw, Bappaw, and her comforter: She can't see Mammaw and Bappaw, but each time she nuzzles or sees her comforter, we are with her; likewise, even though she can't see Jesus, he is always with her. May we remember that as well!

Lord, help us not to keep you out of mind as well. Remind us that wherever we are, you are always with us.

Read Matthew 4:16; 5:14-16.

Today has been a bad day, beginning with a sudden snowstorm and the news that one friend lost her job, another has cancer, and the brakes on my car need replacing. It feels like winter in my soul—a reflection of the chilled world hunkered down in defeat outside my office windows.

Peering closer, though, I see tiny green "fingers" poking through the snow. When the dog and I investigated, we discovered crocuses pushing toward spring. Suddenly the day seems manageable, even if not cheery.

That winter doesn't last is a fact known by grandmothers who record many seasons of change between the lines on our faces. This is why we take our grandchildren along to plant bulbs in the fall and why we show them how to "force bloom" pussy willows and forsythia. They need to know from the depth of our laps that it is okay—even essential—to cherish what is good in our own lives even while others are hurting.

I think today of Elie Wiesel, a Holocaust survivor, who, in the face of his own and others' suffering, said, "Nevertheless, I will dance." On days such as this, the best thing I can do is dance by making angels in the snow and simmering chicken wild rice soup to take to those in pain. With a grandchild on my coattails, I will carry soup in one hand and God's promise tucked away in tulip bulbs in the other: Spring will come.

Darkness, even in the thickest snow and troubles, cannot put out the Light that, even as I write this, is lengthening into spring days.

Lord, may we be help to shed your light in the snowy, dark days that will come in our grandchildren's lives; let them remember that we carried tulips.

Read Psalm 74:17.

Where has this month gone? I asked my winter-morning reflection today. Spring *has* inched a bit closer, but today it's hunkering down again beneath the freezing storm. I'd hoped to take a hike with the grandchildren when they come later today, but I doubt if the little one could stand in the wind.

Where I live, March is neither fully winter nor fully spring. Today, the month's last, is stale—a day when we need something exciting to do. If we can't go outdoors to do it, we will go *really* indoors and make a city of blanket houses in the living room. There we will eat supper and perhaps tell bedtime stories and jokes as we get ready for tomorrow, April Fools' Day.

Yes, tomorrow is April, and I grin at the prospects ahead. April even sounds more sprightly, adding spring to our step as we plot some jokes to play on one another.

As we anticipate a good laugh, we also are anticipating spring. The squirming grandchildren in their tent homes, like we older folks, too, have a hard time waiting for anything. It's been fun building a tent city today. A good place to wait out a final winter storm; great company, too.

Thank you that the long winter days are giving way to spring's light, Lord. Be with us as we wait for the dawn of a new month.

A Season of Rebirth

Margaret Anne Huffman

 April 1

Read Proverbs 17:22.

I've got some bananas ready for April Fools' breakfast—peeled, filled with cotton, and reassembled. The grandkids will get a laugh out of them, and then, I suspect, I'd better be on the lookout for "shoelaces untied" warnings!

This is a day for jokes, and grandmothers can be counted on to laugh at even the most lame joke and homemade riddle—and to laugh again and again as the grandchildren tell and retell them.

I don't mind, really, because we are teaching them the healing power in a good belly laugh, a small chuckle, and even a slight smile, as perhaps Jesus did when he told stories. Just try to think about camels going through eyes of needles without smiling!

The world of medicine is catching on, too. Some hospitals are adding "Good Humor" rooms because scientists have finally gotten the punch line: A good laugh is good medicine.

And so I will serve my silly, stuffed bananas, calling out just in time, "April Fools!" and be ready to tie my shoelaces when warned. Nothing like a laugh to get the day and the month going right!

Lighten us up, Lord; turn our frown lines into laugh lines. Help us see humor almost everywhere and not take ourselves so dreadfully, drearily seriously. One of your best creations in our bodies is the "funny bone."

🍎 April 2

Read Romans 8:28.

The Easter basket blowing in the brisk spring breeze as it hung from a branch in the crab apple tree was the first thing our grandson spied as he and his family drove down our lane. Later we colored Easter eggs as we sat around the kitchen table—the little one loving to splash more than dip!

Far more than tradition and decorations, this ritual blends our lives into a swirling mixture of all colors. Our family, like a rainbow-hued egg, is created by second marriages, stepfamilies, stepgrandkids, and three generations all learning to become one.

The Easter egg, with its promising reminder of re-creation—even an ordinary egg can be transformed with loving attention and creative tending into a masterwork of art—is just like our family busily dyeing, blowing, drying, decorating, hiding, and finding.

True, Easter eggs are traditional, cultural, and societal trinkets; yet they also are marvelous opportunities for giving us a chance to believe.

Remind us, Lord of all seasons, that even the frivolous can be used to send a message of renewal.

🍎 April 3

Read Hebrews 11:1.

This Easter I put a clove-studded ham in the oven, set sweet potatoes to bake, and "nested" marshmallow chicks at each place along our outstretched Easter family dinner table. It was almost like a reunion, for kids, grandkids, and cousins came from everywhere to join hands on this special day.

In the midst of it, I was thinking about the ways we celebrate Easter—"bunnies" hiding the eggs we had colored and angels rolling away stones. On one hand, the two seem contradictory; on the other, they make perfect sense: Resurrections come in the midst of our routine, here-and-now lives, no matter how unrelated they may seem at that moment.

Perhaps the children's games and fun on Easter can serve to remind us that God is the master of unexpected appearances; that spring is the season of rebirth. What better reminder of the nourishment and new life to be found inside after the old has been taken away than brightly-colored eggs!

Lord of Easter surprises and spring renewals, as we hide colored Easter eggs for the grandchildren this year, help us to understand what Easter really means.

🍎 April 4

Read Psalm 90.

It's too rainy to work outside today, so I am working on a patchwork quilt for my granddaughter, starting with scraps of clothes I sewed for her first birthday. Overalls, lace-encrusted paisley dress and bloomers, pinafore, and hooded cape—these pieces will forever remind me of the early summer mornings I spent sewing on my screened porch, a tree house on our wooded riverbank. The bluebirds came by, a papa wren flew over with news of babies, and Mama Woodchuck and her two lumbering toddlers came up from the woods to sample my herb garden.

To be honest, I am making the quilt for myself so I can keep track of where I've been with her, what I've done alongside her. I'm weaving all our many selves into it, for we will never be the same as we were at any given moment, except as one of my patches. I am stitching these first scraps, with others added as we go along, with fine threads of wisdom, a fancy way of saying lessons learned, for parents and children raise one another! And before we have time to apply that knowledge, we are suddenly a Mammaw sewing a seam in the fabric of family with a new generation snuggling beneath our efforts, a counterpane of love.

Guide our hands, Lord, as we "piece together" these awesome grandmother days.

❦ April 5

Read Exodus 20:12.

Art imitates life in a mug sitting on my desk: "If Mother Says 'No,' Go Ask Grandma."

I had forgotten these tactics of children, so I was caught off guard when I innocently gave my granddaughter "a popsicle, please." I was so impressed by her "please" that it never occurred to me to suspect the request, one her mother had just firmly refused until after lunch.

Mammaw was had.

That such manipulations exist is proven by the success of the mug. My own kids tried this regularly. Yet how diligently we must avoid being the point person in a generational triangle, no matter how tempted we feel to take sides on little issues; serious ones are another matter.

Mom and Dad must be respected and obeyed, beginning with us; it's difficult enough maintaining authority without Grandma undermining it—as I recall, having been ambushed myself.

So at the next request from a little angel, I simply asked, "What does Mommy say?" Her brokenhearted sobs were my answer. Together we talked to Mom, asking what she could have, if not a popsicle.

Apple slices were a tear-stained second choice, but were at least the result of honest negotiation. One stuck in my throat, however, along with a chuckle, when she asked oh, so innocently, "Mammaw want a popsicle? I get it for you."

Some of us never give up; it's in the genes.

Lord, help us grandmas to respect our children's authority as parents and to teach our grandchildren to respect that authority as well.

April 6

Read Romans 8:24-25.

Aloft over Glasgow, Scotland, in thought, I was "awakened" by our two-year-old granddaughter: "We're here, Mammaw, Bappaw!" Joy overflowed from her jet-lagged voice. We had been looking forward to the visit.

I had been watching scenes from our vacation video as an antidote to this rainstormy day. There her older brother was, leading us up mountains, explaining, asking, laughing; there she was, discovering, exploring; there we all were, raincoated. Though wet, we saw and heard with their perceptions things our tired selves trudged past. And once, when I was ahead of her as she rode in her Daddy's backpack, she exclaimed with arms stretched to a suddenly blue Scotland sky, "Sun! I need to be naked!" Indeed she was, having stripped off her T-shirt! With her, we felt sun on our upturned faces and laughed in delight at being together in the same ancient street.

On that note and with the realization that if this were a rainy family vacation day, I wouldn't be indoors whining, I am lacing my boots and unfurling an umbrella. Grandchildren are teaching me that only by going out into whatever kind of day it may be is there the possibility of being surprised by joy. I will splash in a puddle in their honor.

Send us outdoors, Lord, regardless of the showers of rain or spirit drenching us. It is better to walk in the rain than wait inside for it to stop. Come splashing with us!

🍎 April 7

Read Ephesians 2:19-20; Galatians 3:27-29.

"This," my son-in-law quipped to the grandkids as we climbed from our vacation van, "is where your grandmother was a little girl." He pointed down the Scottish seacoast to my four-hundred-year-old ancestral castle.

And it felt like it, too—mother-in-law jokes aside! As I wandered among the ruins and listened to the surf pounding the cliffs below, as it had when my ancestors built and tended this fortress, I felt Scots blood stirring within me. It was a family legend underfoot—a rock-and-mortar legacy—to pass on to the grandchildren who were exploring Scotland with me.

This passage from Ephesians also reminds us that we belong to a family, a larger family: humankind. Re-creating family trees is "in" these days. But as I see children in stores being spanked or yelled at for minor whining, on television being carried away in bags from abusive homes, and in the news being shot by peers on city streets and in city schools, I wonder what kind of family I and my grandchildren belong to.

Even as we, the fortunate, enjoy family vacation castles and family reunions and scamper about excitedly in family trees, we also must spread our branches to include *all* children; they are of our house and lineage, too. All of us spring from a common Root.

Remind us, Lord, that we have ample means to help our "other" children, if only an hour spent volunteering at a domestic violence center or a dollar sent to vaccinate some other grandmother's wee one. We are one.

🍐 April 8

Read 1 Peter 5:7.

My voice is recorded for all time in its worrisome insistence: "I don't want them at the edge." There I am, fretting just out of video camera range, in our Scotland vacation memories; and I cringe in embarrassment at how fearful I sound. Granted, the cliff's edge is something to fear, for it leans out into sea-space down to foaming surf. But, to be honest, the grandkids are yards away; the toddler is secure in her daddy's backpack. It's just Grandma worrying.

I never used to worry so much when my trio were young. Now I fret about things I ignorantly blissed through then. Grandparenting, however, like my cliff perch, is life from a totally different perspective. As a friend and I agreed, it's as if we grandmothers have had x-ray vision bestowed upon us as we cover outlets, hide cleansers, and install door latches.

It's just that we want so much to protect these young treasures. Yet I know in my worrying heart that I need to turn down the volume of my concerns. In addition to not being helpful if I am so shrill that they tune me out, I don't want to be a faceless worrywart on all our vacation tapes. I want to be a pathfinding grandmother who shows them where to place their feet along cliff edges. The former is a bad memory; the latter is lasting safety.

Join my adventures with my grandchildren, Lord, and help me to cast my unfounded cares on you.

🍐 April 9

Read Isaiah 25:4; Genesis 9:8-17.

Without missing a beat, Nutmeg Dog leaped into my grandson's lap as she fled the ferocious spring thunderstorm. It had driven the rest of us in as well, and although we were more sophisticated in our expression, we shared the mutt's fears.

Silently the grandbaby climbed into my lap, as worried about the frightened dog as she was about the lashing rain. I assured her it would soon be over. I intentionally avoided hollow promises such as "It'll be okay," because a few weeks ago several houses in our county blew away—literally. Storms are not always "okay."

So the boy held the dog, and I held the baby. Soon the sky cleared itself of troubles. New grass seemed to sprout before our eyes as we returned outdoors. "Okay? Mammaw?" the little one asked. "Okay," I assured.

Storms are a natural occasion to talk to kids about fear; Grandma's lap is a good place for the conversation. There, she helps the grandchildren stand lookout for rainbows, for she knows there can't be one without the other. Children are able to understand two things simultaneously, such as their fear *and* curiosity about storms—which is why we are building a child-sized weather station.

Even in the stormy, uncontrollable moments, to name a fear is to befriend it, or at least to tolerate it, especially if there is a lap nearby.

Lord, calm our fears of all kinds of "stormy skies"; tilt our gaze for rainbow searching.

April 10

Read 1 Kings 7:46-51.

We finished remodeling our kitchen just in time for the grandkids' most recent visit. All cupboards and drawers were filled, including my "everything drawer." Crammed with tools, hardware, candles, crayons, jar lids, egg beaters, and stray buttons, this oversized drawer is the best I can do for a pantry.

My Mammaw lived across the street from us, which gave me easy access to her pantry, a life-sized "everything drawer" with treasures stashed from floor to ceiling. From them I learned to use a brace and bit, churn butter, measure and weigh, sew on buttons, and save string and foil. From that pantry, I emerged equipped to do many things, including tinker, a skill homemakers need as we improvise and create with "what's on hand." Tinkering is a pastime grandchildren need even more today.

So it was without a moment's hesitation that the first new kitchen drawer I refilled was this "pantry" jumble where grandchildren can tinker and make special rubber band airplanes or cork snowmen, a necklace of washers and nuts strung on twine saved "just in case." A place from which to launch improvisations as creatively as did King Solomon in that seemingly useless path of clay ground long ago.

As I close the drawer, tucking in loose ends from the tools of my trade, I glimpse again the rich potpourri of Mammaw's life. Like her pantry, her life held treasures for me, preserved alongside her watermelon rind pickles lined up on sticky pantry shelves of memory.

Bless our tinkering, Lord; it yields discovery and accomplishment.

❧ April 11

Read Matthew 11:28-30.

"Wix it, Mammaw," my granddaughter pleaded with great assurance that I could fix her dolly. She held its head in her right hand; its body in her left.

And Mammaw is trying—with rubber bands, glue, pliers, and sheer determination—not to let her down. As children do—at least in the beginning—she believes that big people are super people and can "wix" everything, especially grandmas. Sometimes we can; sometimes we can't.

Whether anything else gets broken—such as children's hearts and faith—is all in the response. We must at least try, never pooh-poohing their requests even if the dolly is beyond repair.

How easy it is not to try, though, for we often feel we are asked to "wix" it all—pollution and recessions included! We're tired after years of being asked to "wix" the wallpaper the baby pulled loose, the tree the lawn mower nicked, the frosting wilting from the cake, the overloaded family schedule, the kids' broken hearts and skinned knees, the husband's burnout, the neighbor's loneliness, and the stray cat's anxiety. "Wix it" is a familiar summons.

Today I was able to answer the request happily: I "wixed" the doll. Better keep these handy, I thought, smiling to myself as I put my "wixing tools" away. Looks like my repair shop has reopened for business.

We come, Lord, asking you to "wix" our tired spirits; they sometimes get weary from "wixing" everything else.

April 12

Read Matthew 25:14-30.

Neither of us is sure what it is, but my granddaughter's invention of blocks and foil to hold her tiny cars follows in a long line—a sometimes invisible line—of women inventors.

What roadblocks lie ahead for this little grandlady and her peers? Are times changing rapidly enough so that they will escape gender prejudice? As I research and write a worship service celebrating women, I wonder if in the parable of the talents someone hasn't also been sitting on the talents of women.

We enlightened grandmothers can release these buried

talents from obscurity so they may inspire granddaughters to invent and grandsons to applaud. For God has always worked through women to heal, teach, feed, lead, and clothe our world.

Inventions and discoveries of women recorded at the U.S. Patent Office:
- cotton gin — Catherine Littlefield Greene
- dandruff shampoo — Josie Wanous Stuart
- disposable diapers — Marion Donovan
- DNA — Rosalind Franklin
- elastic bathing suit — Rose Marie Reid
- electronic Bible — Helen Gonet
- internal combustion engine — Mattie Knight
- paper bags — Mattie Knight again
- satellite propulsion system — Yvonne Brill
- smallpox inoculation — Mary Montagu
- usable penicillin: terramyacin — Gladys Hobby
- windshield wipers — Mary Anderson

The list goes on and on, Lord, with perhaps the best yet to come; for when women get inventive, anything's possible! Thank you for our talents.

🍎 April 13

Read 1 Peter 1:22; Revelation 21:5.

We made—and ate—dog food during today's visit with the grandchildren. A brown-eyed beggar dog sat trustingly at our feet as we mixed broth, flour, and oats and shaped the mixture into "bones."

The kitchen was dusted with flour and paw prints, and the table was sticky with leftover "People Chow," a cereal-and-powdered-sugar concoction for the owners of pets. In the midst of it, grandson and dog were content in each other's love; the cats were disdainful, as usual, but I saw Abigail cleaning a canine mustache.

Pets are stepping-stone bridges for our family, and this grandson has a dog at each of his homes: mom's, dad's, and grandparents'. Walking the balance between homes is like making it from sink to stove in a sugary mess without getting sticky: a precarious trek!

Yet, rather than accenting the seams of differences that exist, we can meld together the parts of his life by finding special things we can do together. The stronger our family is, the more surefooted are his steps.

It was with a light heart and sticky smile that he took some doggy biscuits for his "mom-house" dog and some People Chow for Mom. There is always enough to go around when love is the main ingredient!

Sometimes we are messy, Lord, in building family. Be present at our sticky table where we join hands in praise for the trying.

🍎 April 14

Read James 5:9.

The classroom teacher blotted her copybook tonight, as oldtimers say, and I am still angry and hurt for myself, my husband, my daughter, my son-in-law, and especially for the small boy who wanted only to take his "other" family to third-grade open house.

I also feel sorry for his teacher, who through her narrow definition of "family" missed meeting some great people. Any anger I feel is being replaced by concern as I write: How can someone so narrow as to not accept stepfamilies teach about the expansive world in which we live? What color is her world? What language does it speak? Who sits around its kitchen tables?

Naively, I had thought she would greet us at the classroom door in appreciation of the child's fine work, sense of humor, and, most of all, kind heart. I also had expected applause at how involved we all are in his learning. Many parents were absent, yet we had driven more than an hour to get there; his father had driven four hours. How about a little partnership celebration here? Instead, we played "Keep Away" and "I Dare You to Come Over."

So I wrote to her and her principal, urging them to decide who they *do* hope to see at Family Open House; it was a closed door for our family.

Lord, help us to be accepting of all kinds of families—and to forgive when we are excluded by others.

April 15

Read Proverbs 15:27a.

Thoughts of money abound today, and my granddaughter is no exception. Her mother reported the story to me.

"I buy it!" she happily shouted at the bookstore, with rainbow bookmark in hand. "I buy it for Mammaw!" (She and I have this thing for rainbows.)

Such generosity from a child. She knows the joy of receiving mail surprises, for Mammaw frequently sends them. She's also discovering the joy of buying something she wants, or as she is apt to correct, she *needs*. How quickly we learn there is a difference between want and need, setting out, whenever possible, to get both!

She is learning, too, that she has power to meet some of her own needs, including the need to buy for someone else. That it takes money is as tricky to teach kids about as sex. Our next step is teaching her to save, and then to pool her coins with Mammaw's for something better. Her brother already saves—some for today; some for tomorrow.

Saving is only part of the point: What do we teach about spending? Today's grandchildren are bombarded by many things to buy, even for others. How can we help them learn that enough is a feast when it is a lesson we acquisitive adults have never mastered?

Tend old and young, Lord, as we shout in unison, "I BUY IT!" For children, it is cute; for us, it is greed. Forgive us for our greed, and help us to teach our grandchildren to be good stewards.

🍎 April 16

Read Matthew 10:42.

Grandchildren are exposed to so much misery these days. As I see it, however, we'd better take them along with us as we tend the sufferers in this world they'll inherit—rather than hiding the suffering as if that would protect them absolutely.

And so our toddler granddaughter "fixes" a friend's failing kidneys with a kiss, a toy, a bright bandaid. Prayer and conversation are prime ingredients in the healing prescription for AIDS concocted by her older brother, who has accompanied his pastor father to visit AIDS patients.

Both grandchildren live daily with knowledge of suffering; both seem undaunted by it, because, in some mysterious way, they understand what Jesus meant when he talked about offering a cup of cold water. Feeding the hungry, visiting the imprisoned, tending the sufferers: small things, really. Children understand this; they know that bandages do help, even if they don't "fix" things completely.

Grandchildren are teaching me about faith, reminding me that small things do make differences—maybe not curing differences, but healing ones just the same.

Send us with bandages, Lord, to tend the ailments around us. We have been waiting for gigantic breakthroughs, magic bullets. But the grandkids know that from our small bandaid beginnings, you can create great big happenings.

114

Read 3 John 2.

I'd forgotten until I became a grandmother that there is more than one kind of lap needed to make this new role a pleasant one. In my mistaken fantasy, I'd seen myself rocking and singing and reading to a cooing, placid infant on my soft, cushiony lap. I should have been out taking a lap around the block, for it is the energetic lap that is most needed to be a grandmother.

First we crawl in the wake of infant grandbabies; then we hustle after the older grandchildren, who are inviting us to pick up our feet and come along. Yet some of us had let inertia take over after our children grew up and left home, and we'd become as soft as pillows. Now at the hands of our grandchildren we are back sitting on bleachers, beaches, and baby blankets—all places where flexibility, if not agility, are needed just to keep up.

Although I am creaky about the ankles and knees, I intend to do just that: move from making only a soft, lullabying lap into taking a long, deep-breathing training lap around the neighborhood. I've a baseball game to attend and a stroller to push around the diamond; and I want to be in shape!

Give us the energy, Lord, to "catch up" to the fit grandmas we intend to be.

❧ *April* 18

Read Romans 14:14.

We sent a strap-around-the-neck reading light as a traveling companion for our grandson's spring break trip. He loves to read, to be read to, and to read to others. And his baby sister is following in the family bookworm's footsteps. What joy to introduce them to my favorites and be introduced to theirs! But will they get to read some books that have made their way from my childhood to banned book shelves? I hope so, for isn't reading about exercising the mind?

My answer is found in The Book—with its message to love God and love others as ourselves in ways that bring us the well-being God intends for us. That God resources us to be able to make choices on how to do just that is comforting as we guide our grandchildren's explorations. *Guiding* choices is not censoring them; it is, rather, a chance to share how we make choices—and how they can.

To sample is not to establish tastes for the lurid, profane, or trashy. Exercising curiosity, rather, is like turning a page, moving to somewhere else.

Lord, help us identify dangers that interfere with who you know us to be: Strong, capable and created in your image. May our choices reflect that view.

April 19

Read Job 11:18.

Silly, surprised robin! There he sits, shivering in our snow-crusted holly tree. What's he doing here now? Can't he tell time?

Perhaps better than we.

As I rest for a minute during this grandchildren weekend, I am caught—like the robin flying crosswind in the swinging moods of spring—in the joy of grandmother time. It is filled with moments that restore my soul, my sense of wonder, my sense of humor. Grandmother time, like early robins, also restores my sense of hope. These days feel like one of my favorite paintings: a fern unfurling in snow.

Sure, the robin can tell time—hope time, that is, as I tell the grandkids as we bundle up to go outdoors to hunt for hope. There are hope-full signs all around: that robins tell time as do swallows of Capistrano and migrating geese; that Native Americans called the asters I planted last year, "It brings the snow," knowing by first blooms when the first snow would come. We've just forgotten how to tell hope time, where to watch for it.

So today we went hunting for ferns along the snowy riverbank. There they were, beneath icy leaves compressed into shelters, uncurling just a bit. Green, green against the slick-black leaves and white snow; heralds of hope. Springtime always comes. Nearby, a shivering robin trills a tentative greeting, an echo of fern truth.

Our hope is strengthened, Lord, by taking time to follow your footprints and a robin's song in the snow.

🍎 April 20

Read Matthew 28:20.

"Bappaw there?" her little voice asked as we played the answering machine back. "Mammaw? . . . Bappaw's coming," she assured someone in the background of her attempted telephone visit.

"Bappaw there?" she asked again. "Bappaw be back," she concluded before hanging up the receiver on her end—a long distance away from a Bappaw and Mammaw who were heartbroken to have missed her call about seeing zebras at the zoo.

It was more than a little sobering to understand her first assumption that Bappaw would be there, and when he wasn't, her second assumption that he would return to talk to her. I think, in great humility, that we are the foundation and the roots of her faith as she learns to trust her "special people," extending beyond Mommy and Daddy to a brother, grandparents, aunts, uncles, and eventually to a God who is so steadfast and everpresent that this is who we model ourselves after.

May we be worthy of the example, never being too busy to want to hear about those zebras; God always does.

Lord, as we strive to be examples of your love, please be a steadfast presence with children who have no grandparents on the other ends of their lives; no parents as conduit between their children and you. May we help you make the stretch.

🌿 April 21

Read Ecclesiastes 3:1-8.

I bought paper cups today so the grandkids and I can plant parsley, dill, and carrot seeds in them this weekend. In a few weeks, when the grandkids come back, we will transplant our seedlings outside. I'm still working on a child-sized explanation of how herbs and veggies create butterflies.

A camera will help, and I plan to record the journey from seedlings to butterflies. If caterpillars eat all our parsley, as has happened in the past, so much the better; for, as I will explain, soon they will make "little houses" from which will come swallowtail butterflies fluttering past to say "thanks" for their parsley feast.

I am looking forward to this planting, for all winter we have been cocooned in tight winter homes, safe and secure against blizzards and darkness. But now, as buds on the trees remind us, it is time to uncurl and head for the garden.

Seasons of butterflies, and of ourselves, are connected in intricate links of God's wisdom. Spring to fall, stillness to flying: Knowledge that is a savory tidbit of spring pleasure, like a first bite of fresh parsley.

Lord of springtime delights, send us from our snug routines into the wakening world to play in your earth.

April 22

Read Psalm 104; Genesis 1:27-28*a*.

We gave donations to the local wildlife society, not appliances, as bridal gifts and tossed birdseed, not rice. It was the thoroughly modern wedding of a friend's grandchild, and I had a wonderful time at the dual celebration: marriage day and Earth Day—a good union itself.

Dare I hope they are representative of today's young people leading the older, more pollutive and nature-squandering generation down new paths—even on the way to the altar—in order to protect the old paths? Yes, and in the face of their efforts, it is my turn to say, "I do"—have hope, that is.

Such efforts are cause for celebrating with a wedding toast to their courage—courage not only to risk getting married in a world that gives marriage bad press, but also courage to link their union of faith with a pledge to do something about redeeming the earth.

And so I called out, "Happy Earth Day!" as they left the church in a shower of birdseed—robins and sparrows already hopping about. May no one cast asunder the commitments they asked us all to make today—not only in marriage vows renewed but also in pledges to be better caretakers of the generations we've begat.

Lord of creation, strengthen all our commitments to love one another and honor the world we share; it can be a happy ending love story we write for our grandchildren, and theirs.

April 23

Read John 15:12.

The heirlooms from my Mammaw that I cherish are likely not what she would have guessed: the smell of spice inside a walnut cupboard; a green glass tea set; a pansy-embroidered handkerchief.

So, too, am I unaware of the memories my grandchildren are gathering in their hearts. Memories are selective; each person attaches importance to some symbol of happy childhood moments. As my grandchildren weave like cats around my ankles, I can only guess what trinket is important to them to have.

So I am asking. Their answers are as amazing as I am sure mine would have been to my grandmother and mother: a swing.

I keep swings on front and back porches from early spring to late frost. Like memory, swings travel back and forth, connecting me to a mother's lap, where I first swung; to a grandmother's lap; to a "solo" in grandmother's swing, where I measured my bravery by how high I would go before leaping from it; to my own lap as a mother; and now, as a grandmother, to both lap and leaping.

Through all life's moods, may movement—the kind first found in a swing—be one heirloom my children and grandchildren have from me.

Give us a push, Lord, as we swing in the rhythm of love passed on.

April 24

Read Galatians 5:1; John 8:32.

Within the lively, unborn mound cradled on her mother's lap coursed my genes, and I wondered as I helped fold baby-in-waiting clothes who the child would be, what to expect from him or her.

It was a logical question, for my grandfather was a dairy scientist, and I grew up knowing about bloodlines and good breeding. But other than my chin and curiosity, what of me should I want to be growing—then and now—in this grandchild?

A yen for God's freedom.

This is my desire for all global grandchildren: to be free to follow where God leads—free from tyranny of government, religion, society, family, fear, obligation, genetics, and prejudice. Free even from my vain desires.

It is one thing to *want* a child to be a certain person; it is another to reshape a child into it. As I patted my squirming unborn heir, I vowed not to follow the example of a friend who is doing just that with her grandson; for he is likely lost to whomever he might have been.

Whether they be the first or the twenty-first grandchild, they are mysteries to be appreciated, not programmed. Like daffodils opening in today's warming sunshine, they are best left unburdened by our expectations, however loving those expectations may be. Instead, let's follow their lead, expecting from them only that they become all God intends them to be.

Endow all children with courage, Lord, to seek your freedom.

April 25

Read Isaiah 41:6.

His carrot-colored hair was trimmed into a spring buzz; last year's too-small shorts testified to a winter of growth. It was an unseasonably warm spring day, and we were all prematurely outdoors in last season's clothes, putting aside for a moment the likelihood that harsh weather might not be through with us.

As I watched from my vantage point of leaning on a garden rake, the neighbor child steered his bike on a wobbly course down the lane; his grandmother ran alongside.

It wasn't the first time I'd seen him and his bike; last year, though, it had needed training wheels. Now, a grandmother's presence was enough to keep him upright and pedaling.

What a place of honor: beside our grandchildren as their training wheels. What a responsibility. Sometimes I fret about my limitations of both knowledge and energy, for there are many bumps in the road, many moments that will puncture their dreams.

Yet, once we learn it, bike riding is a skill we never forget. Perhaps this also is true with living: The grandkids we are steadying on bikes today will remember in the tomorrows what it felt like to have Grandma running alongside, giving encouragement and holding them upright until they got the hang of it.

Help us, Lord, to keep up with our grandchildren's journeys so that we are only a mere wobble away.

🌳 April 26

Read John 11:35; Revelation 21:4.

My heart has room only for a prayer today, Lord, for ordinary words just won't do.

Today Jake, a friend's grandson, was born. All her grandmother dreaming did no good, for there is to be no red wagon, no tractor, and no football in a toy box. Instead, there are feeding tubes, pain medications, and sleepless nights beside a grandchild who will never venture outside infancy, no matter the size of his body.

So many people suffer from never having suffered, Lord, or they wouldn't say such dreadful, silly things: "It's God's will; God never gives what you can't bear; God is testing you; God wants you to be stronger."

At which do you cry hardest, Lord, the tragedies or the explanations made in your name? You will healing and wholeness for all of us, and I know you were the first to cry over this broken child.

But you also gave him a grandmother whose love and imagination are endless, just as yours are. And she is tuned to your ideas, Lord, as she searches for ways to tend her grandson—and her own child. It is hardest to be the third generation removed, Lord, having to watch her daughter gather strength to be a different kind of mother. Be with her as she sets aside her own grandmothering grief to be a mother, too.

I am humbled as she graciously laughs at my grandchildren's antics even as we both cry at the pain in her stories. Help me listen with a whole heart to her grandmothering tales; and keep her sharing them, for hers is a grandson who needs us all gathered 'round.

🍂 April 27

Read Habakkuk 3:2*a*; Matthew 18:3.

"Does God have a grandmother?" my grandson asked. It's a question I've never considered; its answer eludes even my best guess, but the asking of it spawns all sorts of wondrous wondering.

I have decided that along with questions such as "Why are all snowflakes and fingerprints different?" and "Why is the sky blue?" and "Why are there rainbows after rain?" I really do not want to actually know. Nor do I want to know how television and computers work, how airplanes fly, why butterflies migrate, how a cat purrs, how a baby knows its parents and a lover his or her mate.

Not having to absolutely know puts me closer to the childlike faith we are urged to have. We are to ponder, not process; to be content in mystery. For not knowing, like faith, is a kind of knowledge itself, and it gives a certain peace of mind.

So it was with great pleasure that the grandkids and I tiptoed to see the amazing architecture of a tiny wren's nest today. How do they know where to place the next twig? Only God and wrens know, leaving us standing below the nest in awe and wonder, a comfortable place to worship amidst daily miracles.

O Lord who created everything for wonderment, thank you for minds that poke and pull and speculate. Keep us open to children's questions and remind us to go easy on the answers; it is the questing that draws all of us to you.

🌷 April 28

Read 1 Peter 4:10.

Her grandchildren are in the gifted programs at school, she sniffs, implying that there are those *with* and those *without* gifts. Humph!

That her attitude misses the point of wonderful gifted programs is irrelevant, because seeds of doubt are cast: Are there only so many gifted grandkids? So many gifts? Has our family missed out?

I shake my head in sadness at the early competition that evaluates "gifts" and divides children long before schools can take even a creative turn. We are a competitive, highly polarized society: gifted, nongifted; winners, losers; in, out; on, off; for, against. And we love it: pushing our kids and grandkids not only to excel but also to surpass others. Where is the leeway of process, of becoming and evolving, of discovering gifts other than winning?

If nowhere else, it can be in a grandmother's heart as she takes the grandkids on adventuresome "scavenger hunts" in search of their unique gifts. As grandmother and grandchild read, travel, talk, and explore, the child can discover how he or she is gifted.

For some children, giftedness may be in how good a searcher they are—the specific answers not yet clear. But isn't that the form of the scriptural verbs *ask, knock, seek*—the implication being that there is an answer? Perhaps, as we search, we grandmas can lead in unison recitation, "I am gifted." That's God's promise!

Guide our searches, Lord, for you have blessed each of us uniquely.

🍂 April 29

Read Ecclesiastes 3:1-8, 4:9-12; Psalms 126:2-3, 100:1-2; Philippians 4:1.

I've wondered all winter as I watched her dine at the bird feeder if the lady redbird would return to her hatching tree outside my office windows. Today, here she is, with twig in mouth and a bright red companion checking out nest possibilities in the same hawthorne tree.

I am going to assume she is the same bird the grandchildren and I watched last spring and summer. She was a downy youngster of flyaway topknot feathers—hatched and raised in a nest perched precariously within sight of the cats, dog, and people who sometimes forgot to tiptoe past.

Like exploring grandchildren, she knew no fear and relished being able to fly. Feeling a little cocky one day, she landed on the slanted metal roof of the covered bird feeder and, with an amazed tilt to her downy head, slid off! Now here she is all feathered out and going to be a mamma herself.

I am fortunate to sit at the windows of grandchildren's and redbirds' lives, delighting in their swooping, darting games in the springtime now revealing itself in my woods. It is a privilege, and I sit oh, so still, so as not to intrude in their exuberant flights.

Thank you for the perch we grandmothers have, Lord, for it is a gift to watch in wonder as the seasons bring their changes in young lives.

125

Read Matthew 13:18-23.

A carpet of violets covers my yard; a bouquet on my desk inspires me for the day's tasks.

Is there a more beautiful flower in the hands of grand-children than these, delicately airbrushed with scent and color? Before the grandchildren began to bring questions about the flower along with the bouquet, I didn't pay much attention to the violets other than to smile when they reappeared—more in relief that winter was over than delight in their miraculous message.

Their name means "remembrance." Butterfly larvae feed on them, and cooks stir them into jams and jellies. The grandchildren and I, though, are watching them aim at our hearts; violets are sure shots, we have discovered.

After the flowering phase, the fruit capsule—filled with tiny seeds—dries, compressing the seeds and shooting them several feet. What wisdom in creation, I marvel as I kneel in the dirt. As violets scatter seeds in assurance that some will take root, so, too, can we spread hope.

Grandmother sisters, let's join hands like violets gracing the woodland's edge and huff and puff and laugh our seeds of hope aloft on springtime breezes. May we remember that we are passing on our essence like so much violet scent; that what we are, do, and believe is spread like violet seeds all around us.

There is no more fertile ground than the hearts and minds of our grandchildren; let us scatter happily and wisely.

Lord, may the "seeds" we sow in the lives of our grand-children fall on good soil.

A Grandmother's Love

Betty Steele Everett

May 1

Read Matthew 19:13-15.

My husband and I are grandparents who live far away from our grandchildren. It is hard for me not to watch them grow up; Sundays are especially hard. Sometimes I dread going into church and seeing others my age with their grandchildren. Some hold tiny babies; some grip the hands of toddlers; some sit with fidgety preteens.

"I feel so out of it," I told my husband one Sunday afternoon. "It's like we don't have grandchildren. We don't know what things they're doing at certain ages as we would if they lived around here."

He came up with an idea that helps us get over some of the loneliness we have for our grandchildren. It was simple, and it took only time, not money. We looked around the church and chose youngsters who are the same age and gender of each of our grandchildren.

Now we watch each week for these particular children. We note how they are growing; we ask them about their schools, music lessons, and other activities. We tell them about our grandchildren living in Rhode Island and

Florida. Sometimes, when we look at their school portraits, we show them our grandchildren's pictures.

Naturally, we would prefer to have our own grandchildren closer to us, but since that's impossible, we can watch their progress through these church-related youngsters. Perhaps we can help these children someday, in some way. And we can pray for them every day when we pray for our own grandchildren.

Lord, help me remember that regardless of the distance between me and my grandchildren, you are always with them—and with me.

🕊 May 2

Read Matthew 7:9-12.

More of our family's birthdays fall in May than any other month. Our own two children, Dave and Jean, were born in May, as were both of Jean's children, Lincoln and Suzanne.

When my children were small, my mother began a birthday tradition that I am continuing today. In the big box that came in the mail on a child's birthday, she had packed two colorfully wrapped gifts for the "birthday child." She also had included another gift—of lesser value but wrapped just as nicely—for the "nonbirthday child." While there was no doubt in either child's mind as to who was the real honoree of the day, the other child was not completely left out. He or she had something to open, too. When my grandchildren were born—one right after the other, it seemed—my daughter reminded me of what her grandmother had done.

"I always felt good, even when it wasn't my birthday," she said. "Would you please do the same thing?"

We all want to be noticed, singled out. I have heard "experts" say that a child must learn to be left out—such as not getting gifts when it's not his or her birthday—but I don't agree. Neither do my children and grandchildren! I am sure they will continue the tradition when their turn comes.

I don't think God agrees that we should learn to be left out. With Jesus, none of us is ever left out. He is always with us, giving us wonderful gifts every day.

Lord, help me make each of my grandchildren feel "special," not only on their birthdays but always—because I know we're all special to you.

🍎 May 3

Read Matthew 25:23.

We were keeping our granddaughter Molly while her parents were at work and her older sister was at school.

"Take her to the mall," my daughter-in-law suggested. "She loves to ride the escalators."

As soon as we got inside the mall, Molly headed for the moving stairs. Up we rode. We hurried around the stairs' opening, and then rode down. Off, around the opening, and up again. After several rides, I noticed people staring at us. We were moving, but we weren't getting anywhere! Most of the people who noticed us smiled; many were probably grandparents, too!

That experience made me think of my Christian life. It seems that I always am busy doing something in the church: serving funeral dinners; giving a program for the women's association; or attending a committee meeting. Yet I often wonder if all of this "busyness" isn't a little like riding up and down the escalators with Molly. I keep moving, but am I getting anywhere?

When I start thinking this way, I remember the end of my day with Molly. With eyes sparkling, she looked up and said, "I had fun on the escalators! Thank you!"

Sometimes the little things we do don't seem important;

but when someone comes back to the kitchen to thank me for serving a meal for a bereaved family, or someone else says they "got something" from a program I gave, or my committee begins a new program in the church, then I know that even little things count big with God.

Thank you, Lord, for giving me the chance to serve you, even though the "jobs" I do are small ones. Help me remember there are no small jobs.

🍂 May 4

Read John 10:16.

Walking with a grandchild is not only a happy experience; it also is an education. When our own children were small, we were younger and wanted to keep moving. With grandchildren, we've slowed down to their pace, and we find it's a better one.

Suzanne was walking a couple of steps ahead of me in the park. Ever so often she stopped kicking through the crisp brown leaves to bend down and pick up an acorn.

"Look, Grandma," she'd say, thrusting her latest find into my hand. "Look at this one." Then she would show me how it was different from the dozen or so I already had. One was bigger, one greener, one had a red tip, one had a "hat," and so on. To her, each one was distinctive.

I have seen acorns all my life, but for the first time, through her eyes, I saw the differences among them. Suzanne was right: Each one had a quality of its own that made it unique.

We get so busy with the details of living that we often miss the subtle differences in people: the things that make them individuals. We tend to lump everyone into groups: "those people" or "them." We lump by color, religion, age, and sex. Yet, like the acorns Suzanne picked up, all people are different, and those differences make them individuals.

130

Help me get to know your other sheep, Lord, and accept them as my Christian brothers and sisters—even when they are different from me.

🐦 May 5

Read 1 Peter 2:2-3.

I was in a meeting when the president said, "I always said I wouldn't be this kind of grandmother, but . . . well, I have some pictures."

We all laughed. She was a first-time grandmother.

"I never thought I'd be this way," she said again, as if still amazed by her reaction to being a grandmother.

Before you become a grandmother, you shake your head at the women who have a gallery of photos to show, or a new story about their grandchildren to tell. I felt that being a grandmother would not be important to me, and I thought I'd never be like the others.

"No one can tell you how it will be," a friend told me then. She was right. As all grandmothers know, being a grandmother is an experience no one can prepare you for. Friends just have to be patient until you "experience" the grandchild's birth for yourself.

I find it hard to understand Christians who don't want to go to church or be part of a Christian group. I can't explain to them how much these experiences mean to me. No one can tell these name-only Christians how much they are missing when they don't go a step further in their faith. I just have to pray they will have their own special experiences soon and discover the joy and peace that come from being with other Christians in worship and fellowship.

Lord, help me to be patient with those who don't seem to need to be closer to you. Give me the wisdom to understand and to help them long for the pure, spiritual milk that you give.

🍎 May 6

Read 1 John 4:7-9.

When your grandchildren live far away, as ours do, you look forward to an occasional letter from them. The grandchildren's letters come on a variety of papers, from a lined notebook sheet to a pale-colored page with a dozen stickers pasted on at random.

The first letters we got were a series of run-together letters that had to be de-coded into words. As the children grew, their printing yielded to cursive writing that stayed within the lines. Their spelling also improved. Although the form of the letters changed, one thing has always remained the same: Somewhere in each letter are the words "I love you."

It is important to our grandchildren that we know they love us, especially because we see them so seldom. It also is important for them to know that we love them. Loving and being loved are vital to true "living."

Often it is hard for us adults to tell others we love them—even our mates, sometimes. But it comes naturally to children. They instinctively know the value of love and are not embarrassed to talk about it.

God loves us, too, but I often forget to include in my prayers an "I love you" for God. I'm trying to remember, though, because I believe God must appreciate me saying it as much as I appreciate reading "I love you" from a grandchild.

I do love you, Lord, but sometimes I forget to say it in words or actions. Forgive me for being too busy or forgetful to tell you of my love.

🍎 May 7

Read John 8:32.

Our grandson, Lincoln, had offered to get us sodas from the refrigerator. Soda is a rare treat in his house, and someone had always rationed it out to him. "Should I shake the can?" he called innocently from the kitchen.

"No!" his father called, dashing to the kitchen to explain what happens when a can of soda is shaken.

"Wow! Lucky I asked you!" Lincoln said as he poured the soda into glasses. "That could have been an awful mess to clean up!"

Lincoln had learned a painless lesson because he asked someone he trusted for help before he acted.

As a Christian, I often want to "shake the can" rather than ask for advice from friends or from God. I don't like to admit I don't know all the answers; I don't stop to go to the Source for help. As a result, I often make "an awful mess" that has to be cleaned up by making an apology, spending extra time on a job, or missing out on something I had looked forward to.

Learning without pain or problems gives me a thrill like Lincoln's thrill in realizing he had done the right thing and saved himself a lot of trouble. Lincoln will never again think of shaking a soda can; likewise, there are spiritual lessons I'll never forget, either. Learning the truth can set us free from worry and mistakes.

Lord, help me learn more about you and your ways every day. Show me your will and help me grow and mature in my faith as I struggle to learn the truth that will set me free.

May 8

Read 2 Peter 3:15.

The voice on the answering machine was definitely not the one I had expected. "Grandpa and Grandma can't come to the phone now," the high-pitched voice told me. Each word was spoken carefully, as though struggling to be sure it came out exactly as he had been told to say it.

"Please leave a . . . a . . ." There was a hesitation, then came the triumphant gasp, "message!"

I smiled as I left my message and hung up. As I went back to my work, I thought about that grandchild leaving the taped instructions on the answering machine. The child must have been thrilled and proud to be trusted with such an important job.

Then I wondered, how many tries had it taken before he got the short greeting right? It would not be easy for such a small child. His grandparents must have had great patience. Yet he finally had gotten it right, and now my friends have a delightful little "secretary" when they aren't home.

Sometimes I don't get things right for God the first time. I think I have faith until something happens to strain it, and I realize how fragile it is. But God is patient with me, just as I'm sure my friends were patient as their grandson worked to get the message right. God gives me another chance to do it right!

Be patient with me, please, Lord. I need your help to keep my faith strong and do what you want me to do.

🌰 May 9

Read 1 John 2:7-8.

When our granddaughter Sheila was visiting us last summer, she spotted my typewriter on the office desk.

"Can I type, Grandma?" she asked eagerly.

I gave her paper, and she began. To my surprise, she was not using the "hunt and peck" method but all her fingers.

"I didn't know you could type, Sheila."

"Oh, they taught us the keyboard in computer class. I really like computers. We have one at home now, and Molly and I use it a lot."

I sighed. I know nothing about computers; I love my old typewriter. But Sheila and my other grandchildren are of the computer generation. They know how to play games on them, how to move paragraphs around, and how to use a modem. They think of a typewriter only as a way to practice their computer keyboard skills.

It's hard to admit I can learn from my grandchildren, whom I diapered not so long ago. It's hard to admit that times change and the world my grandchildren know is far different from the one I grew up in.

One thing stays the same, though: God and his love for us in Jesus Christ. My grandchildren say the same Lord's Prayer my own grandparents prayed. They sing many of the same hymns, although they know many new ones, too. They read the same teachings in the Bible, but in modern English.

Things do change, and we each have to decide whether we want to change to the new or stay with the old.

Lord, give me the insight to know which of the "new" I should accept and which I should reject. I thank you that you never change.

May 10

Read Exodus 20:12.

May is the month for celebrating motherhood. Now that I am a grandmother, I share Mother's Day with my daughter and daughter-in-law. And that sharing has brought some nice surprises.

Becoming a mother has given my daughter an understanding of many things that happened in her youth that were puzzling to her then. She agrees with some of the things I did in raising her that she once disagreed with. She now realizes the great responsibility—and sometimes hurt—of raising children.

Her own motherhood has given us a closer bond than we had before. We laugh at many of the same things now, and I can sympathize—and help now and then—with the problems of having young children to care for.

We are grandmothers because someone else became a mother. But we were mothers ourselves first of all. This makes Mother's Day mean even more as we share it with those other, younger mothers whom we have loved so long.

Jesus doesn't need a special day to love us—as mothers or just as his children. His love wasn't shown with a card, candy, or carnations. It was shown many years ago on a rough, wooden cross. And we all are alive with him because he was willing to die there.

Be with the mothers of our grandchildren, Lord, today and every day. Give them the patience, the wisdom, and the skills to be good mothers now—and good grandmothers, in time.

❦ May 11

Read Mark 10:13-14.

My friend sat across the kitchen table from me, nervously rubbing her coffee cup.

"I love Stacy, and she'll make my son a good wife," she said. "But . . . well, she has two children from her first marriage, and they'll probably have one or two of their own, and I already have some grandchildren. . . ."

"You're afraid you won't love her other two children?" I asked.

"And that they won't love me! They already have two grandmas. Why should they love me as much? And how can I love them as much as I do my own biological grandchildren? Oh, they're good kids, but it's just not the same!"

Love is the main theme of Christianity, but sometimes even grandmothers have trouble loving a stepgrandchild, an adopted grandchild, or even a biological grandchild who has not reached his or her full potential.

I reminded my friend of some advice I had read: "Go through all the motions of loving them. Treat the new grandchildren as you do your own. Remember their birthdays and other big events. Go to their ball games and music recitals. Encourage them in whatever they do."

"Oh, I'll do all that!" she said.

I smiled. "Then 'love' will come. In fact, I think it has already started."

It's hard to love people who are different from us, yet Jesus loved everyone. He did not love the great religious leaders more than the "sinners," or the Jews more than the Gentiles. And they responded by loving him, too.

Be with all grandmothers everywhere, Lord. Help us to love all of our grandchildren and to enjoy their special gifts.

May 12

Read Matthew 6:19-21.

"My grandson wants a special shirt that costs fifty dollars," my friend told me. "His folks can't afford it, but he wants it so badly. . . ."

"But you can't afford it, either," I said. She is a widow living on not much more than her Social Security.

"But if I don't get it for him, his other grandmother will. She already sees him more than I do. I don't want him to forget about me! I'll manage OK."

Being a grandmother can be competitive sometimes. One grandmother may have more money and be able to give more expensive gifts. To a child, gifts often represent love; so we try to go "one up" on each other. The child ends up with toys and clothes he or she shouldn't need to be happy—and the wrong idea of love.

Getting into a "bidding war" for a grandchild's attention is easy to do; getting out is harder. My husband and I decided to set a price limit on birthday and Christmas gifts. We spend more time now trying to get each grandchild exactly the right present (or sometimes presents), but within our budget.

Christians sometimes seem to be in this same kind of competition. We give, not because we love the Lord, but because we want to make sure we're known as the biggest contributors or the busiest workers in the church. I've stopped trying to "win" here, too, thanks to what I've learned from my grandchildren.

I'm sorry, Lord, if I've given my grandchildren too many "worldly" things. I'm sorry, too, if I've done things for you for selfish reasons and not from true love. Help me know that what I give or do—for you or for my grandchildren—is from love, not from competing for favor.

❦ May 13

Read Mark 9:36-37.

When we cleaned out my in-laws' home, we found in my mother-in-law's special box a paragraph cut from a letter I had written to them years ago. It told about our son buying popsicles from the ice cream cart by himself. He had used the money they had given him that was supposed to last all week!

Until I reread this paragraph, I had forgotten the incident. To me, a mother, it had been a frustrating experience. I had to find room in our small refrigerator's freezer for extra popsicles—all of one flavor! But to a grandmother, it was a memory to be cherished.

Now that I am a grandmother, I understand this. As parents, we often were too busy, too caught up in the details of life, to truly appreciate the clever things our children said or did. We didn't seem to have time to enjoy every moment with our children.

As a grandmother, I am learning more about children than I did from raising my own. I keep all the cards, pictures, and school papers my grandchildren send me. Sometimes I wish I could have been a grandmother before being a mother. It would have helped me be more understanding and forgiving.

Thank you, Lord, for the good memories I have of my children, and forgive me for sometimes having been too busy to "welcome them" as a gift from you.

🍃 May 14

Read Isaiah 40:31.

When grandmothers get together, part of the talk is bound to be about babysitting. Many grandmothers feel they are "on call" every day, and some resent the long hours they have to spend with their grandchildren. They feel more like parents than grandparents. Others say, "It's nice to have them come, but it's nice when they go home!" Still others who live far away from their grandchildren, like me and my husband, look forward to the relatively few times each year when they are alone with the children.

No matter how much time a grandmother spends babysitting, we all can agree on one thing: The Lord knew what he was doing when he gave children to the young! Our grandchildren remind us that we have lost a lot of the energy and athletic abilities we had when our own children were young.

Yet there is nothing like a dizzy game of ring-around-the-rosy or a one-on-one basketball shootout to keep you young! Sometimes I surprise myself at what I can still do. And it never seems to occur to my grandchildren that I can't do everything they can. That's a real boost to my ego, even though I know that in a day or two I probably will feel the effects of trying too hard to keep up.

Please give me the strength to keep up with my grandchildren, Lord, so that I can enjoy these years with them to the fullest—years when we are still young enough to play together.

🍂 May 15

Read Jeremiah 29:12-14*a*; 1 Thessalonians 5:17.

Becoming a grandmother brings us into a whole new sphere of life. We love these little ones, no matter what they look like or what they do. When we visit them or when they come with their parents to visit us, we immediately want to hold them, play with them, or talk to them. We often rush past their parents to get to the grandchildren.

"Sometimes," my daughter laughed, "I think you'd be just as happy if we stayed home and only the children came!"

Her words made me think that perhaps we had been ignoring our own children and children-in-law when we were with our grandchildren. We just assumed they know we love them, too.

Since that conversation with my daughter, I have tried harder to show my love for the "sandwich generation": my children. I try not to give all of my time and attention to the grandchildren, but to give some of it to the adult "children" to strengthen those relationships.

Often I assume God knows I love him, and I rush through my prayer time to get to another activity or meeting. God knows I love him, but I need to spend time with him—not to build his love for me but to bolster my love for him.

I want to spend more time in prayer and Bible reading, Lord. I want you to know I love you, and I want to keep that love strong. Help me to see through my excuses for not showing my love for you and to find ways to grow closer to you.

🍂 May 16

Read Matthew 7:7-8.

One of the women in our church circle meeting was close to tears.

"My granddaughter bought her wedding dress this week," she said. "I was at her house after it had been delivered, but she never offered to show it to me!"

This grandmother was hurt by what seemed to her to be a lack of thoughtfulness. She had wanted to see the wedding dress, but she had not been invited.

"Did you ask to see it?" someone questioned. "Did you tell your granddaughter you wanted to see it?"

"No! If she couldn't realize that I was interested. . . ."

"Ask your granddaughter to show you her dress," the other woman continued. "She's just waiting for you to ask!"

Later we found this was true. The granddaughter had expected her grandmother to ask to see her dress and had assumed that she was not interested when she didn't ask.

There are times I act toward God the way this grandmother acted. I want something, or help in understanding a situation or making a decision, but I don't ask the Lord. I want him to make the first move! Jesus said we have to ask. He is ready to answer, but we do have to ask. Then we will get an answer, just as this grandmother found her granddaughter eager to show off her wedding dress.

So often, Lord, I don't come to you immediately for advice or help. Help me remember the grandmother and the bridal gown and be willing to ask you quickly.

141

May 17

Read John 15:13-14.

"I have a new friend," Sheila told us over the telephone. "It's Micah."

"That's nice," I said. "Why are you friends now with Micah?" Second grade seemed way too soon to have a boyfriend, I thought.

"He needs a friend," Sheila said. "No one is Micah's friend. But he's really nice. He can't help it if he doesn't have a daddy or nice clothes. I told him I'd be his friend."

I have often been proud of my grandchildren, and this time I was especially proud of Sheila. She had seen someone who needed to know he was not alone; someone who needed a friend but didn't have one. She had the courage to break through the wall that others had put up around Micah. Now maybe some of the others in her class would follow her lead.

I thought of the times I have "followed the crowd" when they were leaving someone out because that person was not like the rest of us in some way—not only when I was in school but also now as an adult. It's so much easier not to draw attention to ourselves. At one time or another, haven't we all been afraid to stand out from our friends and speak up for a cause, an action, or a person?

Please forgive me, Lord, for being too timid to be willing to stand alone for something or someone. Keep my grandchildren strong in their willingness to be friends with those who have no friends.

May 18

Read Proverbs 10a.

One thing grandmothers are good at is making memories. The problem is that what we think will make good memories is not always what the children will remember when they are grandparents themselves.

When Sheila and Molly were visiting us one summer, we planned a lot of activities. Some were costly, such as going to the lake; others, such as playing tennis in the park, were not. One morning we announced we were going to pick blueberries. I wanted to make a pie before they left. We did not think of it as a "fun time"; picking blueberries can be hard work.

To our surprise, the girls started right in when we reached the patch. After a quick lesson in how to spot ripe berries, they went to work, dropping blueberries into their coffee cans. We chatted across the bushes, but mostly they discussed together what they would do with the berries when they got them to their own home.

Six months later, Sheila told us on the telephone that she had used the blueberries to make muffins to take to school.

"Don't you remember, Grandma, that Molly and I picked *four pounds* last summer to bring home?"

Sometimes God wants me to do things that don't sound like much fun. Yet I find, sometimes years later, that those are the things I remember and cherish. Grandmas may not always know what makes good memories, but God does.

Teach me to listen to you more closely, Lord, so that I will know that you want me to make only good memories. Give me the wisdom to follow through when I know you want me to do something for you.

May 19

Read Titus 2:3.

I have a neighbor, Emma, who is ninety-four years old and likes to talk about her memories of childhood. One of her most vivid and treasured memories is of her grand-mother, who was blind.

143

"Part of my job was to take her outside every day," Emma says, "and lead her around for a walk. She was so interested in everything. I would tell her about the trees and flowers, and she would want to touch and smell them. She taught me so much while we were walking together, even though she couldn't see a thing."

A few of us who are now grandmothers will live to be great-grandmothers. But most of us know our grandchildren are probably the last generation we will see grow up. Yet the memories of grandmothers live on—for almost a century in Emma's case. We should remember that what we are teaching or experiencing with our grandchildren now will be the memories they will share in years to come. Had Emma's grandmother complained about her blindness, Emma's memories would be different today—and a lot less enjoyable. We can't be sure which events and experiences our grandchildren will remember most when they are grandparents themselves, so we must be sure to help them make good memories!

I want my grandchildren to have good memories of me, Lord. Give me patience and joy and help me to show them that my strength is in you.

May 20

Read 1 Peter 5:7.

Do grandmothers worry more than mothers do?

When I was a child, I often was told by my mother, "Don't tell Grandma about this; it'll just worry her."

Everyone knew that my grandmother was not a well woman. And she had experienced some deep grief in her life. So I grew up knowing we should not "worry" Grandma—although the things we were not to tell her did not seem to bother my mother that much, and seemed unimportant to me.

144

As a young mother, I had an older neighbor who confided that she loved having her grandchildren come to stay for a few days but that she worried about them getting hurt.

"I didn't worry about my own children," she said. "But I do about my grandchildren."

Back then I didn't understand these worries, but now I do. As we get older, we do see more of the dangers in life. We also know we have less strength to fight them or to defend ourselves.

Should grandmothers worry more? I don't think so. We have grown older and more aware of the dangers around us, but we also have grown more mature and secure in our faith in God. We know that God watches over his children; and no matter what happens, he loves us and cares about us.

I will always be concerned about my grandchildren, no matter how old they are. But I also know they are in God's hands—the best and safest place anyone can be.

Keep me calm and secure in knowing that you love me and my grandchildren, Lord. Don't let my concern for them turn into worry or fear.

May 21

Read Matthew 7:16; John 13:35.

Ahead of us in the fast-food line was a young mother holding a baby in a pink sweat suit. As the line inched forward, the infant looked at me over her mother's shoulder.

"Hi, there," I said, smiling.

The baby grinned back, showing her teeth. She made a low sound, and I smiled again.

"Who's that?" her mother asked as she turned. Upon seeing me, she nodded. Then she said to the baby, "But

145

that's not your grandma." She started to turn the baby around, but the child twisted her head to keep watching me.

I think babies sense a grandmother when they see one—whether it's their own grandma or not. And because they recognize us, they are relaxed with us, knowing they have nothing to fear from us. They sense our love and care. Christians, Jesus said, can tell one another by their love and by their fruits. We are to recognize one another, just as the baby seemed to know me as a grandmother and responded to my greeting.

Help me to know your people, Lord, and to let them know me and my love for you by my love and my fruits.

May 22

Read 1 Chronicles 29:13.

"My grandchildren don't write thank-you notes for my gifts," I heard a grandmother complain on TV one day. "So I've decided to stop giving them anything—even on birthdays and Christmas!"

Most of us have given gifts to our grandchildren that were not acknowledged with a thank-you note. The gifts may have been money, or clothes, or something else the child didn't really appreciate. Or the child may have been too caught up in his or her own activities to write a note to thank us.

But I question the TV grandmother's decision to stop giving gifts. I don't think I could do that. We give our grandchildren gifts because we love them and want to share special times with them, even from a distance. If we stopped giving gifts, it would be like saying we loved their thank-you notes more than we loved giving gifts!

Many times I forget to thank God for his gifts—big gifts such as a fine husband and family, or little gifts such as a break in the rain long enough for the picnic we've planned. But God does not stop giving me gifts. God is still there for me; he still shows his love for me every day.

So even if there were never another thank-you note from a grandchild, I would keep on giving gifts. I would know they understand I still love them.

Forgive me, Lord, for not taking the time to thank you for the wonderful gifts you have given me all through my life. I know these gifts are from you, yet I have failed to say thank you so many times. Right now I want to say thank you for all your gifts!

🌱 May 23

Read Proverbs 7:2.

On a visit to our daughter's home, my husband found our grandson, Lincoln, waiting outside the bathroom door when he came out.

"Grandpa! You didn't put the lid down on the potty!" Lincoln scolded. "You have to put the lid down!"

"Oh?" my husband said. "Why is that?"

Lincoln frowned in thought. If he had any idea that putting the lid down would keep his younger sister from playing in the water, he did not mention it. "Because Mom says so!" he responded triumphantly. Obviously, this was an argument that had no way of being "topped."

My husband grinned. "That's a good enough reason for me. I'll remember next time."

I laughed when I heard the story, but I also thought about occasions when God seems to be telling me to do something that doesn't make much sense to me. And God seems to be telling me to do it "just because I say so!"

My husband wanted to please Lincoln by doing what Lincoln's mother had told him to do. I want to please God by doing what he has led me to see as his will. Often I fail, but I intend to keep trying. "Just because God says so" is reason enough for me.

I do want to do what you expect me to, Lord. Help me to understand exactly what those things are and to see clearly how to do them.

May 24

Read Isaiah 65:24.

We grandmothers do a lot of talking to our grandchildren. But sometimes the best thing we can do for them is listen, not talk.

When we were visiting our grandchildren, Sheila wanted me to go for a bike ride with her. We rode slowly, side by side, enjoying the weather. We talked about many things, with her doing most of the talking.

Sheila told me what she liked about school, her family, and her vacations. She told me about the books she likes to read, what she was "collecting," and her new doll. It was a happy time of closeness.

Later, Sheila told her mother eagerly, "Grandma and I just talked and talked!" She was enthused and happy because I had listened to her talk on and on as much as she wanted.

I remember once asking my daughter to please be quiet "just for five minutes." As a mother, I got caught up in so many details; as a grandmother, I had the time to listen. God has the time to listen to us, too. He will spend as much time with me as I let him. It's up to me to begin the conversation, however, just as Sheila began the one with me.

Don't let me forget, Lord, that you are always there, ready to listen to my problems, my pains, and my joys and triumphs. Forgive me for forgetting that I need to talk to you more often.

❧ **May 25**

Read Matthew 28:20b.

It was a major catastrophe! While visiting our grand-children, we were taking our kindergarten granddaughter, Suzanne, to school, and she had forgotten "Teddy." Teddy is the small bear with a checked hat and dress who lives in her backpack. She had taken Teddy out of the backpack the night before and had forgotten to put her back.

"I can't go without Teddy!" she sobbed. "I need Teddy! I have to have Teddy!"

I wanted to cry, too. Grandmothers never want to see their grandchildren sad and in tears. I was about to offer to drive the five miles back to get Teddy when Suzanne spotted a friend and her mother. She ran to them. The mother, sensing something was not right, hugged Suzanne close. Still choking back sobs, Suzanne followed her friend into the school.

All morning I worried. Should I have taken the small bear to Suzanne? Would she still be crying when we went for her at noon?

Later I waited at the school door. Suzanne came out, smiling and waving a paper she had completed.

"I made it without Teddy," she told us solemnly, "but I thought about her a lot." I thought of the things I think I can't get along without: car, telephone, washer and dryer. Yet if they were gone, I could "make it" without them for as long as necessary. The only thing I can't get along without is knowing Jesus loves me. I have to have that every day!

Please don't let me get so caught up in the world's "things," Lord, that I forget about your love. Help me to show that love to others, including my grandchildren.

Read John 6:35.

We had taken Lincoln, Suzanne, and their parents to dinner. It was the first restaurant Lincoln had been to with an all-you-can-eat salad bar. Following the adults example, Lincoln opted for the salad bar buffet. He brought a full plate back to the table and began to eat.

When he had cleaned his plate, his dad said, "You finished, Lincoln?"

"I ate it all," he replied.

"Do you want to go back for more?" his father asked.

"You mean you're allowed to go back?" Lincoln said suspiciously.

"As many times as you want," we assured him. "That's what all-you-can-eat means!"

Lincoln's eyes widened, and he grinned. "I'll be right back!"

The restaurant may have made money on the rest of us that night, but not on Lincoln! He made several more trips to the salad bar, taking a clean plate each time as instructed and returning with a serving of just one item. He enjoyed every bite. And the next time we visited that restaurant, he asked if we could sit near the salad bar!

Too often I view God the way Lincoln first viewed the salad bar. I forget that, as a Christian, I can come to God as often as I want. I'm not limited to one "trip" per day—or even per hour. I can come to God for help, strength, and love as often as I want—every day. Like the salad bar, God keeps his table filled for me.

Thank you for always being there for me, Lord. I know I forget to come to you sometimes, trying to do everything on my own. Forgive me for not remembering to talk everything over with you before I make a decision or act.

🍓 May 27

Read Psalm 119:10.

Our children have laid down different "rules of the house" for our grandchildren. In one home, each person at the table carries his or her own dirty dishes to the kitchen to be washed. In the other home, school clothes must be changed immediately upon getting home in the afternoon.

These rules, and others like them, are made to keep things running smoothly in each household—where the mothers as well as the fathers work outside the home. When the rules are broken, things become more disorganized, more chaotic, and more difficult.

When we go to visit either home, we have to remember to obey the rules of that house, too, as much as possible. The rules often are strange to us—different from those we had for our own children when they were young.

I often think about God's rules. Sometimes I don't understand the reasons for them; they seem strange to me. Yet when I break one of them, I see pain, despair, and confusion.

I know my children's rules are good for my grandchildren. And I know God's rules are good for me.

I know your rules are necessary for me, Lord. Please forgive me when I don't take them seriously. Help me to stand firmly by these rules, even when others say they are not for today's world.

🍓 May 28

Read Psalm 119:105.

It was our first visit to our son's home since he and his family had moved to Florida. Molly, then age three, wanted to show us around the neighborhood. Many of the trees, birds, and flowers were new to us. In answer to our questions, Molly's reply was usually, "We have a book at home that tells." When we heard a bird singing in a nearby tree, I said, "I wonder what bird that is."

Molly looked at the tree and concentrated. Then, with all the confidence of a three-year-old, she said, "Maybe it's a mocking bird!"

I never did find out what bird was actually singing that day, but Molly's answer, and the certainty in her tone, seemed a lot like my relationship with God's Word.

There are many scriptures I don't understand. But rather than admitting this to myself, and to God, I often rush in to give a possible answer. I try to convince myself—and others, if I'm in a group—that my interpretation is right, even when I am not sure.

I often do not want to take time to search for the answer; I want to sound as though I already know. With this attitude, I won't grow in my understanding of God's message in the Bible. Sometimes I have to be willing to say, "I don't know" and seek help in finding the answer.

Lord, I want to understand what you want me to know from your Word. Help me to study your Word in order to learn the real meanings in your teachings.

May 29

Read Luke 11:13.

On a visit to see our daughter and her family, we planned to go the next day to a nearby state park. We would hike the trails, feed the ducks, and eat our picnic lunch beside the beautiful lake. We all were excited, and the grandchildren were planning what play equipment to take with them.

Then the TV announced a very good chance of rain for the next day.

"Oh, no!" I moaned. "It can't rain!" I thought of what a downpour would do to our picnic plans.

Lincoln, then five years old, interrupted my complaining. "But, Grandma, if it rains, there could be a rainbow!"

That brought my grumbling to a screeching halt. I had thought only of my wants, but Lincoln had seen beyond our possible disappointment to recognize the beauty that could come with the rain.

Since then I have tried to be more intentional about watching for the good and the beautiful that God sends after the harsh and unhappy times. Often, like the rainbow in the rain, the good is easy to see right away. Other times, the good is much harder to find, and may not show up immediately. Yet I am finding that God is faithful and that the good always comes—even if it takes me a long time to discover it.

I know that "bad" things happen to us, Lord; some that make us unhappy and disillusioned. Help me remember that you are still there, walking beside me through all the shadowy valleys.

🌿 May 30

Read Luke 2:52.

It was unusually hot one weekend when we visited our grandchildren. They had a wading pool on the patio, filled with water and their best-loved boats, ducks, and other bath toys. It was their favorite place to be that day.

"Come on and get in with us, Grandma," Lincoln called. "We can splash each other."

Comparing my size to the size of the pool, I knew that if I got in, there would not be much room for play. I had outgrown a wading pool long ago.

"I'll sit here by the pool, and you can splash me here," I told him. Disappointment clouded his face. "Don't you want to get in the pool, Grandma?"

Of course, I would have loved to get into the cool water. But I needed a much bigger pool. He could still enjoy the little pool; I could not.

We settled for my staying on the cement patio and our splashing back and forth. My "hits" on him were rewarded with giggles; his on me with squeals.

As adults, we have outgrown some of our early religious beliefs, just as we have left behind our childhood toys. But we must guard against trying to outgrow the basic beliefs of Christianity. They are for all ages. May we, like Jesus, increase in wisdom as we increase in years.

Lord, help me to "act my age" in my Christian faith. Let me learn more about you and your will for me in my mature years.

🌺 May 31

Read Luke 14:18a.

As usual, our daughter had set out four-year-old Suzanne's clothes the night before. This morning, however, Suzanne objected to the choice.

"I can't wear that!" she told her mother.

"Why not?" her mother asked. Our daughter was hurrying to get everyone ready for work, school, and day care.

"I don't have any jewelry to go with it!" Suzanne's tone left no doubt that no one could argue with that calamity.

Later my daughter told me, "I doubted whether it was a good reason or just an excuse to wear something else."

Whichever it was, Suzanne's explanation worked; she wore another outfit, complete with jewelry.

My excuses to God probably sound as weak to him as Suzanne's did to her mother. I excuse not being in church by saying that I'm too tired or I have to go somewhere else at that time. I excuse not giving as much as I could by

154

reminding myself that I have to buy a car this year. I excuse not taking time to pray or read my Bible because God already knows what I'm going to pray and I have read the Bible through before.

Suzanne's excuse sounded good to her, but her mother, while letting her have her own way, was not fooled. Likewise, God does not force his way on me, but neither is he fooled. I am only fooling myself with my excuses.

Help me to see the excuses I give you as what they really are, Lord—weak reasons for doing what I want to do or what is easiest and most comfortable for me. Give me the strength to stop making excuses and do your will.

Grandmother Days

Betty Steele Everett

🍂 *June* 1

Read John 15:13-14.

Every grandmother needs a special "grandma friend." This friend is another grandmother whose grandchildren are near the ages of your own.

A "grandma friend" is someone you can brag to about your grandchildren at any time, and she will not try to "top" your story by telling something smarter, cuter, or braver that one of her grandchildren did or said. A "grandma friend" will listen to all your grandmother stories, then compliment you and your grandchildren highly and sincerely. She will look at all your photos, admiring the grandchildren and finding something good to say about the photos—even when they are poor pictures. And you will do the same for her.

My "grandma friend" is Katie. We have been walking together several times a week for more than twenty years—long before we ever thought about being grandmothers. We have plenty of time to talk about our grandchildren as we walk our five miles. We agree completely that our grandchildren are the best in the world in every way. Privately, of course, we each continue to think that our own are just a shade better. But we never, never say so!

Jesus is a special friend, too, but in a different and deeper way. Although he listens to us as other friends do, he has done for us what no human friend can do. He died for our sins and opened the door to heaven so that we may go in.

Thank you, Jesus, for being my friend. Show me how to share your friendship with my other friends. And thank you for my special "grandma friend."

🍂 June 2

Read John 14:1-3.

The grandchildren are coming to visit! They will be with us for a whole week! It is a chance to make new memories that will warm us through the coming years. It is a chance to get to know them all over again.

We've been planning for "the visit" for more than a month. Each time I go to the grocery store, I add one or two extra items to my cart. One time it is a six-pack of soda; another time a package of ice cream bars. Sometimes it is one of their favorite cereals.

As I put these "goodies" away in the cupboard and freezer to wait for "the visit," I think about how Jesus said he was going to heaven to prepare a place for us there. Just as we love our grandchildren, so also God loves us—only much, much more. God has prepared for our coming, too. We can only imagine the delights in store for us. We do know they will be to our liking—as tailored to our desires as we have tailored the buying of treats according to what our grandchildren like. Heaven will be . . . well, just heavenly!

There is one big difference, though. In a week, our grandchildren have to leave us. In heaven, we won't ever have to leave; we can enjoy it for eternity.

Lord, thank you for the opportunity to spend time with my grandchildren. Even more, thank you for preparing a place for me in your heavenly Kingdom.

June 3

Read Ephesians 1:4-5.

My friend's only son and his wife cannot have children, so they have begun the mountains of paperwork to adopt a baby.

"It was their decision," my friend told me, "and they are so excited. But I can't forget that this won't really be my grandchild. It will be someone else's."

"But you'll learn to love the child," I assured her. "And the child will have a good, Christian home—something he or she might not have had without your son and his wife."

"But it won't have any part of *me* in it. Not my eye color, hair color, or love of music. And what if . . . well, the child has "bad genes"?

"No baby comes with a guarantee," I replied. "And your own biological grandchild might have brown eyes instead of blue—and love art, mechanics, or sports more than music."

"But it won't have my blood," she said as she shook her head. "It won't really be mine."

When my friend had gone home, I thought about the grandchild she someday would hold who would not be of her blood. In my heart I knew she would love it, regardless of physical characteristics or personality traits.

Then I remembered Moses, the adopted son of Pharaoh's daughter, who was used by God in such a powerful way. My friend's grandchild might never be famous, but he or she could become an adopted child of God. And Grandmother could help!

Lord, please help those who have adopted grandchildren to love them as though they were of their own blood; to love them as you love us.

June 4

Read 2 Timothy 1:5.

I know I am important to my grandchildren. They look forward to the letters I write them each week, and to the riddles I enclose. They watch for their birthday packages, knowing I have made a special effort to buy the gifts they want. They wait on that birthday night for the special telephone call that is just for them. And I look forward to all these things, too.

Recently a friend pointed out that only once in the Bible is the word *grandmother* used. I was skeptical. How could anyone as important as a grandmother be neglected in the Bible? I checked my concordance, and my friend was right.

But in referring to Timothy's grandmother, Lois, Paul gave all grandmothers a definite idea of our role and responsibilities. We are first to teach our own children about the Lord. For us, that time has past. There is a new generation of mother and child. But Paul says we are to help with teaching the new generation. Not to do it all—that is up to our children. But we can be a Christian example to our grandchildren. We can let them know we go to church and take part in its ministries. We can mention our prayers for them. We can be there for them, and for their parents, when they need encouragement or advice. If we do this, someday our grandchildren will remember us as true Christian role models.

Lord, I thank you for letting me be a grandmother. Help me be the kind of grandmother that Lois was, always putting you first in my life.

159

♥ June 5

Read Exodus 3:13-15.

When my daughter-in-law was expecting her first child—and my first grandchild—she asked, "What do you want our children to call you?"

I had to smile. Despite all my mother could do to persuade me otherwise, I had called my grandmother "Knee" until I was in school. I assume it was because she always held me on her knee. With her arms around me as I leaned against her, I felt very safe—and special.

"They'll probably come up with their own name for me," I said. "But just 'Grandma' or 'Grandma E' is fine."

Like all children, my grandchildren started out calling me by a simple name. I was just "E" at first. As they got older, it became "Grandma E," and now it's just "Grandma."

Whatever our grandchildren call us, it sounds wonderful to us. Grandmothers have many different names, and the names really don't make any difference. Talking with the children is what matters.

I call God by different names, too. Sometimes I follow Jesus' example and call God Father. Sometimes I use Lord, or Master, or God. Regardless of what we call God, I'm sure the most important thing to God is that we call him by name and talk to him in prayer.

Father, thank you for the chance to talk to you whenever I want, wherever I am, and to know that you hear me and love me.

♥ June 6

Read Matthew 5:9.

June 6, 1944 was D-Day, the day Allied troops, many of which were American, landed in France for the final assaults against Hitler.

I was finishing my sophomore year in high school. My friends and I were excited. We did not think of the men, some only a few years older than we were, who would die. We thought only that at last the "good guys" would win over the "bad guys."

While we are not in the midst of a world war today, there are smaller wars all around us. Even our streets are battlegrounds. The world my grandchildren live in is far scarier than the one I lived in then. We did not know about AIDS, and even the atom bomb was a secret. "Drugs" meant aspirin, and teenage pregnancy was rare in our neighborhood. Only dedicated hunters owned guns—and kept them locked up tight.

My grandchildren are facing perils I never dreamed of at their age. Yet some things have not changed. As Christians, we still believe that God is in control and loves us. We still believe in our families. My grandchildren are being taught the values that time can never change. I don't know what the world will be like next week, let alone when they are grandparents, but I pray and trust that they will be peacemakers and that you will be with them always.

Please, Lord, don't give up on our world. Help us make it safe for our grandchildren and their grandchildren. Don't ever let us forget that you are in control, even when others tell us that you don't exist.

June 7

Read 1 Corinthians 12:4-6.

School's out! That means that sometime in the next three months many of our grandchildren will go to Vacation Bible School for a week. It's a time of activities, crafts, and learning about Jesus.

Our church is a large one, and children come to our

Bible school who attend our church, other churches, and no church at all. The teachers are young mothers, but we grandmothers have a job, too. We bake the cookies that are given out at "treat time" each day. Many grandmothers are known for baking cookies, even if some of them start out at the supermarket dairy case!

As I bake chocolate chip cookies (Is there any other kind?), I think about my role. It's not highly visible, but it's still important. Cookies bring a special mood and feeling—a feeling of security, of caring, and of love. It is a feeling we all want to give, not only to our grandchildren but to all children.

Jesus knew how important food is. There was a small boy with a small amount of food—only five loaves and two fish. But Jesus used this small amount to feed five thousand people!

As I pull the cookies from the oven, I wonder if somehow Jesus will use them, and those cookies baked by other grandmothers, to "feed" children more than a sweet treat. I may never know the answer, but I don't need to. I only need to do what I can today.

Lord, please use my skills and my life to influence my own grandchildren and others, too, for you.

June 8

Read Nahum 1:7.

We were talking to our grandson, Lincoln, on the telephone. He had just finished second grade, and I was asking about his plans for the summer.

Unknown to me, he had handed the receiver to Suzanne, his four-year-old sister, for her turn to talk to Grandma. I continued with my questions to Lincoln.

"What books are you reading now that school is out?" I asked.

There was a brief pause. "Oh, Grandma! I can't read a word!" Suzanne said. "Don't you know that?"

I quickly apologized, explaining that I thought Lincoln was still on the line. "Don't worry," I assured her, "you'll be reading one of these days—when you get to school."

"I know," she said confidently. "I'll read real good then."

I admired her certainty. She was sure not only of her own ability to learn but also of the ability of teachers to teach her to read. She trusted them with her future and looked forward to school with no doubt that it would be a good experience.

Just as Suzanne trusts her future teachers to teach her to read, so also I trust the Lord to take care of me. I believe my future with the Lord will be good—both for the rest of my time in this world and for eternity in heaven.

Lord, I trust my present and my future to you and your promises. Give me grace to trust you even more.

June 9

Read John 10:14.

My husband and I talk to our grandchildren on the telephone often. When they were young, it was hard for me to tell their voices apart.

"Hello, Sheila," I'd say, only to be met with a giggle and an "Oh, E, I'm not Sheila! I'm Molly. Didn't you know that?"

I had the same problem with the other set of grandchildren, too, and often had to admit my mistake. The children took it as a big joke on Grandma and laughed at me.

Now that they are older, though, I have no trouble telling them apart. Their voices have taken on individual characteristics. Molly's voice is soft and quiet; Sheila speaks quickly so she can tell me everything she wants to in the few minutes she has. Suzanne speaks very distinctly, making sure I understand each word. Lincoln speaks slowly, as though pondering the exact answer to my question. In a few years, of course, his voice will deepen and be even more distinctive.

Jesus knows our voices, too. No matter how many of us are praying at the same time, he knows who is who, and he does not get confused. It is reassuring to know that he knows my voice even better than I know my grandchildren's voices.

Thank you, Lord, for listening to me and knowing my voice among the many others praying to you. Help me always to be open to hearing your voice speaking to me.

June 10

Read Matthew 11:29.

When Molly was born, Sheila became "Big Sister." Her parents explained that she would be Molly's first teacher, because the younger one would look to the older one as an example of what to do and how to do it; and that as "Big Sister," she must do all she could to help and protect Molly.

Sheila took her job seriously. When her parents warned her about playing too roughly with Molly, she tried to be more gentle.

As I sat on the floor with Molly on a blanket and Sheila lying beside her, Molly suddenly grabbed Sheila's hair. A baby's grip is frighteningly tight, and it doesn't take much of a pull on the hair to cause pain.

"No, Molly!" I said almost sharply as I saw Sheila grimace. "You can't pull Big Sister's hair. That hurts Sheila."

"It's OK," Sheila said quickly. "She's just a baby."

"But she has to learn not to hurt people." I gently removed Molly's fingers from Sheila's hair.

Sheila looked at me in surprise, and I realized it was the first time since she had become "Big Sister" that anyone had protected *her* instead of the baby.

Then she smiled at me and touched Molly gently. "It's OK, Molly. You just have to learn."

All our lives we have lessons to learn, and the lessons sometimes can be painful. But just as Sheila forgave Molly and tried to comfort her, so also God forgives us and wants to give us peace in our lives.

Thank you for being there for me, Lord, when the lessons I have to learn are painful and I feel deserted by everyone.

🍂 June 11

Read John 14:13-14.

When Molly was approaching two years of age, we were visiting in her home. As she struggled to put on her coat, my husband moved to help her.

"No!" Molly said, giving him a withering glance and pulling away from his reach. "Me do own self!"

She wasn't sure of the full sentence, but she knew her own mind. She wanted no help! She was independent, and she was going to prove it. She wanted no assistance. Eventually, of course, she got the coat on all by herself, although it took a lot more time and struggle than it would have if she had accepted her grandfather's help.

The words "Me do own self!" have become a sort of slogan between my husband and me when we don't want any help. It always makes us laugh as we remember.

I wonder, though, if I often sound to God like Molly did to us. I know God can help me, but I don't want to admit I need God's aid. I continue to struggle along on my own, too proud and independent to ask for God's help. Like Molly and her coat, I could solve my problems a lot faster with God's help—and that help is as close as a prayer.

Lord, help me to be less independent and more dependent on you. Give me the meekness to admit my needs and ask for your help.

June 12

Read Matthew 7:12.

My husband is a semiprofessional photographer. When our granddaughter Sheila was about six years old, he wanted to take pictures of her that would be artistic, rather than mere snapshots.

"Sheila, will you be my model?" he asked her seriously. "You'll have to stand like I tell you and be very still and patient. Do you think you can do it?"

Sheila was thrilled to be singled out as a model. "Will you come, too, Grandma?" she asked me.

"Sure. I'll be your 'makeup lady.'" Since she wore no makeup, my job was to make sure her hair was not too wind blown and her dress collar was straight.

The photo session went well. Sheila obeyed every instruction, and my husband ended up with several very good portraits, as well as action shots.

"Can I be your model again sometime, Pa?" Sheila asked eagerly on the way home. "It was fun."

We all like to be asked to do something special. We like to be treated like "professionals"—even in areas where we know we're rank amateurs. We treated Sheila that way, and she responded.

As grandmothers, we have to remember that although our grandchildren may be young and far from being expert in anything, they should be treated with respect and love—as should everyone we come into contact with in church, school, or elsewhere. Respectful treatment *of* others results in respectful treatment *from* others.

Help me remember, Lord, that how I treat my grandchildren will make a lasting impression on them and their lives. Give me the patience and wisdom to know what to do to give them self-confidence for life.

June 13

Read 1 Corinthians 3:7-8.

In a recent letter my daughter told us that she had been trying to teach traffic safety lessons to our youngest granddaughter, Suzanne. She began to wonder if she had overdone it, though, when Suzanne told her solemnly, "Jesus died on the crosswalk."

"But," my daughter assured us later in her letter, "as soon as she said it, she knew she had the wrong word and corrected herself."

We laughed at the remark and shared it with friends. I even sent it to *Reader's Digest.* But the most important part of the incident was the proof to me that my grandchildren are being taught about Jesus.

No child is born knowing about the Lord. At age five, Suzanne does not understand all the words and their meanings, but the ground has been prepared and the seed planted. It will take time and many people to water and nourish that seed into full faith. Parents cannot do the job alone. Many Sunday school teachers, pastors, and youth leaders will eventually take part in my grandchild's Christian growth.

My part as a "long-distance" grandmother is not as direct. I can pray for my grandchildren and for those who teach them about the Lord. I can remind the children that I am praying for them, and I can share my experiences as a Christian and a church member.

Be a real presence in my grandchildren's lives, Lord, and show me how to help them grow as your children.

June 14

Read Luke 11:11-13.

A special June holiday is Father's Day. On the second Sunday of the month, fathers all over the country are honored and remembered.

We all are here because of our fathers (and our mothers, of course), and we all have been shaped by our fathers as we have grown. I thank God that my father was a good father, as was my husband to our children. I also thank God that both sets of our grandchildren have fine, loving fathers. My son and son-in-law are good examples for the children of what a father should be.

No matter how good earthly fathers are, though, or how hard they try to do what is best for their children, the only perfect example of a father is God. In Jesus' descriptions of God, we find what a true father should be to his children. And this is the example I pray my son and son-in-law will follow as they are fathers to their own children on earth.

Lord, I thank you for all the good and loving fathers in the world. I pray that my grandchildren will continue to live and grow under the guidance of their fathers.

June 15

Read Philippians 4:8.

When our grandson, Lincoln, was still the only grandchild old enough to sit and eat at the table, we took him and his parents to dinner. Lincoln chose the restaurant and made his own choice from the children's menu.

Lincoln worked his way to a clean plate, enjoying every

bite. He also enjoyed talking to all of us and looking around at the other diners. We were eating our desserts when two older women at a neighboring table rose to leave. As they passed our table, one of them bent down to speak to my daughter.

"Your little boy is so well behaved. It was a pleasure eating near him," she said.

Flustered, my daughter murmured a thank you, and the woman was gone. But as I looked at my daughter's and son-in-law's proud faces, I saw a new glow and confidence there. They had been complimented on their child, but they also had been complimented on their job of parenting. This woman had made two parents happy and had given them assurance that they were doing something right!

I thought of all the times I could have said something nice to a parent about her or his children but had not. Since that night, I have tried to offer assurance when I feel others deserve a pat on the back. It makes me feel good, too. I think Jesus probably smiles to see us making others happy.

Lord, I want to help others feel good about themselves. Give me the shove I sometimes need to tell them they are doing a good job.

❧ June 16

Read Psalm 103:17.

I sometimes think about my grandchildren's future weddings and wonder if I will be there. Then I remember an older Quaker lady with whom I had a correspondence for a short time before her death.

"My grandmother prayed for her descendants down to the fifth generation," she once told me. "She prayed for them even though she knew she never would see them.

And she prayed for the ones they would marry. She prayed for good Christian marriages for each one."

Five generations! Yet the time passed quickly. My friend was the second generation; her grandchildren were the fourth.

"After Grandmother died," she said, "I began praying for five generations. And someday someone else will be praying for five more."

I liked the idea. Now I pray for my children, for my grandchildren, and for their children and grandchildren—even though I have no idea what sex they will be, what they will look like, or what they will do with their lives. I also pray for those they will marry.

The Bible mentions "children's children" often. I know God will take care of them!

Lord, please bless my family for many generations. Lead them to the right people to marry, and teach them to honor you in all they do.

🍂 June 17

Read Matthew 5:14-16.

Anyone coming into our kitchen, living room, or bedroom instantly can tell we are grandparents! There are snapshots stuck to the refrigerator with magnets, studio portraits in silver frames on the living room tables, and a gallery of other poses on our dressers. Actually, our home is not much different from the homes of my friends who also are grandparents!

Being a grandparent means wanting to have reminders of your youngest family members close by. It means wanting to share with friends these pictures and the stories of what these precious people are doing. I love my grandchildren, and sharing their pictures and talking about them is one way I show it.

I love the Lord, too, but as I look around my house, I'm not sure a visitor could tell it. There are several versions of the Bible, but they are shelved on an out-of-the way bookcase.

Talking about my grandchildren is easy to do; talking about the Lord is not. Do I know the Lord as well as I know my grandchildren? Do I think about him and talk to him as much? Do I tell my friends what he's doing in my life the way I report on what my grandchildren are doing?

Help me, Lord, to let my light shine for you. Bless my family and remind me that you will always be with each of us.

🍂 June 18

Read John 3:16.

Equality is a word we hear often in many different arenas today. A grandmother knows what equality means! It means being sure that each grandchild is treated as equally as possible as all the others. It means making sure that Christmas, birthday, and other gifts are similar in price and importance. It means giving the grandchildren the same amount of time and attention.

When we got a new car, I wrote about it in my weekly letter to my granddaughter Sheila. Because I try to give the two sisters different bits of news, I did not mention it in Molly's letter. Later, Molly said to me, "You didn't tell *me* about your new car!" The fact that I had told her sister and had expected her to share the news made no difference. I had not told Molly personally about the car. She felt slighted and left out. She wanted to feel as important as her older sister, and Grandma had let her down!

It's hard sometimes to keep things equal, but we grandmothers know how important it is. And so does Jesus. He died for anyone and everyone who will accept his gift. We all are equal in his sight. It is a comforting thought—and an ideal for me to aim for as I relate to my grandchildren and others.

Lord, help me treat my grandchildren as fairly and equally as possible in worldly things. Please let them know I love them all equally, which is the most important thing.

June 19

Read 1 Corinthians 3:1-2.

Molly taught herself to read when she was four. None of us knows how she did it; even she does not know. She says, "I just saw how the words looked."

Because she began to read so early, Molly probably has read more books for her age than my other grandchildren. She began with the usual simple books and has gone on to progressively harder and more interesting ones. She reads several grade levels beyond her own.

When I mentioned some of the books I had seen children reading in our library, she said, "I call those 'baby books'! I don't read them any more!"

I tried to explain that these children were "baby" readers. They could not read as well as she could and were right to choose "baby" books. They would not always read them, I assured her.

Sometimes, as a Christian of mature faith, I get impatient with newer Christians. I forget they are "babies" in the faith and will grow. Like Molly and the "baby books," these newer Christians will want to grow beyond their early "baby" ways of faith. I must remember that it's my job to help them grow, not to be impatient with their growth.

Give me patience, Lord, and the insight of your Holy Spirit so that I may help new Christians grow in faith, whether they be children or adults.

June 20

Read Mark 10:15.

In the fall, our youngest granddaughter, Suzanne, was to start kindergarten. Early in June, before school was officially out, she went to a "new student" orientation. The teacher she would have in the fall talked to the children in the kindergarten room. She showed them everything in the room, explained the basic rules of the class, and told them what supplies they would need. She also showed them where the restrooms were.

This last thing impressed Suzanne the most. She excitedly told us about it on the telephone that night.

"There are two restrooms," she explained eagerly. "One is the 'Ladies' Room' and one is the 'Men's Room'." She paused to be sure we understood and then continued. "Grandma, you can come with me to the 'Ladies' Room,' but Grandpa has to go to the 'Men's Room'."

We laughed, but we understood that this was new information to Suzanne and that she wanted to share it with us because she loves us.

I know about Jesus and his love, but my zest is no longer that of a child. I rarely mention the Lord unless I am talking to other Christians. Yet if a child can be enthused about something as mundane as restrooms, why have I lost my enthusiasm for telling others about Jesus? Jesus said that unless we become like little children, we will not be able to enter his Kingdom. Enthusiasm may be part of what he meant.

Forgive me, Lord, when I let my enthusiasm for you and your Word become a mere routine instead of a marvelous miracle. Help my eagerness to tell others about you be like the ardor of a little child.

🍂 June 21

Read Matthew 6:34.

My daughter and son-in-law go regularly with their children to a cottage in Maine, which is about a four-hour drive from their home. On one such trip, the children naturally were excited, knowing some of the fun things they would be doing in the next few days.

"Are we there yet?" Lincoln, then age seven, asked every few minutes.

At last, his patience wearing thin, Lincoln's father said, "Lincoln, we're a long way from Maine, and I don't want to hear you ask again if we're there yet!"

For several miles there was complete silence in the back seat. Then in a timid voice came the question, "Are we halfway there yet?"

All of us measure our progress in time and distance. Is it time to go to work, to go home, to eat? Have we gotten as far on our trip as we wanted to by this time?

On this earth, everything can be measured by some method. And by the measurement of years, I am more than halfway to heaven. It is a sobering thought. Have I accomplished all I could have, or should have, in this time? Or should I try to do better? Like Lincoln and the trip to Maine, I know there is "fun" awaiting me in heaven. Unlike the trip to the coast, however, I will not have a chance to come back and live any part of my life again. Today is truly the first day of the rest of my life—and the last day of the past.

Show me what you want me to do for you today, Lord, so that the rest of my "trip" in this life will be made living even closer to you.

174

❦ June 22

Read John 14:8-9.

Our two sets of grandchildren live almost the length of the Atlantic coast apart. Two are in Rhode Island; two in Florida. They rarely see one another, and at their ages, they are not very interested in writing letters.

As "Grandma" to all of them, I try to help bridge the miles for them. When I write to one child, I mention by name one of the faraway cousins. I mention schools, activities, or weather, trying to show that they have many of the same interests. I do the same thing when we talk on the telephone.

My husband and I also try to have both families visit us at the same time during the year. Then we try to leave the children and grandchildren alone to get to know one another again. In a short time, the grandchildren are playing together as if they had lived next door to one another all their lives.

I love all my grandchildren and want them to know one another. It is not easy to keep in touch with someone you seldom see. But I am praying that, with my help, they will work it out on their own—so they won't feel like strangers all their lives.

Jesus wanted his followers to know his father, although they were in different worlds. Jesus made himself the "bridge" between us and the Father.

Thank you, Lord, for giving us grandchildren. Please help me to help them know one another despite the distance between them.

❦ June 23

Read 1 Corinthians 12:4-6.

Both sets of my grandchildren are fortunate to have another living grandma. Both of these other grandmothers

175

are clever with their hands. They knit, sew, and do fancy needlework. The children proudly wear sweaters, caps, and tops made just for them by these two grandmothers.

I have no skill in this area. When I sew—which is as seldom as possible—I can count on sticking myself at least once with the needle. And I don't know knit from purl. For a long time I felt left out when these grandmothers talked with my daughter and daughter-in-law about their current projects.

Then I wrote a book. Since it was about being a grandparent, I dedicated it to my four grandchildren and "any that may come after." My grandchildren can't wear a book, but they can take it to school and show it to their classmates. It's debatable whether a book is as wonderful to a child as a hand-knit sweater, but it taught me a valuable lesson.

We grandmothers do not have to have the same skills or talents. Our grandchildren benefit more from grandmothers who are truly different from each other. Some grandmas can bake blue-ribbon chocolate chip cookies; some can tell original stories; some can teach a foreign language; some can show grandchildren how to hit a golf or tennis ball. The important thing is that we each use the gifts God gave us to help make life better and more enjoyable for our grandchildren.

Keep reminding me, Lord, that my skills are important. Help all of us to use the talents you gave us to help our grandchildren grow "in divine and human favor."

June 24

Read Jeremiah 1:5a; Romans 5:6-8.

When our first grandchild, Sheila, was born, we were unable to make the trip to see her for almost three weeks. When we got there, we found a beautiful baby with her

176

father's blue eyes. Her "just born" wrinkles were filled out so that her skin was smooth and soft.

My husband has never been a big admirer of babies. He prefers them old enough to talk and to respond when you play with them. But as I watched him hold this tiny baby, I looked at his eyes. They were moist and soft as they looked down at the small face that looked back, almost unseeing.

"You love her already, don't you?" I whispered in surprise.

"Oh, yes!" he said. "I sure do!"

At this point we could not be sure this grandchild would be a loving person when she grew up; yet despite not knowing, we loved her. Of course, Sheila is now growing into a fine young lady whom we are proud of, but that was not a "given" when she was born.

Jesus loved us before we were born. He loved us enough to die on a cross for our sins. Just as we unconditionally loved our just-born grandchild, so also Jesus loved us before we knew him as Savior.

Thank you, Lord, for loving me even before I knew you as my Savior. I need your help, though, to keep growing in my faith. Stay beside me all the way.

♥ **June 25**

Read Galatians 5:13*b*.

I have found that being a grandmother has changed the way I look at things—and the things I am willing to do that would not have appealed to me before grandchildren.

Two of my grandchildren decorated a white sweatshirt for me. They put their handprints up and down the sleeves and across the front in bright red, blue, orange, and green. With special paint they added their names and "We ♥ Grandma" on the front. The shirt can be seen from far away; I will never be lost in a crowd while wearing it!

I'm a quiet person who does not dress to be noticed. In the past I would not have worn such an unusual, attention-grabbing outfit in public. Now, however, I wear the shirt proudly because I'm a grandmother, and my grandchildren made it especially for me. And it makes them happy to see me wearing it. Every other grandmother I've talked to understands.

Just as we appreciate the gifts of our grandchildren, so also God appreciates everything we do for him. It may be a small job, such as cleaning cupboards in the church kitchen. Or it may be a big job, such as leading a meeting or singing a solo in Sunday worship. But to God, all we do for him is valuable and appreciated.

Help me remember, Lord, that what I do for you is as important to you as what my grandchildren do for me is to me.

🍃 June 26

Read Psalm 119:105.

During a visit to our son's home in Florida, Molly, then six, and I were alone. At her suggestion, we started on a walk. It ended in the large cemetery in their town.

As we walked, it seemed to me that Molly noticed everything. Suddenly she stopped and looked up at a big oak tree.

"Look, Grandma!" she said, pointing excitedly. "There are ferns growing on that tree!" She looked at the tree, studying the green, lacy ferns that grew on the branches and in the niches where branches joined the main trunk. Then Molly shook her head. "They've been there all the time, and I never even noticed them before! And I've been here a lot, too!"

It's always exciting to learn something new. Sometimes it is a new fact; sometimes just an observation that we have somehow missed before.

I remember Molly when I walk in the cemetery near my home—and when I read my Bible. Like the trees she had seen so often, I have read the Bible often. Yet like the ferns she had not noticed before, almost every time I read familiar passages, I find a new message in them. It's something that always has been there, but I have missed it before. It's a good reason to reread what I think I already understand!

Lord, help me and my grandchildren to learn what you want us to know from your world and your Word.

June 27

Read Matthew 11:29.

One thing many grandmothers can count on is seeing their grandsons—and perhaps granddaughters, too—in "Little League" uniforms. The baseball may sit on a "tee," or it may be lobbed in by a coach, but the uniforms usually are professionally designed and tailored.

"And here's my ball card, Grandma," Lincoln told me.

The card looked like those collectors buy. His picture was in color: a steely-eyed batter facing an unseen pitcher. The look was worthy of a Cecil Fielder or a John Kruk. On the back of his card were his "statistics," including age, height, and weight.

It was all very grown-up. As I watched the young players warm up, I listened as they called to one another. They all talked like the professional players they had seen on television and the local minor league team. They were mimicking adults.

We're all in a hurry to grow up when we're young. As we become "grown-up," however, we find it's not quite as thrilling or liberating as we had expected.

Growing up will come naturally for my grandchildren. My own physical growth has peaked, but my mental and spiritual growth can continue to grow. For a greater spiritual life, I can copy the model of Jesus and his followers through the ages.

Even in the last quarter of my life, Lord, I want to keep growing in my faith and knowledge of you. Give me the wisdom to learn from you and from those who have been close to you over the centuries.

❦ June 28

Read Proverbs 22:6.

Being a grandmother is usually a fun thing. As one ad on TV said, "After they give me all this joy, they go home." But there are times when it is hard to be a grandmother.

A friend discovered that her daughter and son-in-law were not taking their children to church or Sunday school because they came from different religious backgrounds. Quietly talking to her daughter about it did not change anything; the children still were not going to church.

With her daughter and son-in-law's permission, this grandmother took it upon herself to take the children to church. She got up early so she could pick them up at their house and drive them to church. She attended her own Sunday school class while they attended theirs.

My friend has not seen a change in her own daughter or son-in-law, but she keeps on taking the children to Sunday school and church—through rain, snow, and ice. She talks to them about their lessons each week and urges them to show their parents what they have drawn and to sing the songs they have learned. She also continues to pray for the whole family, confident that one day the Lord will become a part of their lives.

Lord, please help us grandmothers know how to help our grandchildren come to know you as their Friend and Savior.

🍃 June 29

Read Luke 12:27-31.

Each morning I put my wedding band on my left hand. On my right hand, I slip a gold band with four colored stones: a garnet, an emerald, a ruby, and an opal. Each stone represents a grandchild, and the ring is called a "Grandmother's Ring."

The children gave me the ring almost five years ago, and each time I slip it on I think of the child each stone represents.

Whenever I am with a grandchild, he or she asks to try on the ring. In the past, after letting the ring turn around on their small fingers, the inevitable question would come: "Which one is me?" Now that they are older, the children know which stones are for them, and they touch them saying, "This is me."

The ring helps me remember each child and bring back happy memories. The same ring reminds the grandchildren that they are individuals yet part of a larger family.

We all get lost easily in today's world. We need to know "this is me." God doesn't need a special ring to remember us and know us, his children. God never forgets his children or our needs.

Thank you, Lord, for always knowing who I am and what I am. Help me live up to what you expect of me—as a Christian and as a grandmother.

🍃 June 30

Read Proverbs 17:6.

One of the dangers I've found in being a grandmother is that I want to tell everyone what to do! I want to tell my children how to raise their children. I want to tell my grandchildren how to act. I want everyone to do everything "right."

When I catch myself falling into this trap, I remember what my father told me when I had my first child. "It's your duty to raise him and teach him about the Lord," he said. "That's what your mother and I tried to do with you." Then he grinned and said, "But it's a grandparent's duty to spoil and enjoy the children!"

My father never "spoiled" my children, if that means giving them everything they want without asking anything in return. But he did enjoy them! He enjoyed playing with them, going on short walks with them, and taking them to restaurants. He died when our older child, Dave, was a high school freshman. Jean, two years younger, does not remember much about her grandfather; but Dave says the sight of round, pink lozenges still reminds him of his grandfather, who always had some to share with him.

It may be hard not to "butt in" sometimes, but God has given us grandchildren for another chance to enjoy all the stages of childhood.

Lord, give me the wisdom to keep quiet about how my grandchildren are being raised when it is different from the way I raised my children. Give me the ability to enjoy them at all stages of their growth.

Our Beloved Grandchildren

Marilyn Brown Oden

---❦---

❦ July 1

Read Ephesians 4:1-6.

Once when I telephoned my three-year-old grand-daughter, Chelsea, who lives 1,400 miles away, she greeted me with: "Hi, Grandmom. I'm afraid of the dark."

We are all afraid of the dark, of those times when we feel the absence of Light. Henri Nouwen speaks of "the darkness of not feeling truly welcome in human existence." He says, "Self-rejection is the greatest enemy of the spiritual life because it contradicts the sacred voice that calls us the 'Beloved'" (*Life of the Beloved*).

Our task "to lead a life worthy of the calling" (Eph. 4:1) takes on new meaning when we become grandmothers. With this gift comes the responsibility of a significant new vocation, regardless of our geographical distance from our grandchildren and the marital situation of their parents. This vocation consists of "grand" parenting, of modeling the Christian faith, putting faces on the past, and making memories that ripple into the future. But there is something more, something deeper. It is truly welcoming a grandchild into human existence, day after day and year after year, echoing God's soft, gentle voice that calls this child "Beloved." In so doing, even across the miles, we bring Light into the darkness.

Loving God, thank you for the joy of "grand" parenting. We pray that our relationship with each grandchild may whisper "Beloved."

🍎 July 2

Read Ecclesiastes 2:9-11.

I stood under the sun in the village of Greystones on the bank of the Irish Sea. The waves swelled rhythmically, as if the earth were breathing, in and out. As I listened to their song, I thought about all the words I had written, wondering if the time and toil were merely vanity, a chasing of the wind, if "there was nothing to be gained under the sun" (Eccles. 2:11).

Suddenly I became aware that I was not alone. From under the brim of a pink-trimmed straw hat, a little lass smiled up at me, one baby tooth missing.

"See my new hat?" she asked, holding it on her head with both hands. Her eyes danced with glee, and her blond curls blew in the breeze of the sea.

"There's my wee girl," called her grandmother, stepping from the shop nearby. "I'm a bit mad—" she said, a lilting common phrase, "buying us both new hats!"

The child giggled. Grandmother took her small hand. "On our way now, that's you."

The little girl brushed against her, and the sunlight caught their smiles—the child so clearly *beloved*, the grandmother so clearly delighted to give this greatest gift of all.

Perhaps—if we open our eyes to the wonders of the world and the preciousness of the people who wander through it—perhaps each new sun offers an extraordinary day waiting to be received.

Dear God, thank you for each new day. Help us to glimpse the sacred in the ordinary.

🌱 July 3

Read James 1:19-27.

It had been a day of college memories—holding hands with my husband, Bill, and walking once again beside Theta Pond, sitting together for a moment in the chapel where we became engaged, driving past his old student church where we were married. Now, we sat at a Wesley Foundation reunion banquet in the Student Union ballroom, filled with grandmothers and grandfathers.

Many persons in this room had been involved in bringing change, change historically long overdue: integration of the university and Wesley Foundation, affirmation of women's full responsibility in and for society, actions for peace and poverty programs. Our beloved grandchildren do not experience the old world we knew. That world is gone. The part that was worse. The part that was better.

The grandparents around us had reason to feel proud of their tiny thumbprints in reshaping the clay of history. But as I listened, I heard the past tense—recalling bygone days, redecorating old milestones, deceiving ourselves that past actions sufficed for today. The window of vision for a new future, once so important, had been painted by time into a mirror of the past.

James says to "be doers of the word" (there is no age limit—until age 40 or 60 or 80), "and not merely hearers who deceive themselves," for people who are only hearers "are like those who look at themselves in a mirror" (James 1:22-23). As grandmothers, how tempted we are to look into the mirror instead of through the window! Yet, James still calls us to service and action, to be doers of the word.

185

Eternal God, thank you for opportunities to reshape our tiny space in your world. Help us not to fill our tomorrows with our yesterdays.

🍃 July 4

Read John 3:19-21.

Independence Day. Fireworks day. Traditionally, a family holiday.

Grandmothers across the country join grandchildren to watch fireworks displays. Communities hurl bright lights into the night sky, like shattered neon signs. Colors and patterns splash across the domed canvas, lasting only seconds in time. Below, our quilts spread in the darkness, we watch the distant light.

Says John, "The light has come into the world, and people loved darkness rather than light because their deeds were evil" (John 3:19). We feel separated from the light, hide from it, fear exposure of our real selves, our true hearts, our faithless deeds. We live from below, in the darkness.

Yet, we are mesmerized by the light, longing for spiritual life. Henri Nouwen (*Life of the Beloved*) tells us that everything changes radically "when the totality of our daily lives is lived 'from above,' that is, as the Beloved sent into the world." With this radical change, we live life as an unceasing "Yes" to "the One who calls us the Beloved." He reminds us that all people want more than survival, and through our "presence among them" as "one who is sent" they "catch a glimpse of the real life"—like glimpsing the light of fireworks in the sky, from a space in the darkness on life's patchwork quilt.

If we, as grandmothers, can "come to the light" (John 1:21), perhaps our presence with our grandchildren will help them to catch a glimpse of the real life in the Spirit and to rise from the crazy quilt of today's world.

186

Dear God, thank you for bringing light into the darkness. May we live in that light and help light the way for our grandchildren.

♥ July 5

Read Revelation 1:8 and 21:5-7.

One month ago today, my husband's father died. The family came together to celebrate his 94-year life. Informally, we gathered for lunch and shared memories about him. Formally, we gathered for the memorial service at his church, where my husband—still called "Billy" by the older members of that church—had preached his first sermon.

Our three-year-old granddaughter wiggled between Bill and me in the pew at the service. She didn't really understand why we were there. But she knew it was a place for worship. She knew to fold her hands and close her eyes for prayer. And somehow she knew it was a time to show care. At one point she crawled up into Bill's lap and said, "I love you, Granddad."

Her attendance and that of her sleeping baby sister were surprising gifts of ministry to the family. Their presence evoked hope in the midst of heartache. It shouted life in the face of death. It manifested the mysteries of God, the Alpha and the Omega, the One "who is and who was and who is to come" (Rev. 1:8), the Giver of Life who—even in death—makes all things new.

Thanks be to God!

Eternal God, thank you for new life in the face of death. Help us to grow in our trust of you—even in death.

♥ July 6

Read 2 Timothy 1:7-10.

Joan, whose grandchildren lived far away, decided to become a surrogate grandmother for eight-year-old

Tommy. He had no local grandparents, no church home, and very few privileges. Joan agreed to assist with a church day-trip to the zoo in another city if Tommy could go along.

The children stopped for breakfast at a restaurant. Tommy had never seen a breakfast bar before. His eyes lit up when he saw all the food, and he heaped some of everything on his plate.

Another sponsor watched him and said to his surrogate grandmother, "He'll never eat all that!"

"Let it be," Joan responded.

Tommy stuffed himself and finally looked up at her. "I can't eat all this."

"You took too much?" asked Joan.

Tears came to his eyes. "It all looked so good."

"Yes. Next time you will know that you don't have to take everything."

How we gobble life! We have trouble learning that just because something is available, we do not need to take it. Just because something is faddish, we do not need to do it. Just because something is beautiful, we do not need to possess it. An important aspect of the faith is developing the self-discipline to do without when we don't have to—remembering that God gave us "a spirit of power and of love and of self-discipline" (2 Tim. 1:7).

Dear God, thank you for your bountiful gifts. Help us to remember the children with less and to broaden our "grand" parenting to include one of them.

🍎 July 7

Read Galatians 6:7-10.

My friend is called "Puddin." I winced at her pain as the message stabbed her soul: Her daughter was dead. Left behind, motherless, were an infant and toddler.

Puddin could have let depression disable her. Instead, she peeked through the tears in her heart and focused on her grandbabies and son-in-law. Steadfastly, she offered comfort and love, care and support to that grieving little family.

A few years later her son-in-law became engaged to a widow with two small children. Puddin could have stepped back into the shadows and resented those strangers who would move into her daughter's home. Instead, she wrapped her arms around them. After the marriage, Puddin could have fostered suspicion that her grandchildren might be mistreated by this new stepmother. She could have exclusively favored her biological grandchildren with attention, presents, and invitations. Instead, she broadened her circle of love and took the whole new family of six to her heart, accepting as a gift from God this new daughter-in-love and the doubling of grandchildren.

Within each of us is the strength of a "Puddin," capable of sowing seeds of love and saying a beautiful yes to the opportunity—even opportunity born of tragedy—to "work for the good of all" (Gal. 6:10).

Loving God, thank you for the Puddins among us. Help us to rise above our human vulnerabilities and work for the good of all.

🍂 July 8

Read Colossians 1:24-29.

The day ended with a call to my granddaughter. "Where are you?" she asked.

"In Arkansas."

"Your house is in Louisiana."

"That's right, Chelsea."

"You are all mixed up!"

Indeed, we are all mixed up. The spiritual, physical, mental and emotional rooms of our "house" feel as disconnected as separate states. Our mornings begin with moments of prayer, scripture, and meditation in the early dawn light. Next we charge into the physical regime of exercise. Then we pass through the mental door and begin work: outside the home or inside it, volunteer or paid, full time or part time. Afterward we move into the emotional arena, sharing our joys and concerns with family or friends or a support group. (I noted in a small city's Calendar of Events in the Sunday paper that 78 support group meetings were listed for the week!) Holistic living seems impossible. We are all mixed up!

John Wesley wrote: "Let every action have reference to your whole life, and not to a part only." As we struggle toward wisdom and maturity in Christ, we begin to discover that spirituality is the center room of our house, with each of the other rooms connecting to it. The "mystery which is Christ in [us]" (Col. 1:27) unifies all our actions—no matter where we are.

Dear God, thank you for the Christ. Help us to be centered on that mystery wherever we are and whatever we are doing.

🍂 July 9

Read Matthew 18:1-5.

As a school counselor, I meet with the parents of physically challenged children, including preschoolers. I had read the description of this eighteen-month-old I was about to meet: Only the thighs of his legs were formed, his handless little arms were developed only to the elbows, and he was blind. I entered the room expecting to find him lying helpless in a crib.

But not this delightful child! He was playing on the carpet, contentedly manipulating a soft squeaky duck between his arms. His grandmother, who babysits while his mother works, introduced herself. "And this," she said, "is little Robert." Her voice rang with love—not a hint of pity. Hearing his name, he smiled and scooted himself toward his grandmother's voice. She leaned down and gently caressed his cheek.

I picked up the duck left behind, sat down on the floor, and spoke to him. Curious rather than frightened by a strange voice, he moved himself toward me. I sat him on my lap and squeaked the duck. As we played, he was alert and responsive, with an incredible ability to use his limbs. His wonderful laugh still echoes in my ears.

His eyes did not see, and his limbs hung incomplete beneath his short-sleeved shirt and denim shorts. Yet, he had been loved into wholeness by his grandmother.

I continue to recall little Robert when I think about the disciples' question: "Who is the greatest in the kingdom of heaven?" (Matt. 18:1).

Creator God, thank you for making each life sacred even though all of us are imperfect. Help us to love one another—especially our grandchildren—into wholeness.

❦ July 10

Read Romans 8:35-39.

"My grandmother has Alzheimer's," said my young friend. "The last time I was home, I spent a day with her. She doesn't know me, but she's delightful."

My friend told me about that day:

"Grandmother showed me a wedding picture of my mother. That's my daughter," she said proudly.

"It's my mother too."

"*Really*?" She was so surprised and pleased.

Some of her friends came by that afternoon, and she performed as the hostess she'd always been as the wife of a university dean. She told little jokes and made sure everyone had a good time. She wore her robe and her hair was a mess, but she didn't know it. Finally she told them she had no idea who anyone was, but she was so glad they had dropped by.

My friend went back in time to her childhood and the week she spent with her grandmother each summer. "She was always so much fun. So creative. We could enter into fantasy together." Her eyes twinkled with fond memories. "I still have the queen-to-princess letters she wrote me—complete with dragons."

Her smile faded. "Now—" she reflected a moment, then smiled again. "Now, I guess we can still be together in fantasies. I will always love her."

I heard the gospel in her words—that nothing "in all creation, will be able to separate us from the love of God in Christ Jesus our Lord" (Rom. 8:39), a love manifested in our love for each other, even in changed situations.

Loving God, thank you for steadfast love in changing circumstances. May our play with our grandchildren now make a lasting impact that will strengthen them in the serious times.

July 11

Read Isaiah 1:21-23.

During my second visit to Ekaterinburg, Russia I stood behind the church pulpit to bring greetings from Louisiana. Galina, a member of that church, had helped me prepare the greetings in Russian.

Galina and I share a deep friendship. Her granddaughter, Katia, the one child of her one child, and my granddaughter Chelsea are the same age. We dream that these two beloved little girls will meet someday and also become friends. As I looked at the congregation, saying the words she had taught me, my eyes met hers and she smiled.

It was the last time Galina would smile for a long, long time. Two days after my visit, little Katia's father disappeared. Galina learned months later that her son was murdered.

Ekaterinburg has a history of violence. It was the site of the executions of the last Russian czar and his family. Renamed Sverdlovsk to honor the Communist who approved the murders, it became a city of military weapons production and secret biological warfare research. Today, like most large cities, it fits Isaiah's description: a place of murderers and bribes, where orphans and widows are ignored.

But the church is now present, filled with members of honesty and integrity, who offer a strong and faithful ministry to the city. The church cannot restore Galina's only child, but it offers Light in the darkness, supporting and assisting little Katia and her mother.

As committed Christians, we cannot restore what is lost, but regardless of the environment surrounding us, we can be present with the Light of Christ's love.

Creator God, thank you that each congregation is a family all around the World. Help us to remember that every child in our congregation is in a way our grandchild and needs to hear the word "beloved."

🌿 July 12

Read Ezekiel 47:6-9.

On this day—Bill's and my anniversary—I sat beside a window high above the Mississippi River in New Orleans. God tossed the sun into the sky and splashed color on dawn's gray canvas, then painted a crimson stripe along the horizon and touched the earth with a strip of blue. A sliver of yellow peeked at me. The river rolled along, reflected the colors of the sky, and shaped an "S" around the French Quarter. The city slept, missing this cosmic ritual that began the day.

Other rituals flashed in my memory: our wedding ritual so long ago when I vowed to love and to cherish Bill, the baptisms of our four children, the weddings of our grown children with our old vows repeated by them (and my silent vow to love and cherish these new family members), and during the last three years the baptisms of our two grandchildren. How easy it is to sleep through the deep meaning of these rituals, these reflections of our commitment, these "S" points in the stream of our lives. Ezekiel asks, "Mortal, have you seen this?" (Ezek. 47:6). Grandchildren are gifts that teach us to see anew, that reawaken us, that send ripples of fresh water into our life stream.

As I glanced from the window to Bill, rejoicing in our marriage and our children and their marriages and our grandchildren, a salty tear of gratitude splashed into the cosmic river of time.

Dear God, thank you for rituals in the river of time. Help us to see the Son rise in each new day and stage.

❦ July 13

Read Matthew 7:24-28.

My young friend told me about her grandmother, a staunch Episcopalian, a "southern lady" (meaning, I've found since living in Louisiana, that she fit the "steel magnolia" metaphor—very feminine and very strong).

My friend spoke of the beautiful live oak trees at her grandmother's home and the gardens that allowed nature some freedom but not chaos. "Grandmother treated us like her garden, giving us space but also supervision."

She recalled her grandmother as a person in control of situations. "Only once as a child did I see her vulnerable side. Soon after my grandfather's death, she phoned us and said she was lonely. She sounded like she was crying and asked if anyone could spend the night." My friend paused, remembering. "I stayed with her several nights. Then she began managing things again."

She shared her sense of loss when her grandmother's home was sold. "I didn't expect to miss it, but I do. I miss her beautiful antiques arranged so nicely. I miss the pretty flowers, the smell of the roses. I miss the backyard where we used to play." She turned wistful. "My grandmother's house was the one place of continuity for me. I just assumed that it would always be part of my life."

It still is, I thought; it's tucked away safely in the heart. Over the years her grandmother, now in her nineties and still a southern lady, heard the words of Christ and acted on them, withstanding torrential rains, bayou floods, and hurricane winds—built, like her house, on a rock.

Strengthening God, thank you for opportunities to provide continuity for our grandchildren through the home of relationship. Help us to build those tender relationships on a rock that can withstand turmoil.

July 14

Read John 6:28-34.

My friend Anne knelt at the altar beside her little granddaughter during Holy Communion. A change of preachers had brought a change in communion from a baked loaf of bread to stiff round communion wafers. When the pastor offered the plate to the child, she took the flat white wafer, looked at it carefully, and with a frown whispered softly to her grandmother, "Are we supposed to eat this plastic?"

Henri Nouwen (*Life of the Beloved*) says, "We are called to become bread for each other—bread for the world."

How different is the image of being called to be bread from the image of being called to be plastic! Plastic people: cool and flat, hard to the touch, rigid and stagnant, mass produced and packaged for marketing, unbreakable, and melting in the heat of trouble. No! We are called to be bread for each other: warm and stirred by life, vulnerable to the touch of another (perhaps reshaped by a squeeze), rising with courage and growing in faith, unique and authentic, giving pieces of ourselves yet retaining our wholeness, and scenting the air with hope in the heat of trouble.

Like communion bread, we are blessed and given— blessed with God's love, like yeast in our lives, and called to respond by giving ourselves to each other, to the world. "For the bread of God is that which comes down from heaven and gives life to the world" (John 6:33).

Loving God, thank you for the bread of life. Help us to accept fully your blessing and to give ourselves fully to others.

July 15

Read Romans 7:4-6.

Tears pooled at the corner of my friend's eyes as she talked. Her beloved grandbaby would be a year old next week. But there would be no celebration. They had lost him.

The loss of a child and also children's loss of parents are heart-wrenching tragedies in the human family. Our hearts ache especially for a little one who loses both parents simultaneously and has to be placed with strangers.

Yet, the legal system pronounced this sentence on my friend's innocent grandbaby and his adoptive parents. It snatched the baby from the arms of the real mother and father—"real" defined as the ones he knows as parents, who cherish and care for him, who would die to protect him. It placed him with a stranger whose womb had sustained him but who did not welcome him, adopting him out at birth, then changing her mind nearly a year later. It removed him to an environment ranging from unstable to sordid. Biological roots are important, but it is the relationship that gives life.

As my friend shared her pain, I thought about the new law and the old: "But now we are discharged from the law, dead to that which held us captive, so that we are slaves not under the old written code but in the new life of the Spirit" (Rom. 7:6). The legal system is not an "it" but a "we." When we, as Christian decision makers and jurors, find severe discrepancies between moral and legal action, the new life in the Spirit calls us to discernment and courage, and perhaps to uphold the moral code instead of legal loopholes.

Loving God, thank you for adoptive parents who take unwelcomed children and call them "beloved." Help us to recognize that love takes precedence over all else in the new life of the Spirit.

❦ July 16

Read Matthew 13:31-32.

My friend Lydia told me about her grandmother's having her baptized as a child—secretly, in Russia, during the Communist regime, when imprisonment threatened the practice of religion.

In 1990, Louisiana pastor Dwight Ramsey visited Ekaterinburg, Russia and met grown-up Lydia. Because of her baptism—kept secret all these years—she was very interested in the faith, asked many questions, and listened intently to his answers. For the first time, she realized fully the meaning of her baptism.

Lydia Istomina helped him start the first legally registered Methodist Church in Russia in seven decades and became its pastor. From a small mustard-size seed sown in a field of turmoil and transition, this church in Ekaterinburg has grown to a thousand members. It has become a tree whose branches reach out to the city, ministering to widows and children, the ill and imprisoned, and extend beyond the city, helping to start other churches in Russia.

For Pastor Istomina, Ramsey's words touched the spiritual seed she had felt but did not understand, the seed planted by her grandmother's witness to the importance of the faith. The seed grew, and ultimately history was changed—that of United Methodism, of Ekaterinburg, and even of Russia.

Our circumstances as grandmothers are radically different from Lydia's grandmother, but we too have opportunities to witness to our faith, to sow a tiny seed that will grow in our grandchildren's lives, so that one day others will find shelter and comfort in the branches of their love.

Creator God, thank you for the potential of tiny seeds. Help us to plant seeds of faith and love in the lives of our grandchildren.

🍎 July 17

Read Genesis 9:12-17.

Early one morning I drove westward along Interstate 40 across the flat Texas panhandle on the way to visit my granddaughters. A rainbow arched across the highway in the distant western sky, reminding me of God's covenant: "I have set my bow in the clouds, and it shall be a sign of the covenant between me and the earth," which includes "every living creature of all flesh" (Gen. 9:13, 15). Joy replaced boredom as I drove toward this vivid symbolic gateway of care and love and hope—the only morning rainbow I have ever seen.

Mother Teresa of Calcutta dreamed that all people would know that they are loved before they die. My image of this is persons' experiencing pieces of God's rainbow falling like colorful confetti upon them, surrounding them, softening their outer journey, brightening their inner journey—knowing before they die that they are unconditionally loved by God. This experience may come late in life, like an evening rainbow; or in younger years, like an afternoon rainbow; or in childhood, like a rainbow in the morning.

One of our joys as grandmothers is relating to a grandchild as Beloved. Another joy is to become surrogate grandmothers for children who have no one to teach them of God's unconditional love. What a joy to welcome them into our lives, "adopting" them as Beloved and dropping the colorful confetti of God's love around them—showing them a rainbow in the morning.

Dear God, thank you for the rainbow of your love. Help us to see opportunities to share that love with a child who would otherwise not know to look for it.

July 18

Read Exodus 20:1-6.

I stood in my son's home, staring at the meaningless random pattern in the frame entitled "Lady Liberty." Suddenly, the image beyond the surface appeared in this three-dimensional hologram: the Statue of Liberty with the New York City skyline in the background.

My granddaughter snuggled against me, and I thought of how the shaping of a grandchild's character and self-image appears to be a meaningless random pattern of parenting styles. But when we look beyond the surface, we see the influence of our own parenting styles on our children's style of parenting, and in the background lingers the child-rearing pattern of our parents. The old words from Exodus about "punishing children for the iniquity of parents, to the third and the fourth generation" (Exod. 20:5) and "showing steadfast love to the thousandth generation" (Exod. 20:6) took on added meaning; for while some of the generation-to-generation patterns of parenting foster holistic health, others block it.

The past is present in the birth of a baby, not only genetically but also in parenting styles. As grandmothers, we can be a bridge to awareness of past patterns, and set up a detour that frees future generations from ongoing destructive patterns. Like Lady Liberty, we can bring meaning to a random pattern and help pass on holistic health and faith—instead of iniquities—from generation to generation. What an opportunity!

Eternal God, give us the courage to reach beyond defensiveness about our parenting patterns. Help us affirm and assist our children in recognizing the unhealthy dimensions that we passed on, so that they will not carry them forward to our grandchildren.

July 19

Read Psalm 104:1-4.

Colorful clouds danced with the sunbeams in the evening Colorado sky. My granddaughter Chelsea and I took a walk to see them better when we finished our family picnic. We stopped near the bank of a creek and felt the wind blow against our faces. Putting a hand above our brows like a cap bill, we squinted into the western sky. "Look!" said Chelsea excitedly, "Yellow clouds!" She lifted her small hand, pointing, "See! Pink ones!" We turned around slowly to gaze at all of the beautiful light patterns.

The sky was filled with clouds, and gray-blue storm clouds began to roll in unexpectedly. But Chelsea, intent on the beauty of the sun's light touching the other clouds, was not worried about the stormy ones. As we watched them, I realized that when life is filled with clouds and storms blow in unexpectedly, we can recall that the Son's Light transformed yesterday's clouds into beautiful opportunities for us to grow. We can face each new storm with faith and confidence, trusting the Light to touch today's clouds also.

Standing with Chelsea beside the creek, the clouds swelling above us and the wind blowing in our faces, I suddenly felt the joy and praise of Psalms: "You set the beams of your chambers on the waters, you make the clouds your chariot, you ride on the wings of the wind" (Ps. 104:3).

Creator God, thank you for the beauty of your creation and for your presence with us. Help us to feel your closeness especially in the stormy times.

💜 July 20

Read Colossians 3:12-17.

One of our little granddaughters' favorite books is *Where's Spot?* It asks, "Where's Spot?" Then we begin to look for him. "Is he under the bed?" "No!"

While reading this book to them for the umpteenth time, my mind began to wander. I thought about a visit with a friend and his telling me that he and his wife were trying to effect change rather than be affected by the changes in this stage of their lives. I began to reflect on the grandparent stage of life. Where are we, grandmothers? Are we still effecting change? Or have we been so affected by the changes in our lives and the world around us that we are hiding under the bed?

201

Do we clothe ourselves with "compassion, kindness, humility, meekness, and patience"? Or do we hide under the bed stripped of these virtues?

Do we "bear with one another" and "forgive each other"? Or do we hide under the bed in the darkness of judgment and criticism?

Do we let "the peace of Christ rule" in our hearts? Or do we hide under the bed planning revenge?

Do we "sing psalms, hymns, and spiritual songs to God" with gratitude in our hearts? Or do we hide under the bed in the silence of bitterness and cynicism?

Where are we grandmothers? Are we hiding under the bed? Let us pray for a resounding "No!"

Eternal God, thank you for ongoing opportunities to live the teachings of Christ. As long as we have breath, may we draw courage from you so that we do not give up and hide under the bed.

July 21

Read 1 Timothy 6:11-16.

"Start the pictures, Daddy," Chelsea called to my son, a summertime National Parks Service ranger. As we waited for his slide presentation to begin in the amphitheater, jagged white bolts in the dark distant sky provided a cosmic backdrop for the topic: lightning.

Part of Dirk's program included an explanation of how lightning strikes. Though my summary is an oversimplification, he explained how an electric field follows along the ground beneath the storm clouds, and he showed how our common assumption that lightning darts down from the sky to the earth is incorrect. Instead, the leader starts down from the sky and the return stroke shoots toward it from the earth, and they connect.

Lightning is a metaphor for spirituality. For as long as

the earth has been inhabited by humankind, peoples have sought the Creator, calling different names and going about it in different ways, but following along the ground, drawn to the spiritual dimension in our journey through time. A common assumption is that we are simply passive receptacles, waiting for the Spirit to strike our lives. Instead, God has given us the Leader, but the return connecting stroke depends on us. According to the scripture, we connect by pursuing "righteousness, godliness, faith, love, endurance, gentleness" (1 Tim. 6:11).

Lightning is a message written across the cosmos reminding us that the spiritual journey is not passive and private but active and relational.

Creator God, thank you for the Leader. Forgive us when our attempts at reaching toward his teachings are lazy and halfhearted.

🍂 July 22

Read James 4:1-10.

Today we celebrated our second granddaughter's first birthday. The party focused attention on Sarah, a difficult experience for her three-year-old sister, Chelsea—the first grandchild on both sides of the family. At one point when Chelsea gained attention by negative behavior, her daddy commented, "There is much to learn in life, and not all of it is pleasant."

The Scripture calls us "double-minded" (James 4:8). As grandmothers, we are indeed double-minded. We want our grandchildren to be responsible, to share with others, to grow in faith, strength, and courage. But we also want to protect them from potential rejection and painful realities, from difficult challenges and disturbing conflict. We want their maturing to develop without hurt, and their tempering to occur without heat. Edwin Friedman, author of *Generation to Generation*, stated in a workshop that people with small difficulties, who perceive themselves as lacking the inner resources needed to handle their situation, are less likely to cope than people whose difficulties are more serious, but who are confident in their inner resources. Our double-mindedness regarding our grandchildren shortcuts the development of their own inner resources and teaches them to rely on others to solve their problems instead of building confidence in themselves.

An important gift to our grandchildren is to become single-minded in helping them realize that they are Beloved even in difficult times, that God is with them, and that they have the inner resources to handle the challenges that life will inevitably bring their way.

Loving God, thank you for challenges that make us grow. Give us the discernment not to jump in and rescue our grandchildren when they face challenges, but to help them grow through them.

🍎 July 23

Read Psalm 63:5-8.

One morning my husband, Bill, and I hiked in a mountain area new to us. As I followed him on the narrow trail, it blurred, then disappeared altogether. Much later in our journey the trail once again emerged, and we discovered we were right where we should be. Bill commented, "I was on the trail all along and couldn't tell it."

If we grandmothers, in the days of our youth, had peeked through a window into our future, we would have cringed at the shattering of our youthful hopes, at the seemingly lost trail of our life journey—so different from the one we mapped out in our dreams, at the changing face of our loved one wrinkled by the decades. But now we are grandmothers, standing inside that future, and we celebrate the undergirding of hope even when our hopes were shattered. Now, we celebrate the fulfillment of undreamed dreams and the discovery that we are where we should be and were on the right trail all along but couldn't tell it. Now, as we peer into the aging face of our loved one, remembering the way he used to look, we see the lines formed by strength and courage and celebrate the character and beauty that were not there when we first met.

We celebrate our life journey, knowing that each fleeting moment has been and will be sacred, for it offers an opportunity to respond to the presence of God. We praise you, O God, for throughout the journey, "you have been [our] help, and in the shadow of your wings [we] sing for joy" (Ps. 63:7).

Loving God, thank you for our life journey. May we never forget how to sing for joy.

🐚 July 24

Read 2 Timothy 1:3-5.

My son Bryant and I browsed through art galleries in Santa Fe, New Mexico, and I saw a painting by Larry Riley that glued me to the floor before it. Entitled "Grandmother's Doll," it captured a beautiful little Native American girl wearing a red skirt and shirt with a silver and turquoise belt around her waist and a detailed squash blossom necklace. Her dark eyes caught mine and held, drawing me like magnets into the depths of her soul and that of her people. She carried an extraordinary doll dressed in a dark blue dress with long sleeves decorated by tiny pieces of silver and turquoise.

As I looked at the painting, I wondered what her grandmother's doll represented to the child. What kind of feelings between them did it recall? What attitudes of her grandmother lingered in its presence? What values did her grandmother's life demonstrate that the doll symbolized for the little girl?

If we gave a granddaughter an old doll from our childhood, what would her answers be to these questions? The words of Timothy come to me: "I am reminded of your sincere faith, a faith that lived first in your grandmother Lois . . . and now, I am sure, lives in you" (2 Tim. 1:5). Like Lois, do we have a sincere faith? Are we *living* that faith before our grandchildren? Is our faith message so clear in our actions that a passed-on doll would be a reminder of a life lived faithfully?

Dear God, thank you for the artists who speak without words and for Grandmother Lois whose words we did not hear. Help us to speak with our lives a message of faith for our grandchildren.

❧ July 25

Read 1 Peter 5:6-11.

The high desert road from Taos to Tres Piedres, New Mexico, offers easy travel and minor obstacles—until suddenly, without warning, the flat earth divides, gashed by a 660 foot drop, a deep jagged scar called the Rio Grande Gorge, cut by the ribbon of river rushing far below. It is impassable without a bridge.

I stood on that bridge to get a better view of the gorge. Nearby a little girl clutched her grandmother's finger with one hand and a teddy bear with the other. "What holds us up?" she asked, a quiver in her voice. Her grandmother answered, "Our will power, Sweetheart. Our will power." She was half right.

Life rolls along on a high desert road with minor obstacles—until suddenly, without warning, an impassable chasm appears. Perhaps the chasm is carved into our lives by the death of a loved one, the diagnosis of terminal illness, a car wreck with permanent injury, or the loss of a job. We can't leap over the chasm, or buy or bargain our way to the other side. Life as it was comes to a jolting stop.

Recalling the words of 1 Peter 5, that God cares for us and will restore, support, and strengthen us, we begin to build a bridge across the chasm to the other side of life, inch by inch, prayer by prayer, step by step. What holds us up is not just the power of our will but more healing and trusting in the power of the Spirit.

Dear God, thank you for the power of the Spirit. Help us to trust that healing power when we face life's chasms.

July 26

Read Romans 8:22-25.

Mother and daughter sat together in a remote area which, more than any other place, offered them a sense of wholeness. Summer after summer they had hiked here, individually and together, and had sat on this special rock. Over the years it had become a sacred space for healing and renewal. Today a tall spruce tree, so tiny the first time they had come, shaded them from the hot noon sun.

Daughter spoke of a yearned-for unborn child. Tears hid behind her sunglasses and also in the heart of her listening mother, who ached for this month-after-month, year-after-year unpregnant daughter. Apparently, there could be no child—no grandchild. Time had gradually led daughter and mother through the grief process to the stage of acceptance, of sharing a deep reverence for those little lives that would not be. Yet, even in this moment of acceptance, hope swelled in their souls.

In *The River Within*, Christopher Bryant says: "God addresses us through the people we meet and the work we do, through our hopes and fears, through our moods and dreams . . ." God also addresses us through our grandchildren, not only the ones born, but also the ones unborn—for "if we hope for what we do not see, we wait for it with patience" (Rom. 8:25). As we wait, God deepens our reverence for life, strengthens our endurance against despair, and heightens our sensitivity to the pain of all peoples.

Dear God, thank you for hope that sustains even if we wait forever. Help us to use our own grief as a means to grow in our care for others.

❦ July 27

Read Mark 10:13-16.

Several years ago as a school counselor, I worked with a little boy named Tommy. He was a thin, blond-haired, blue-eyed kindergartner whose front teeth were missing and, most of the time, so were his glasses, which were necessary for school work. He got himself into more mischief than any other student. He could grab the fastest, laugh the loudest, move the quickest, curse the worst, and wiggle the most of any kindergartner in the history of that school. He was *always* in trouble.

Despite the difficulties, however, his best hours each day were the ones spent at school. Tommy's mother had been on drugs before his birth, and his home environment after his birth was equally hazardous. Frequently he sat beside me at the small round table in my office. I could help him develop coping skills and appropriate patterns of classroom behavior, but that dealt only with symptoms—like offering aspirin for a headache caused by a brain tumor. His young life was already built on survival, devoid of nurturing and love. What he really needed was someone to fill that void. How he could have benefited from having a surrogate grandmother take him up in her arms and call him Beloved!

One way we follow Christ is to open our eyes and hearts to little children like Tommy, for Jesus took the children "up in his arms, laid his hands on them, and blessed them" (Mark. 10:16).

Dear God, we pray for the Tommys of the world. Help us to respond if you are calling any of us to speak the word "beloved" to one of them.

🐛 July 28

Read 2 Corinthians 4:7-15.

Ludmila and her daughter Marina had become my friends in Ekaterinburg, Russia. They had been "afflicted . . . but not crushed; perplexed but not driven to despair" (2 Cor. 4:8). Now, they were on U.S. soil.

They had come to Louisiana to attend a school of Christian mission and would return home to teach the courses in their own church. They were here to learn Matthew, but they taught us by example the essence of the gospel. These new converts made visible the life of Jesus Christ in their own lives. They touched our hearts and humbled our souls with their faithful witness.

After a few days I asked Marina, who is seventeen, if she felt homesick. She said, "I miss my grandmother and my grandfather. They worry about me here."

I understood. Marina is beloved by her grandparents, and they were taught to fear Americans—just as we were taught to fear Russians.

"Their love for me is big." Marina smiled. "But in our church I have learned that God's love is even bigger."

She said it well. Our deep love for a grandchild is a wonderful mystery—but even that love stands small beside God's amazing love for each of us—life-giving love that will not forsake us. Trusting in that love, we cannot be destroyed.

Dear God, thank you for your perfect love. Help us to teach our grandchildren that your love for them is even greater than ours.

🌰 July 29

Read James 3:13-18.

Two years ago my friend's son and his wife divorced. Their baby daughter, Karen, stayed with her mother during the week and her daddy on weekends. Now, Karen's mother is getting remarried—and little Karen is getting a new weekday father.

My friend shared her anguish. What if this new father feels competition with her son as the former husband and tries to influence little Karen against her daddy? What if he doesn't treat her well? What if his parenting style is detrimental? What if someday his job moves her far away? What if they have additional children, and she is cast into the background? If only her granddaughter had been spared the pain of an unstable marital relationship and its dissolution! If only her son's first marriage had worked out! If only she could have done something to help!

This situation is common, and it is rife with "if only" guilt over the past and "what if" anxiety over the future. God's forgiving grace heals guilt about the past, and trust in God heals anxiety about the future. Our faith helps us ground guilt and anxiety rather than transmit them, and strengthens us to be a source of comfort and wholeness instead of sowing dissension. As grandmothers, the dynamics of divorce and remarriage—perhaps more than any other situation—call us to "the wisdom from above," which is "peaceable, gentle, willing to yield, full of mercy and good fruits" (James 3:17).

Dear God, thank you for your love that sustains our grandchildren in situations potentially destructive for them. Help us to realize that our response can foster heal-ing or further destruction.

🍎 July 30

Read Isaiah 40:28-31.

My young friend Page is a pretty woman with some whim-sical goals—like running a marathon. Recently, after training for the 26 mile race, she started on the run of her life.

She ran mile after mile. One hour. Two hours. Three. Finally, she bumped against the wall—that physical point where she simply could not go on. Her body had given everything. There was nothing left.

A verse of scripture came to mind: "Those who wait for the Lord shall renew their strength, they shall mount up with wings like eagles, they shall run and not be weary, they shall walk and not faint" (Isa. 40:31). The words tolled like a bell: "They shall run and not be weary . . . They shall run and not be weary . . ." Then she thought of her grandfather, who had died some years before—a renowned university basketball coach, a man of honor and courage who loved her dearly. And Page broke through the wall!

With the scripture running through her mind and her grandfather running with her in her heart, she reached the finish line. She crossed the line not with a whimper but with her head high, her body lifted by the scripture and the memory of her grandfather.

One of our opportunities as grandparents is faithful behavior when we find ourselves against the wall. Per-haps those little eyes watching us are taking mental snap-shots that memory will call forth at a needed time, helping that loved one to cross a finish line.

Dear God, thank you for memory, which carries our loved ones with us. Help us to make memories for our grandchil-dren that will nurture, strengthen, and encourage them.

Read 1 Corinthians 15:53-58.

My daughter Valerie, whose grandmother survived cancer of the larynx, chose the oncology unit for her chaplaincy internship.

The sting of death permeates a cancer floor. Paintings hang on the wall to brighten the hall, and the stark white decor of a former day is gone. But not the aura of ebbing life. The future shrinks to days or hours. Tubes abound from plastic bags. Nurses inject needles, give pills. The smell of disinfectant intermingles with coffee and the aroma of a rosebud.

Silence is broken by quick, soft-soled steps, whispers of visitors, patients' muffled moans. The taste of death lingers: if not now, next time; if not here, at a hospice or, for a blessed few, at home. The hands of the big round clock, spinning toward death for the patient, stand still for the family at the bedside.

Valerie walks down this hall into Rosalita's room, expecting to find her in bed. However, Rosalita—eighty years old, diminished in body but not in spirit—is in the chair. Her ten-year-old granddaughter sits in her place in the bed of death, comfortably coloring a picture, very much at home with her dying grandmother. The child is oblivious to the aura of the oncology unit. Her grandmother's presence, filled with a decade of love and trust, supersedes tubes and bags and needles and tall hospital beds and anxious whispers in the hall.

The child knows she is beloved by her grandmother, something death cannot erase. "Where, O death, is your victory? Where, O death, is your sting?" (1 Cor. 15:55).

Eternal God, thank you for the opportunity to call our grandchildren "beloved." Help us not to miss that opportunity, regardless of the circumstances.

A Grandmother's Vocation

Marilyn Brown Oden

August 1

Read Mark 7:14-15, 21.

On the long flight to Singapore, my seat mate was a young businesswoman returning to her homeland. This was my first visit, but the tradition of honoring and respecting the elderly held a prominent place in my images of Singapore culture. The young woman, thoroughly westernized, corrected my assumption and gave an example: "Now, mothers who work hire people to take care of their children instead of leaving them with their grandmothers." With a hint of superiority, she added, "We do not want the old ways to be transmitted." I listened sadly, for both grandparents and grandchildren lose when they are cut off from each other.

Concern about transmitting the old ways brought to mind words from Mark: It is not something "outside a person that by going in can defile" (Mark 7:15). It is important for people to soar toward their lofty dreams for the future. But a kite is carried off by the wind and drifts with the breeze if disconnected from its string. And an airplane must land for refueling. And a bird finds a secure place to rest between flights. As grandmothers, if we are not glued to the past, perhaps we can become a grounding connection for soaring dreams, be available for refueling during the down times, and provide nurturing security that fosters sound character and a strong heart. For it is "from within, from the human heart" (Mark 7:21) that intentions and motivations are born.

Dear God, thank you for the ways of the past and the dreams for the future. Help us to be a source of both roots and wings for our grandchildren.

August 2

Read John 12:35-36.

Upon entering a small church in Berwick, Louisiana, my eyes were drawn to the beautiful paraments. The white handmade cloths for the altar, pulpit, and lectern were unadorned except for the pattern of filet-crocheted crosses. A single large cross was crocheted at the center of each parament, and a row of smaller crosses trimmed the lower border. The beauty was in the simplicity and the perfection of the tiny intricate handwork.

After worship I met Kathleen, who told me she had made the paraments in memory of her deceased husband. With the death of a spouse comes the midnight of grief, and while we "walk in the darkness, [we] do not know where [we] are going" (John 12:35). From her shadowy cross of grief and loneliness, Kathleen began to look toward the light. One stitch at a time, she transformed a ball of fine white thread into something magnificent for God.

Henri Nouwen (*Life of the Beloved*) says: "The great spiritual call of the Beloved Children of God is to pull their brokenness away from the shadow of the curse and put it under the light of the blessing." Kathleen answered this call, casting her grief under the light of blessing. In so doing, she also blessed her three grandchildren. Every time they enter that sanctuary for the rest of their lives, the beautiful paraments will be a special symbol of their grandparents' loving presence and a reminder to carry their burdens into the light.

Loving God, thank you for the light of your presence. Help us to grow spiritually so that we may walk in that light even while we are broken with grief.

🌱 August 3

Read Deuteronomy 32:1-4.

Today is my husband's birthday. A few years ago, our family celebrated his fiftieth at the top of Uncompahgre, the sixth highest mountain in Colorado (over 14,000 feet). As I stood on the summit and looked in awe at the full-circle panoramic view beneath me, I understood why this was a sacred mountain for the Utes before their removal. I thought of the Ojibwa Prayer and the reference to the Creator as "Grandfather" in Native American spirituality.

No single image can capture God, yet the image of God as grandparent is one of the most significant. That image symbolizes respect and wisdom, yet comfort and closeness. When we reach up and take the hand of God as Grandparent while we walk along our journey, we know in the core of our being that God, the Sacred One, calls us Beloved.

This image also helps us get in touch with the kind of grandmother we want to be—evoking respect through our actions, showing wisdom in our words, bringing comfort with our presence, offering closeness of heart even when apart. We offer our hand to those precious ones, hoping that deep in their soul they hear us calling them Beloved.

O Grandfather/Grandmother God, "May [our] teaching drop like the rain, [our] speech condense like the dew; like gentle rain on grass, like showers on new growth" (Deut. 32:2). May we walk together in the Sacred Way.

❦ August 4

Read Colossians 1:15-23.

She told me her story. Three years ago she had gone through an extremely difficult period in her life. It was a time we've all experienced to some degree—when one bomb drops after another, and we stand knee-deep in rubble, our dreams shattered, and we pray with that fervor that desperation always brings. For her, the bombs fell on health, finances, and marriage. And then her grandmother died.

Her grandmother. The woman who had always been there for her when things were bad—to kiss her skinned knee when she fell down, to give her milk and cookies when spats with her best friend brought tears after school, to ceremoniously bring out the two special tea cups when she earned an honor, and to be present without questions when she broke up with a boyfriend.

When she sat at the service celebrating her grandmother's life, she felt numbed by grief and the debris of her own life. As she listened to the pastor, his words faded and into her mind came the oft-spoken words of her grandmother, ringing with conviction: "If you keep focused on Jesus, you can handle everything else."

Now, as she finished her story she smiled, standing on a strong foundation of faith built from the rubble heap, attesting to the scripture: "He himself is before all things, and in him all things hold together" (Col. 1:17).

God, thank you for the Christ. Help us to be centered spiritually and thereby sort out the debris and glue together our fragmented lives.

❦ August 5

Read Galatians 5:22-26.

As I flew northward, I read *Creation Spirituality*, in which Matthew Fox said that if he were pope he "would dismantle the Congregation for the Doctrine of the Faith (formerly known as the Holy Inquisition) and replace it with a circle of grandmothers who would comment on the healthy or unhealthy spirit behind theological ideas."

As I pondered how to discern between a healthy and unhealthy spirit, night began to fall, dividing my view of the earth. The plane window on my right framed the eastern sky, already put to bed under a dark coverlet, stagnant. The small window on my left caught the west view: the sun had journeyed beyond the cloud bank below, but its light continued to enflame the sky with brilliant golds and fire yellows, vibrant and celebrative—like the lingering Light of the Son, glorifying the Creator. Looking from the left window to the right, I saw a cosmic metaphor for a healthy and unhealthy spirit.

Paul speaks of the fruit of the Spirit as "love, joy, peace, patience, kindness, generosity, faithfulness, gentleness, and self-control" (Gal. 5:22). These qualities are fundamental to a healthy spirit.

We are God's circle of grandmothers, invited to nurture a healthy spirit within ourselves and foster that spirit in our relationships with others—placing ourselves in the lingering Light of the Son and producing the fruit of the Spirit.

Creator God, thank you for your magnificent universe. Help us to see the beautiful stories you tell through its wonders.

August 6

Read Luke 15:8-10.

One beautiful aspect of grandparenting is that when we are with our grandchildren, our whole purpose is simply to be *with* them. During these times together, we set aside our harried agendas and are fully present.

When our son Bryant was small, his grandfather showed him how to use a metal detector. They would amble along side by side, listening for the clicking, laughing excitedly when the sound grew louder. Even old rusty nails were a treasure because they found them together.

One morning Bryant and his sister Valerie and their grandmother decided to take a walk. Bryant led the way with the metal detector. As they returned home along the path they had already strolled, Bryant heard them whispering behind him. He turned around and saw his grandmother nudge his sister and smile. He could tell something was up, but he didn't know what. Suddenly, the metal detector went crazy, and there on the path was a silver dollar. He went along with their secret, but he knew that his grandmother had planted the coin.

What grandmother who has silver coins will not give one to her grandchild and rejoice in the gift? The same is true of our time. Presence is more important than presents. Praise God that our gift of time—being fully *with* a grandchild—sends ripples of love far into the future.

Generous God, thank you for your gift of life and the rhythm of family relationships. Help us to be with— wholly present to—our grandchildren when we have the privilege of being together.

🍂 August 7

Read Psalm 37:5-9.

One morning I watched a blue butterfly among the wild flowers in a high mountain meadow. For a while it flew along in front of me. Then suddenly, it became still—while still moving. Without a single wave of its wings, it soared to the top of the ridge above me.

This is like the stillness of spiritual wholeness, which catches the current and glides unmoving to a summit of sacred space. The winds of the spirit buoy us up, and we climb life's next hill while being still. This inner attitude of stillness is not passive but empowering. It permeates and transforms our words and deeds.

The words *holiness, health,* and *wholeness* spring from one root (*hal*) and denote a state of togetherness, as compared with dividedness. Wholeness is a merging of all aspects of the inner life with all roles of the outer life. But in our society, where is the time for stillness? Where is the time for wholeness? The war against them begins so early that even children are fractured, fragmented, and frenzied.

One of our joys as grandmothers is to "be still before the Lord" (Ps. 37:7) with our beloved grandchildren, providing them with opportunities to experience that blue-butterfly kind of stillness.

Dear God, thank you for those precious moments of holy stillness. Help us to know when to reach beyond entertaining our grandchildren and toward empowering the blue butterfly of your spirit within them.

August 8

Read Isaiah 55:10-13.

Looking forward to our three-year-old granddaughter's visit to our old log cabin, I stained a toy bench, made a cushion for it, filled it with blocks and toys, and planned many activities: sifting powdered sugar and making colored icing for graham crackers, playing the game Candyland, reading stories, gathering wild flowers for the table, walking beside the stream, and playing in the "secret" playhouse my own children had built years before in the aspen trees.

When Chelsea arrived, we began moving from one activity to the next. The day was fun and busy for both of us. However, as I thought about it later, I realized what a mistake I had made.

Bill and I like to be at this cabin primarily because it is a retreat from scheduled activity and invites us to reflection and simply to savor life. Even children—programmed for learning activities, lessons, sports, and passive entertainment—rush from one thing to another without pausing for satisfaction and reflection before the next activity. I realized that I had fallen into that trap with Chelsea, scheduling out of our time together a pause for satisfaction and reflection.

Whatever our age, when we meet a need or achieve a goal or complete a project, a pause is in order for a moment of satisfaction, to listen to "the mountains and the hills . . . burst into song, and all the trees of the field . . . clap their hands"; and for a moment of reflection, to "go out in joy, and be led back in peace" (Isa. 55:12).

Eternal God, thank you for the rhythm of activity and rest in your creation. Help us to follow that rhythm and include pauses for satisfaction and reflection, especially when we are with our grandchildren.

August 9

Read Genesis 1:9-13 and Revelation 22:1-5.

My granddaughter and I walked along a trail through an aspen forest. We came to a place where a tree had fallen across our pathway. "The tree died," said Chelsea. She peered at it in serious reflection. "The tree went to heaven." Carefully, we stepped over the aspen trunk. As we started down the trail again, she paused and looked back at the tree, then up at me. "Grandmom, trees make heaven pretty."

"Trees make heaven pretty" is a three-year-old's simple and trusting theology. She had heard the Story, and she related it to her own world, to her present moment. In that Story is the symbol of the tree: "The earth brought forth vegetation . . . trees of every kind" (Gen. 1:12); "On either side of the river is the tree of life" (Rev. 22:2). The first and the last chapters of the Bible. The Alpha and the Omega. The creation story and the story of the new creation.

Children sense the holism of creation. They sense with a kind of curious reverence that all life is a wondrous connection of Oneness with God—not just humankind but also pets and plants. Children sense the mystery that life in its totality, its beginning and its end, is in God's hands.

Over the years we adults tend to *un*learn this sense of reverence and to distance ourselves from this mystery. We complicate theology, forgetting to relate it to our own world and our present moment. Our grandchildren reteach us.

Eternal God, thank you for trees, for trust in you as the Alpha and Omega. Help us to listen to your little theologians.

🌱 August 10

Read Judges 13:17-18.

One afternoon when everyone was napping after a mountain hike and picnic, my year-old granddaughter, Sarah, suddenly startled herself from her nap. Quickly, I picked her up so she wouldn't wake anyone.

I took her into my room, and we lay down quietly on the bed together. She began to study my face, then sat up and looked at me intently. Evidently satisfied, she lay back down. I closed my eyes, thinking that she might close hers and go back to sleep. I felt her little hand gently caress my cheeks and trace my chin. I opened my eyes. She smiled and said, "Mimi."

It was a wonderful, memorable moment, for I felt she had called me by name.

There are wonderful, memorable moments in life when we feel God calls us by name. In those moments we sense a powerful dynamic in our lives. All aspects of our being are unified. We feel in tune with the divine plan, energized by a guiding force, directed by God. In those holistic moments a transformation occurs. We sense that we are more than we are. Our cup runneth over.

That addedness, that consciousness, that energy, that transformation, is the extraordinary spiritual experience of hearing God call us by name.

Loving God, thank you for knowing and loving each of us. Help us to tune out the noise and listen more closely.

🌿 August 11

Read John 1:10-14.

Our family sat on the cabin porch, talking about Christianity in Russia and one fledgling, faithful congregation in Ekaterinburg. My granddaughter Chelsea sat on my lap, seeing pictures of my Russian friends and hearing about some of the children. The church in Ekaterinburg was born in 1990. But this was not the beginning.

There was Sister Anna Eklund who arrived in St. Petersburg in 1908 and kept Christian work alive even through the horrible Stalin era, until illness forced her to leave in 1934. But this was not the beginning.

There was the Reverend Karl Lindborg, who preached there in the early 1880's. But this was not the beginning.

Over a thousand years ago (A.D. 957), Princess Olga of Russia visited Constantinople, was converted, and returned to Kiev a fervent servant of Christ and a future saint. Three decades later her grandson Prince Vladimir was also converted (988), and he proclaimed Christianity the religion of all Russia. Some historians attribute his conversion to the wish of his bride Anna from Constantinople; others attribute it to his being struck by the beauty of orthodox worship. But I have no doubt that his conversion was influenced by the foundation of faith laid by his grandmother. I can picture her holding him on her lap and telling him stories about the Christian faith.

I think of Princess Olga as the grandmother of Russian Christianity.

Dear God, thank you for the faithful grandmothers of the past. May we influence the future of your church in our small way by being faithful grandmothers today.

August 12

Read Matthew 13:10-15.

My three-year-old granddaughter, Chelsea, was building with wooden blocks on the cabin porch while her parents, Dirk and Angela, rocked and read and watched the hummingbirds.

My friend Gerry stopped by. Pointing toward the ponds, she told them about her husband's taking all the grandchildren fishing on her granddaughter's birthday. "They saw a bear!" said Gerry. "A huge black bear! It really scared them!"

Angela asked her granddaughter's age.

Gerry said, "She was eight yesterday."

"Ate by the bear?" asked wide-eyed, terrified Chelsea.

Sometimes we are like three-year-olds in our misunderstanding and resulting anxiety. Busy building secular blocks, we give only halfhearted attention to other matters, especially spiritual growth. Jesus' words fit us: "Seeing they do not perceive, and hearing they do not listen, nor do they understand" (Matt. 13:13). We see the beautiful gold cross above the altar but do not perceive that it symbolizes giving our lives. We hear the words from the Scriptures during worship but do not listen with our hearts and let the words change our actions and attitudes.

Spiritual growth moves us toward deeper perception,

223

closer listening, and clearer understanding. And even when we come face-to-face with the bears of life, spiritual strength can transform our fear into trust in God.

Dear God, thank you for your patience with our misunderstanding and our misdeeds. Help us to see more clearly and to be transformed by the vision.

♥ August 13

Read Ecclesiastes 3:9-13.

High in the Rocky Mountains, my granddaughter and I held hands as we walked along the dam that separates two ponds. Wild flowers from seeds of the rainbow dotted our way. Jumping fish drew circles in the ponds, and the wind blew the water into waves. I realized the present is like that dam, dividing the past and the future, offering opportunities to savor life's beauty and to be stirred by the winds of the Spirit.

We stopped to skip a rock and watched it form new patterns in the original pond. It is possible in the present to skip a rock of reflection into the pond of our past, discover new meaning in old pain, and thereby transform our perspective of the past.

At the edge of the dam, we listened as the water was released in a stream that flowed into the new pond, which peeked at us from around the bend, distant but visible. It is also possible in the present to send currents into the future through our words and deeds—calming the waters that lie ahead or creating potential storms.

The pond of my past is larger than that of my future; for my granddaughter, the opposite is true. As I looked at her smiling face, I thought of how God "has made everything suitable for its time" and "has put a sense of past and future" into our minds (Eccles. 3:11). In that joyful moment, I felt the presence of God and was filled with gratitude that God is and was and always will be present with us.

Eternal God, thank you that we can trust in your presence. Help us to be a healing presence in our grandchildren's lives and to guard against being a source of pollution in the stream that flows into their future.

❦ August 14

Read Psalm 150.

Tomorrow we would go home, but this afternoon we would have a party. With goodies on the table and John Denver songs on a tape, we celebrated the family time we would have shared this summer.

Through his songs, John Denver had been with us in this mountain cabin every summer since "Rocky Mountain High," and now he burst into "I'm a Country Boy." As I looked around our old table at the family members I love so much, joy and gratitude overflowed. Spontaneously, I said, "Let's dance, Chelsea."

We held hands, my beloved granddaughter's little arms moving with mine. We stepped closer together, farther apart. "Do you feel the rhythm, Chelsea?" Of course she did. Her small feet stepped fast with the quick beat. "Just do what you feel like," I said. "Move any way you want. No one can dance wrong." I turned her around, stooped and turned around myself. We laughed and danced on.

We danced in joy for our family. We danced in gratitude for God's bountiful gifts—the physical ones of nature, the emotional ones of love, and the spiritual ones of life. We danced in praise of the ever-living, ever-loving Creator. "Praise him with tambourine and dance; praise him with strings and pipe!" (Ps. 150:4). The joy, the energy of that relationship! I felt it like a laser. The beat of love, the beat of life. Glory be to God!

Dear God, thank you for the dance of life. Help us to dance to your beat.

🍂 August 15

Read Psalm 116:5-9.

O Lord, our Lord, tears fill my eyes. I hide behind sunglasses, the facade of a smile. Dirk, Angela, and my grandchildren drive away—they must not see me weep!

O Lord, our Lord, tears fill my eyes. My younger son, lingering, looks closely at me, undeceived, feeling my secret sadness. I explain: "I'm not unhappy about going home." He nods, "It's hard to leave." We hug each other and part.

O Lord, our Lord, tears fill my eyes. Bill and I drive down the dirt lane, shut the gate to summer sabbath time, and begin our winding descent through the mountains. The memories of these rich days wind through my mind, cling to my heart.

O Lord, our Lord, my tears fall now. They drip down below my sunglasses and drown my worn smile. Bill looks at me, the silent questions of Elkanah in his eyes: "Why do you weep? Why is your heart so sad?" (1 Sam. 1:8). Aloud he asks, "Can I do anything?" Silently I recall Carlo Carretto: "Why, Lord all this weeping? The answer does not come easily." Aloud, I reassure him. "It will be good to get home. It's just that going home requires this to end."

O Lord, our Lord, my tears fall now. Children grow, and I am grateful for their independence. Grandchildren grow, and I am grateful for their solid, happy home. Bill's and my life together is busy, filled with meaning and purpose, and I am grateful for the mission we share.

But O Lord, our Lord, my tears fall now. Not tomorrow. But today.

Loving God, thank you for family and for sabbath times together. Help us to treasure our yesterdays and trust our tomorrows even when we blink at them through the tears of today.

🌿 August 16

Read 1 Corinthians 13:11-13.

In "Circle of Transformation" (*Stories of Dreamwalkers* by Joyce Mills and Frank Howell) a Native American grandmother says to her grown granddaughter: "Earlier today, my beloved Granddaughter, you said that you are a woman now, not a child—that is but a half truth; for in order to be a true woman, you must first embrace the girl-child within. She has not gone away—she is just present in another form."

Our relationship with our grandchildren when they are growing up is not only lodged in their memory, it is also part of their formational experience. Our times together are grains of sand mixed into the foundation on which they build their adulthood.

Grandmotherhood offers spontaneous joy; it also offers responsibility. It is a special vocation that merits intentionality. Our grandchildren's eyes are watchful of what we do, and we can sow the seeds of faith. Their ears are open to the words of our mouths, and we can plant hope. Their hearts are responsive to our gift of belovedness, a gift that continues to be unwrapped throughout their lives. When our grandchildren embrace the child within in order to become a true woman or man, our experiences together—experiences that foster faith, hope, and love—will abide with them always.

Ever-living God, thank you for the connection that exists from generation to generation. Help us to plant the seeds of faith, hope, and love in our relationships with our beloved grandchildren.

August 17

Read Philippians 2:9-15.

The little boy steps between his grandparents on a crisp August night. His eyes stare toward the heavens, watching a meteor shower. Streaks of color arch across the immense dark dome. Suddenly, with awe in his voice he asks, "Are they God's fireworks?"

God's fireworks! We catch the spark. We confess that Jesus Christ is Lord, "to the glory of God." We are baptized in that name, that name "that is above every name," that name before whom "every knee should bow."

God's fireworks! God is at work in us, enabling us "to will and to work" for God's "good pleasure." Setting us afire with hope, faith, love, gratitude, and joy. Asking us to be "without blemish in the midst of a crooked and perverse generation."

God's fireworks! We are God's children. We "shine like stars in the world." We are dots of light offering direction in the darkness of despair. We are signals of hope in the midnight of hopelessness. We are tiny twinkles of joyful spontaneity, open to the spirit, singing God's praise.

Suddenly, with awe in our hearts we realize that our lives are like meteors, colorful streaks across Christendom—we are God's fireworks!

Creator God, thank you for the message of the meteors. Help us to be faithful as your fireworks.

August 18

Read 2 Corinthians 2:14-17.

Missing my granddaughters after being with them during our vacation, I called to check on them. "Hi, Chelsea," I said, recovering from my surprise that she had answered the phone for the first time. "This is Grandmom."

"Where are you?"

"In Louisiana."

"I was in Louisiana," she said, remembering back a year-and-a-half before. "We went to the river. And the boat went HONK-A HONK-A. It scared me."

"It scared me, too, Chelsea."

"And Daddy and Mommy and Granddad."

"We all jumped, didn't we?"

"Yes," she said with her mischievous laugh. "The boat was too loud!"

Sometimes as Christians we also are too loud. We repeat pious words and make grand pretenses of sacrificial gestures, peddling the faith. But Christianity is not spread by the loud tooting of our own horn. That makes the non-Christians and nominal Christians around us want to jump back and hold their ears.

Instead, the people around us are drawn to Christianity through the silent fragrance of a Christ-like presence, like the soft aroma of honeysuckle. Through us spreads "the fragrance that comes from knowing him. For we are the aroma of Christ to God among those who are being saved and among those who are perishing" (2 Cor. 2:14-15).

Dear God, forgive us when our faith is too loud or lacks fragrance. Help us to be honeysuckle Christians rather than HONK-A-HONK-A Christians.

August 19

Read Ezekiel 17:5-6.

I looked at the Aboriginal painting, "*Mininjtjimuli*," named for the edible purple-flowered plant, and recalled: "Then he took a seed from the land, placed it in fertile soil; a plant by abundant waters" (Ezek. 17:5). The artist lives in the Nauiyu Nambiyu community, which is by the abundant waters of the Daly River in the northern territory of Australia. The ancient myths, stories, and symbols rejoice in the plentiful food and water of this lush tropical land. Their spirituality intermingles traditional rituals with recent Christian influence, and their art reflects this complex mix.

The Aboriginal artists in this community are mostly women. They sit together—a circle of grandmothers, mothers, and granddaughters between eighteen and eighty—remembering the ancient stories and preserving them through art. The roots of their heritage remain strong, issuing new branches and leaves on the vine that spread into the future.

What wonderful story gifts would be exchanged in a circle of women, eighteen to eighty! We grandmothers would hold rich memories indeed if we had experienced that kind of intergenerational circle at eighteen, sitting with women born before the turn of the century. Now, our grandchildren could benefit from intergenerational-intercultural circles of women whose task is to remember the past and gain new insight into the present. Perhaps our culture, instead of producing annuals with new seeds planted each season, would begin to develop like Ezekiel's vine, with new leaves reaching out, yet remaining attached to sturdy roots.

Eternal God, thank you for the rich diversity of the peoples of our planet. Help us to honor customs from other cultures and from the past, and to be a link in sharing the stories so they will not be lost to future generations.

🍂 August 20

Read John 21:15-17.

The grandson of my friend Julia was staying with her. He was playing happily, fully attentive to the puzzle before him, so she went upstairs to do some work. After a while, she heard his feet on the stairs. She stepped into the hall and smiled at him.

"You are glad I am here," he said.

"Very glad."

Then, needing more, he came close to her. "Do you love me?"

Henri Nouwen (*Life of the Beloved*) speaks of "the blessings that come to us through words of gratitude, encouragement, affection and love. . . . They are gentle reminders of that beautiful, strong, but hidden, voice of the one who calls us by name and speaks good things about us."

Like Julia's grandson, sometimes we are totally engrossed in the complex puzzles we face. Our attention to spiritual growth wanes. After a while, we become aware of a spiritual void and seek assurance. In whatever words we choose, we pray to God, "You are glad I am here." We feel God's smile. Needing more, we move closer and ask, "Do you love me?"

Through prayer, God's love begins to fill that emptiness. Our cup overflows, and we respond by filling the cup of others. Nouwen says, "The faithful discipline of prayer reveals to you that you are the blessed one and gives you the power to bless others."

Dear God, thank you for loving us. Help us to be so in touch with you that our lives can be a blessing to others.

August 21

Read James 1:17-18.

Catherine de Hueck Doherty explains the concept of *poustinia* in her book of that title. It is a Russian word meaning desert. The essence of *poustinia* is a place within the heart where we contemplate the presence of God. In our *poustinia* we open our eyes and ears to God within ourselves and to God in others. We experience the Word of God as a word of love.

A *poustinik* was a Russian religious pilgrim. When a pilgrim built a shelter, called a *poustinia*, it was always open to the world on one side so the pilgrim could see others' needs and go quickly to serve. In our *poustinia* we learn tenderness to all God's creatures, to all our sisters and brothers, and to ourselves.

We learn that the Word of God as a word of love does not change; it just comes to us in different disguises. One of those disguises is a grandchild. This generous act of giving, this perfect gift of a grandchild, comes from the One with whom "there is no variation or shadow due to change" (James 1:17).

Awareness of God's unchanging love is a life-changing experience for us. The unchanging grace of God redeems us from the residue of guilt about our yesterdays, and the unchanging trustworthiness of God releases us from anxiety about our tomorrows. In joyful response, we open one wall of our poustinia to the world, repeating God's word of love to others through our own words and actions.

Dear God, thank you for safe places. May our grandchildren always feel safe when our arms are around them.

🍂 August 22

Read Psalm 27:1, 7-10, 13.

During his sermon, the pastor told a story about a young man and his relationship with his grandmother. He was gay and had contracted AIDS. Upon learning this, his parents took his pictures out of their house, commanded him never to come back home, and forbade his brothers and sisters ever to see him again. His grandmother could not change his parents' decision, but she herself remained present to her grandson. He died in the arms of his grandmother.

Henri Nouwen (*Life of the Beloved*) reminds us that

232

"there are few places where we can feel truly safe." When a child is small, a grandmother's lap is one of those places. Years later, when the child has outgrown the grandmother, being enfolded in her arms—even if they are frail—can still feel like a truly safe place. As our grandsons and granddaughters grow older, we will eventually grow feeble, but one thing will always remain unchanged: A grandchild does not have to put on a mask to be significant to us. They are beloved just as they are.

That belovedness provides them a place where they can feel truly safe. It is a gift that helps them "see the goodness of the Lord in the land of the living" (Ps. 27:13).

Generous God, thank you for spiritual shelter. When we withdraw to that shelter, help us to remember to keep the world's needs in view.

🍇 August 23

Read 1 Peter 1:22-25.

"Grandmom, you are my best friend," said Chelsea on the phone. My heart did a grandmother meltdown.

That is not an uncommon statement for three-year-olds to make about their grandmothers. Perhaps that is because we do not see them as clay to be shaped at our potter's wheel, but as precious vessels, clear as crystal pitchers, in which to pour our love until it overflows. Perhaps it is because our purpose is not so much to prepare them for the doorway to adulthood as to walk with them through the gateway to the garden of spiritual fruits. Perhaps it is because we are like fireflies in the presence of our grandchildren—the light of our grace shines.

Ann Belford Ulanov (*Picturing Grace*) says: "Grace comes to us in the flesh, through the spaces and forms and contents of our human life." We can enflesh grace for another's life. Sharing grace, we stir the air as we move through space.

The leaves sway, the waters ripple, the kite flies. The light of our grace shines, and the other hears the name, "Beloved."

Through grace we are "born anew, not of perishable but of imperishable seed, through the living and enduring word of God" (1 Pet. 1:23). To live that word before another is to be his or her best friend.

Dear God, thank you for opportunities to be a best friend. Help us to share your word of grace by touching a life that has no friend.

🌰 **August 24**

Read Romans 12:14-21.

My friend Judy shared a story about her little grandson. The firstborn grandchild in their family, he was the focus of attention and enjoyed his status.

It had been that way all his life—three whole years—and he felt this was the way it should always be. Then a baby sister was born. Attention was suddenly divided. He hadn't done anything differently, but his world had changed radically. And he knew the source! Sometimes he did little things to his sister, not mean or cruel, but frustrating things—like setting a toy beyond her reach or giving her an over-enthusiastic hug.

It had been that way all her life—several months—and she feared this was the way it would always be. Then she learned to crawl. She could move on her own! She saw her brother sitting on the floor watching TV and immediately crawled toward him. She reached her goal, and pinched him as hard as she could. She sat back and smiled, quite pleased with herself.

We smile also, for the behavior of those two children is understandable and human. But it reflects a revenge-response cycle of human conflict that can get out of hand—between children, spouses, and nations.

One of our roles as grandmothers is reconciler, to say with our lives: "Do not repay anyone evil for evil, but take thought of what is noble in the sight of all. . . . So far as it depends on you, live peaceably with all" (Rom. 12:17-18).

Dear God, thank you for the Teacher who showed us how to live on a higher plane. Help us to live peaceably even with those who are trying to start a family war.

🍂 August 25

Read Luke 8:11-16.

This is my mother's birthday. Slapped by the Great Depression as a teenager, she has lived her life with patient endurance. To me, the best celebration of her birth occurred last year when she turned 75.

She and I took a trip to see all of her grandchildren and her two great-grandchildren. My daughter Danna Lee and son-in-law Mark hosted a surprise party for her. My mother—who loves to surprise people—was herself surprised. She had fun opening her grandchildren's thoughtful gifts, and with delight she blew out the candles on her cake. We took pictures during the party so she could show her friends back home.

We gathered around her that day as family—the fruit she had borne—ones she has held lovingly in her honest and good heart. The photographs caught the light in her face, a light that lingered, inextinguishable.

Perhaps our vocation as grandmothers is fulfilled when our grandchildren, whatever their age, know that they are beloved—whether, like the parable of this seed, they skim along a path, stand on a rock, fall into the thorns, or plant themselves in good soil.

Dear God, thank you for the grandmothers with honest and good hearts who have gone before us and showed us

the way. Help us, like them, to be channels of uncondi-
tional love for our grandchildren.

🌱 August 26

Read Proverbs 2:1-8.

My friend Ruth, a grandmother, is an elegant lady, the personification of kindness and dignity. One memorable day she shared with me her journey.

The journey. She spoke softly, matter-of-factly about how things were when her children were growing up. About having to buy dresses without trying them on. About camping across the country for vacations because they could not use public restrooms or eat in the restaurants. About not letting her children know they were unwelcome. About not wanting them to begin to wonder if something was wrong with them. About not wanting seeds of hatred to fester in their hearts. The journey. I listened, filled with pain, knowing I was in the presence of grace.

The journey. I thought about my friend Ruth as I stood in a reception line at Dillard University in New Orleans. Students passed by—third generation graduates of this excellent seat of education. The pride these grandchildren had in themselves could not begin to compare with the pride of their grandparents. The grandparents had vision, the parents had determination, and these grandchildren had hope. The journey. Filled with admiration and respect, I shook hand after hand, knowing I was in the presence of greatness.

The journey. The Lord "stores up sound wisdom for the upright; he is a shield to those who walk blamelessly, guarding the paths of justice and preserving the way of his faithful ones" (Prov. 2:7-8).

Dear God, thank you for our brothers and sisters who have met persecution with love and grace. Help us to learn from

236

them to be loving and grace-filled toward people who (in comparatively small ways) make our lives difficult.

🐛 August 27

Read Ephesians 2:1-10.

"For by grace you have been saved through faith, and this is not your own doing; it is the gift of God" (Eph. 2:8). This great verse of scripture tolled like steeple bells throughout the Protestant Reformation.

When priest Martin Luther married nun Katie, one of the reasons he gave (besides opposing the pope and supporting clergy marriage) was that it would please his father who liked the idea of grandchildren. Could it be that the desire for grandchildren played a part in the Protestant Reformation!

In my mind's eye (though not supported by official records) I see a scene in which Martin Luther and his father are talking. His mother is peeking at them from offstage. Just loud enough for her husband to hear, she whispers about the special joys of being a grandparent. Convinced, he begins to tell Martin what a blessing grandchildren would be.

Martin Luther, the Father of the Reformation, also became the father of a dozen children—surely beloved by their grandparents. And the words of Paul in Ephesians still ring clearly in our lives as Christians: We are "created in Christ Jesus for good works" (Eph. 2:10).

Dear God, thank you for the age-old desire for grandchildren and the way that desire has shaped history. Help us to extend our good works to a child orphaned from grandparents.

🐛 August 28

Read Psalm 42:5-8.

Sea foam formed scallops on the sand as the waves rolled in and slid out again on the South Carolina beach.

The full moon played peek-a-boo with the clouds that billowed across the sky and cast their shadows over the sea. The distant lighthouse signal blinked in steady rhythm, and the stars, like spotlights from scattered farms, splayed across the sky. Unblocked, the moon shone in the darkness and bright patterns of light danced with the waters. Waves slapped the shore and the night breeze sang a soft low song.

My feet sank into wet sand and gritty shells. I tasted damp salt air and smelled the mystery of creation in the rhythmic swelling and shrinking of the sea, the ancient in-breathing and out-breathing of the Earth. A sea gull flew past, dipped and soared toward the deeps.

The silhouette of a small boy caught my eye. He waded into the water and played tag with the waves. He chased them onto the sand, and they chased him back toward the sea. Finally growing weary, he drew close to his grandmother who snuggled him in her arms.

Like this little boy, when we grow weary from the struggle of chasing the waves in our lives, we can draw close to the heart of God who rocks us and sings to us the ancient lullaby of the sea. "By day the Lord commands his steadfast love, and at night his song is with me, a prayer to the God of my life" (Ps. 42:8).

Loving God, thank you for the haven of your arms and your midnight lullaby. Help us to be a song in the midnight of others.

August 29

Romans 5:1-5.

My friend and I visited a restored antebellum home in the South. A pair of ornate china vases decorated the mantle of the fireplace in the parlor. Calling our attention to them, the guide turned them halfway around, and the scene changed. "Weekend vases," she said. The picture on the side now facing us was a simple bush.

My friend, who is one of the kindest people I know, said, "If I had a Sunday side and a Monday side like those vases, my grandmother would be ashamed of me."

"Your grandmother?"

She nodded. "She was a wonderful woman."

Paul said, "Thanks be to God that you, . . . have become obedient from the heart to the form of teaching to which you were entrusted" (Rom. 6:17). Grandmothers are entrusted with a teaching responsibility.

We can choose to be negligent in this trust. Like the weekend vases, we can turn ourselves around in different situations to show whatever side we want another to see, thus teaching our grandchildren a form of posturing.

Or we can take seriously our teaching responsibility. We can develop a nurturing relationship with our grandchildren, providing unhurried, undivided attention and non-anxious presence. We can give them the gift of an authentic relationship that reaches deep into our interior and integrates our faith—obedient from the heart in our form of teaching.

If we choose the latter, decades from now when our grandchildren have grandchildren, perhaps they will say, "My grandmother was a wonderful woman."

Dear God, thank you for opportunities to "grand" parent. Help us not to be empty weekend vases in fulfilling the responsibility that comes with that opportunity.

🍂 August 30

Read 1 Timothy 6:17-19.

While sitting in a Florida restaurant, I noticed the people in the booth in front of me and behind me. Ahead of me a man sat beside his grandson and across the table were his wife and granddaughter. All four shared in conversation. Grandmom, smiling and solicitous, leaned over to help the little girl. The boy laid his head against his granddad's shoulder, comfortable and trusting. Their grandchildren's presence was central, a special privilege.

Behind me, a family hurried through dinner because Mom had to get to work right afterward. The couple talked with each other about family concerns. Their preschool son tried to get their attention and failed, then tried negative behavior and succeeded: "STOP that!" said Father. Their child's presence was peripheral, taken for granted.

As parents, we can remember those days. As grandparents, we are now at a different stage in life. Whatever our financial situation, comparatively, it is probably better expense-wise than when we were struggling to rear our children. Comparatively, we better understand the quick passage of time and the importance of wholehearted presence with a child. Comparatively, we are richer now—richer in experience, wisdom, and spirituality.

Timothy admonishes the rich (1 Tim. 6:17, 18) "to do good, to be rich in good works, generous, and ready to serve," and to set our hopes "on God who richly provides us with everything for our enjoyment"—including beloved grandchildren. We are indeed rich. We do indeed have much to give.

Generous God, thank you for the richness of our lives. Help us to share all that we are and all that we have.

August 31

Read 2 Corinthians 6:2-10.

This summer I taught our granddaughter Chelsea how to play the game Candyland. Each time we played she said repeatedly, "I get to win. I want the princess card. Remember, Grandmom. I get to win. I want the princess card."

(It is not difficult, of course, for a child to beat a grand-mother—but assuring who draws the princess can take a bit of card-sharking!)

My son played with us one evening, and Chelsea did not draw the princess, nor did she win. She threw the kind of three-year-old fit that showed me the importance of games (without grandmother card-sharking) in teaching children how to handle situations that do not turn out the way they desire.

We all experience at times the joy of "winning" and get-ting the "princess card"—whatever that represents in our own life. Also, at times we all face difficulties and chal-lenges, and during those times our only choice may be the attitude with which we face them.

In a conversation with Emily Dickinson, who was phys-ically incapacitated toward the end of her life, a man asked her, "Does not your handicap color your life?"

"Yes," she responded. "But I choose the colors."

We cannot select the events that are sketched on the canvas of our lives; that canvas stands on God's easel. But God expects *us* to do the brush strokes. And *we* choose the colors.

Dear God, thank you for giving us so many colors to choose from in difficult situations. Help us not to act like a three-year-old when we don't draw the princess card.

For Everything a Season

Marilyn Brown Oden

---- 🍂 ----

🍂 *September* 1

Read Psalm 149:1-4.

The shadows of the leaves from the trees in the park danced around the grandmothers and their grandchildren. With the first day of September upon them, it would soon be too cold to gather in the city park.

The grandmothers, from many racial backgrounds, chatted with one another and kept a watchful eye on the large sandbox where the children played—a kaleidoscope of the human family, sifting and shifting the sand. The grandmothers cared for these little ones while their parents worked. They shared with one another a thread of love for their grandchildren far stronger than the web of cultural and racial differences separating them.

Thomas Merton (*New Seeds of Contemplation*) said, "If we would let go of our own obsession with what we think is the meaning of it all, we might be able to hear His call and follow Him in His mysterious 'cosmic dance'." These grandmothers were not struggling with finding the meaning of this chapter in their lives. They were simply present to their beloved grandchildren, all dancing together in the moment. The psalmist wrote: "Let them praise his name with dancing. . . . For the Lord takes pleasure in his people" (Ps. 149:3, 4).

Dear God, thank you for our colorful human family. Help us to make meaningful moments as we share in others' lives.

September 2

Read Psalm 18:1-3.

My friend told me about her grandson's helping his mother clean house on Labor Day weekend. As soon as they finished, they were going to celebrate the holiday by going to the zoo. He was usually a cooperative little boy and, eager to get on their way, he had been especially helpful that morning. The kitchen was the last room, and his mother asked him to get the broom from the closet.

"No," he said. "You get it."

Surprised, she asked, "Why?"

"It's dark in there."

"Are you afraid?"

He nodded.

"There's no reason to be afraid of the dark. God is with you everywhere."

"In the dark?"

"Even in the dark," she assured him.

He went to the closet, paused, then slowly turned the knob. Remaining behind the door, he opened it a few inches, reached his hand around inside, and said, "God, if you're in there, please hand me the broom."

How like my friend's grandson we are! We do not trust that God is with us during times of darkness in our lives. We lack faith that God's loving presence in itself gives us the strength to get through those times. We expect God to hand us what we want—to change the situation—rather than opening our own hearts to new courage and deeper faith.

With the passwords, "I love you, O Lord, my strength"

(Ps. 18:1), we can enter the doorway to darkness, confident in God's light.

Dear God, thank you for being with us in the darkness. Help us to have the trust and courage to get the brooms ourselves.

🍂 September 3

Read Matthew 13:33.

My husband's mother died several years ago, but I think of her often, especially on this day, her birthday. Frequently on Sunday afternoons when our children were growing up, we would drive to the farm and have dinner around Grandmother Oden's table. Even now, the smell of baked ham and homemade bread takes me back to those Sunday afternoons.

Dinner can be a time of simply forking food into the stomach for survival or a time of strained and sullen silence. But it can also be a time of sacred space for significant sharing. Henri Nouwen (*Life of the Beloved*) says that "a really peaceful and joyful meal together belongs to the greatest moments of life." These joyful meals are moments not just of communication but of communion—we become bread for one another.

Nouwen tells us that as the "Beloved Children of God" we are called not only to become bread for one another but also "bread for the world." Our table is a global one. Those rare feasts of the human family when we move beyond suspicion and share peace and joy together belong to the greatest moments in history.

Jesus likened the kingdom of heaven to "yeast that a woman took and mixed in with three measures of flour until all of it was leavened" (Matt. 13:33). Just as my husband's mother mixed the yeast of love into her family and leavened each segment, so the yeast of God's love is mixed into the bread of the human family, leavening the whole.

Dear God, thank you for family times around the table. Help us to welcome strangers to our table.

Read Psalm 145:1-9.

I stood on the Moonwalk in the French Quarter of New Orleans and saw the sun kiss the horizon good morning. It hugged the cross on the St. Louis Cathedral before shining on anything else. The old buildings in Jackson Square, the galleries with their hanging plants and fancy iron work, the banana trees by the gates to the park all looked to the cross for the first point of light and watched the sun slide down the steeple before they felt its warm greeting.

Inside, the old cathedral is a holy place of beauty. I recalled a life-impacting experience there when the bells tolled from the steeple and my husband, Bill, knelt before the altar—the first time in history a Methodist bishop was consecrated in a Roman Catholic cathedral. Invisible beside him were all the saints from his past, including his paternal grandmother, who looked on from her small armless rocker, her glasses on her nose, her Bible in her lap.

I recalled another life-impacting experience on a sunny morning before a different church altar. Bill held our granddaughter and asked the traditional baptism question, "What name shall be given this child?"

"Sarah Elizabeth," came the response.

And again the invisible saints were present, especially one: Sarah Elizabeth Oden, his paternal grandmother, who once again sat in her armless rocker, smiled, and whispered, "One generation shall laud your works to another, and shall declare your mighty acts" (Ps. 145:4).

Dear God, thank you for loved ones in the past who lauded your works and whose positive influence remains with us. Help us to send positive ripples into the future through our relationships with young people, especially our grandchildren.

Read Psalm 56:8-13.

Two vases of roses, given by my friend, sit on the altar for morning worship at a church in New Orleans.

A large brass vase contains a dozen scarlet roses interspersed with white baby's breath. They are in memory of her deceased husband who died one year ago. O God, you keep "count of [our] tossings; put [our] tears in your bottle" (Ps. 56:8). In times of sorrow, we draw comfort from our trust in you. We draw courage from our faith. When the sword of death severs the presence of a loved one and we cry out in torment, your loving hand holds us and delivers us from the inner death of the soul. You keep our "feet from falling," so that we may walk "in the light of life" (Ps. 56:13).

On the altar also is a small crystal vase with a rosebud tied by a white ribbon. It is in celebration of the birth of my friend's new grandchild. O God, as life is taken, so is it given. We thank you for new life, for the precious gift of grandchildren, those we call Beloved.

Two vases on the altar: symbols of death and life, the ultimate pain and the ultimate joy. From seed to bud to full bloom to a new seed and a new life. O Creator, we praise you for the cycle. Complete. Beautiful. Eternal.

Creator God, thank you that new life can follow death. Help us to trust your cycle.

❤ *September 6*

Read Romans 6:3-11.

Through holiness of heart and compassion for others the grandmother of Nikolai Aleksandrovich was "alive to God in Christ Jesus" (Rom. 6:11). In the defense of Russia against Napoleon, she lost not only the son who was

Nikolai's father, General Aleksander Alekseevich Tuchkov, but also another son, and her third son was taken prisoner. Amidst sighs of "God's will be done," she pulled herself from her own throes of grief and went to care for little Nikolai and to comfort his mother, Margarita, who was overcome by extreme depression and occasional delirium at the death of her husband.

Margarita had wrapped herself in her husband's life, accompanying him on military campaigns and giving birth to their son while on a long march. After her husband's death, she finally overcame her lengthy depression, built a chapel at Borodino where he was killed, and wrapped herself in her son's life—until Nikolai died of scarlet fever at fifteen.

Lost and bitter, she moved near the chapel. Troubled women began to come to her, and the Borodino religious community was born. Margarita turned no one away, drawing together both rich and poor, unusual for Russia. In time, Metropolitan Filaret suggested she become a professional nun. She was professed by him, given the monastic name "Mariia," and consecrated both as an Orthodox deaconess and abbess of the newly elevated Borodino communal women's monastery.

Like Nikolai's grandmother, through holiness of heart and compassion for others she became "alive to God in Christ Jesus."

Eternal God, thank you for the courageous grandmothers of history. Like them, help us to grow in compassion and holiness of heart.

September 7

Read Isaiah 58:6-9.

"Isn't this fun!" I exclaimed to my daughter. We walked fast toward the Sears Tower in downtown Chicago to catch the view from the top as the sun set and the city lights came on. I started across State Street, suddenly realized we were too late to make the light, and wheeled. My slick-soled shoes slipped. As I sprawled, I caught myself with the palm of my hand. My wrist snapped.

Now I lug a cast that reaches from fingers to shoulder. My left hand takes over, like a faithful second stringer waiting for a chance to star. It produces squiggly scribbles and adapts to one-handed hunt-and-peck on the computer. I work on patience. (And hope the editor will be patient with a missed deadline.) The heavy cast is a constant reminder that for grandmothers, no matter how fit, tomorrow's days are more vulnerable physically than the days of yesteryear.

But Isaiah reassures us: "Then your light shall break forth like the dawn, and your healing shall spring up quickly" (Isa. 58:8). As our own physical sun begins to set, the light of spiritual strength shines in our evening sky. That light casts trust and courage on vulnerable spaces. In that twinkling light, we know a continued sense of joy and gratitude and praise.

Creator God, thank you for physical and spiritual healing. Help us to draw courage as we walk toward sunset.

September 8

Read Luke 8:4-8.

Grandparents' Day is more than a marketing opportunity for card companies. It is a good time to ponder the meaning of grandchildren to grandparents and grandparents to grandchildren.

Sigmund Freud ignored the grandparental connection in his work, but he could not ignore it in his life. His beloved grandson died at age four—the only time Freud is known to have shed tears. Later he admitted to a friend that he had not enjoyed life since that death, and he attributed to it his attitude toward his own cancer of the mouth: "It is the secret of my indifference—people call it courage—toward the danger to my own life."

Grandparent-grandchild relationships are significant not only for grandparents but also for the children as well. The results of an interesting study, reported in *Grandparents, Grandchildren: The Vital Connection*, concluded that grandparents are vitally needed in the lives of children. These relationships affect children's attitudes toward themselves as well as to older people in general. However, only 5 percent of the 300 children in the study saw their grandparents regularly.

Throughout history until recent decades, the human family was three-dimensional, including grandparents. Now the family in the Western world is viewed as two-dimensional—parent and child. Though the pattern has changed, the need for connection between grandparents and grandchildren is deeply rooted and has not changed.

Grandparents, surrogate if not familial, can help nurture the small seed and tuck good soil around it.

Dear God, thank you for the vital connection between grandparents and grandchildren. Help us to connect to our grandchildren in a healthy and loving way.

September 9

Read 1 Thessalonians 5:14-19.

I met my friend Eleanor in July, 1988; her grandson was a tot of two. But before I knew it, Eleanor's beloved grandson celebrated his seventh birthday. Time is a trickster. Measured in the crowded calendars of adults, it sneaks away season by season. Measured in the growth of children, it mounts by visible inches and skills. Nine weeks is a couple of rounds of bills to us. To children it's the entire span of a report card. Adult weeks and years blur by while child weeks creep by.

249

The time between grandparent-grandchild contacts feels much longer to grandchildren than to us. Time tends to get away from us, but it mounts to grandchildren, and they can begin to feel unimportant to us.

Does time also get away from us in our prayer life? How is the time span between our contacts with God measured by God? We are taught: "Rejoice always, pray without ceasing, give thanks in all circumstances; for this is the will of God in Christ Jesus for you" (1 Thess. 5:16-18). In other words, we are to live our whole lives—every moment of every day—joyfully and gratefully in touch with God.

Loving God, thank you for each day. Help us not to lose the experience of the precious moment in the passing blur of the month.

September 10

Read Psalm 42:1-4.

My friend Evelyn was talking on the telephone to her beloved little granddaughter who lives in another city. It had been a long while since they had been together— especially from a child's perspective of time. Evelyn's granddaughter missed her presence and wanted to be with her. Through the phone came the soft appeal of a sweet little voice: "Oh, Mema, my heart hurts to see you."

The plea of Evelyn's little granddaughter is our plea also: "As a deer longs for flowing streams, so my soul longs for you, O God" (Ps. 42:1). Just as beloved young grandchildren yearn to be in our presence, so we yearn to be in the presence of the One who calls us Beloved. And just as we enfold our precious grandchildren, so God enfolds us. Our praise and gratitude overflow as that One puts loving grandmother arms around us, accepts us as we are, and rejoices in us.

Loving God, thank you for calling us Beloved. Our hearts praise you in gratitude.

🌿 September 11

Read Psalm 139:7-12.

On a lovely summer morning as I walked toward the Black Sea in Varna, Bulgaria, I saw a park where elderly women gathered. They crocheted intricate lace patterns with nimble fingers. Beautiful table cloths and scarves lay at their feet like giant snowflakes scattered across the green grass.

Though we did not speak the same language, I felt communion with them. I bought some tablecloths and took pictures of the Varna grandmothers who created them. One day the artwork and photos will be gifts for my granddaughters, and I will tell them the story of another day, another land. And with my payment these grandmothers would buy needed things for their grandchildren and tell them the story of this day and the grandmother from another land. It was a good exchange.

For half a century these women have experienced the darkness of communism. "Surely the darkness shall cover me, and the light around me become night" (Ps. 139:11). But midnight had passed. Thomas Merton (*New Seeds of Contemplation*) said that "no despair can . . . stain the joy of the cosmic dance which is always there. Indeed, . . . it beats in our very blood, whether we want it to or not." I felt the beat of that dance in the rhythm of the rolling sea nearby and the cosmic song of rising and falling voices of the needle artists of Varna whose fingers danced in a new dawn.

Creator God, thank you for the new dawn. May we, as grandmothers around the world, join in your cosmic dance.

❦ September 12

Read Psalm 101:1-3.

Neither could walk very well. The toddler was just learning; his grandmother used a cane. But they were having a wonderful time making their way along the sidewalk in front of her apartment house in the Hyde Park area of Chicago.

The grandmother's joy-filled face broadcast her delight in her beloved grandson. His little white teeth flashed a smile against his dark skin, and his black eyes were bright with pleasure. Despite her cane, his grandmother's short, quick steps kept stride with his, and she chuckled in harmony with his laughter. They were a duet, a song to the Lord, so in tune with each other that the colorful movement of Hyde Park's human kaleidoscope did not distract them.

To watch them was to "study the way that is blameless," the way of attentive and active love. In that grandmother, I saw a demonstration of the psalmist's words: "I will walk with integrity of heart within my house" (Ps. 101:2). She is a model for all of us.

Dear God, thank you for opportunities to be a duet with grandchildren. Help us walk with integrity of heart before them and before you.

❦ September 13

Read Leviticus 19:11-18.

The Israeli-Palestinian Peace Accord was signed on this day. Leaders of two families of humankind took a step toward peace and inched away from historical hostilities dating as far back as Old Testament times.

As grandmothers we too, in our small way, can step toward peace and inch away from historical hostilities within our own immediate and extended family. The ancient concern for family peace is seen in Leviticus: "You shall not hate in your heart anyone of your kin" (Lev. 19:17). Yet, that hatred of kin continues even today. Unresolved family disagreements can grow into hostility that is perpetuated from generation to generation. It is very difficult for grandchildren to learn to follow the relational wisdom of Leviticus and live peacefully in the world family if that wisdom is ignored within their immediate family. A significant gift to our grandchildren is the healing of family relationships. As grandmothers, we can be reconcilers. We can try to mend the tears in the family fabric and to file off the sharp points in family triangles. Holding our grandchildren in our hearts, we can strive to be peacemakers among our own kin.

Loving God, forgive our hatred of kin in our family of birth and our family of Earth. Help us to be reconcilers and peacemakers.

September 14

Read Psalm 78:1-4.

Birthdays were always significant celebrations when our children were growing up. Even now, though it's just the two of us, we still celebrate each other's birthday in a special way. My birthday comes during an annual fall meeting that Bill attends, and he gets my present early and takes it with him. This year, all prepared, he kept seeing the gift hidden in his office, and watching my struggle with the broken wrist at home, and he decided to give it to me early. It was a timely gesture!

The gift was a silver bracelet of storyteller dolls. A storyteller, usually a piece of pottery, consists of a Native American woman with small children attached to her, who are obviously listening to her story. To me, she is the wise grandmother passing down the family and Spirit stories to her grandchildren.

As grandmothers, we too are storytellers. Sharing the stories "of old, things that we have heard and known, that our ancestors have told us" (Ps. 78:2-3) is an important part of grandparenting. What a joy it is to gather around us all our grandchildren—biological, adopted, blended-family, and surrogate—and tell the colorful stories not only of extended family experiences, but also of faith journeys and spiritual roots. "We will tell to the coming generation the glorious deeds of the Lord, . . . and the wonders he has done" (Ps. 78:4).

Dear God, thank you for stories and the Story. Help us to tell them joyfully and faithfully.

September 15

Read Isaiah 40:3-5.

My three-year-old granddaughter and I were talking on the phone. She wanted me to come to Colorado to see her "tomorrow."

"I wish I could, Chelsea, but I'm in Louisiana."

"That's okay. You can come."

"Oh, Sweetie, it's too far away."

"No, it isn't," she said. "Just get in the car. Buckle the seatbelt. And drive down the road. And when you come to a juncture, just turn toward our house."

How I longed to make that journey!

"You can do it, Grandmom!"

Another voice cries out to us, giving us directions: "In the wilderness prepare the way of the Lord, make straight in the desert a highway for our God" (Isa. 40:3). We've been given the directions for our faith journey, but sometimes they are hard to follow.

When we feel we are wandering through a wilderness, without a sense of purpose, it is hard to buckle the seatbelt of spiritual discipline and prepare the way for the Lord in our lives. When we experience the desert times, like a drying up of the waters of the Spirit, it is hard to drive on down the road and head straight along the highway of faith instead of meandering miserably through self-pity. When we come to a major juncture in our lives, tempted by selfishness and expediency, it is hard to turn toward the house of the Lord. Yet, how we long to make that journey!

We can do it, Grandmothers!

Loving God, thank you for the directions. Strengthen us for the journey.

September 16

Read Psalm 55:6-8.

On the other side of the world, my friend Gerlinde in Moscow talked on the telephone with her beloved three-year-old grandson in Germany. He told her, "Tomorrow I fly to Moscow." It was a wish, a dream, a longing to see her. "O that I had wings like a dove! I would fly away and be at rest" (Ps. 55:6).

Many children, like Gerlinde's grandson, are well loved and cared for by their parents. But they still need a grandmother's lap—a special place of rest and unconditional affirmation where they feel wrapped in emotional warmth and sheltered from whatever tempest they perceive in their lives. Mobility has removed most of us from our grandchildren geographically, but despite this obstacle it is important not to abandon them emotionally.

Many children around the world, unlike Gerlinde's grandson, have difficult family situations. They especially need a place of rest and a shelter from the raging storms around them and within them. Becoming a grandmother figure to these children—being the face of Christ for them—can give them "wings like a dove," and they can fly into the presence of love and hear the song that calls them Beloved.

Dear God, thank you for places to be at rest. Help us to provide those places for your little ones.

🍂 September 17

Read Psalm 3:3-5.

During the children's sermon at worship, the pastor talked about his beeper. Afterward, during Sunday dinner, my friend's grandson asked, "Can we beep God?"

Pondering that, I found myself wondering what would happen if for a whole hour no one "beeped God"—if all prayer ceased simultaneously all around the planet. Would the chalice clatter from the communion altar? Would the anointing oil leak from the sacred vial? Would the wings of doves stop shimmering across the blue sky? How would the wind feel if suddenly no prayer was falling from the lips and heart of anyone under the sun or moon across the entire earth?

Martin Buber tells the story of Rabbi Barukh's grandson, who ran crying to him because in a game of hide-and-seek he had hidden himself and waited a long time to be found—then realized his playmate had not even looked for him. Rabbi Barukh listened to the story, and his eyes filled with tears: "God says the same thing: I hide, but no one wants to seek me."

What happens without prayer is not the absence of God, but the absence of seeking God. Through prayer we make ourselves present to God's presence, feeling God's "shield around [us]," hearing God's voice "from his holy hill," and trusting that "the Lord sustains [us]."

Almighty God, thank you for being present even when we are absent. Help us grow in the discipline of prayer until it becomes our daily anticipated privilege.

September 18

Read Matthew 6:9-13.

Yesterday we reflected on what would happen if moments passed with no one in the world in prayer. Perhaps that could never happen, however, because of the prayers of children.

My friend Retta drives twice a week to another city to take care of her beloved preschool grandsons while their mother works outside the home. Getting the two-year-old down for his nap is quite a challenge! Curious and rambunctious, he doesn't want to miss a thing. One afternoon the nap time struggle required exceptional persistence. Finally, Retta got him settled down and quiet. She tiptoed from the room feeling relieved—and weary.

But soon she could hear him again. Listening outside his door, she heard his little voice saying the Lord's Prayer, repeating it again and again.

It was as though he was taking responsibility for being sure someone in the world was in touch with God during that rest time. We can guess that Retta did not interrupt him. And perhaps we can also guess that God rejoiced in the music of a little boy for whom prayer is such a common part of his life that he can babble the Lord's Prayer at two!

Dear God, thank you for the innocent and mischievous lessons of children. Help us learn from them.

September 19

Read Matthew 14:19-21.

My friend Gayle kept her eighteen-month-old granddaughter for a week this summer. She and her husband habitually hold hands at the table and say grace before each meal, and they included their beloved little granddaughter in that time. When she returned home, she would reach out with her small hands at the beginning of each meal and say, "Gae. Gae." Of course, her parents complied with her desire for a table grace.

Gayle shared with me this story of her prayerful grandchild the day after I had seen a TV documentary on gang violence. One member of a girl gang who was interviewed wore a chain with a decorative cross. How different would the young lives of gang members be today if at the table—or in front of the television set—they had held hands with a grandparent figure and said "gae" at eighteen months? Or if they had experienced an opportunity to understand the cross as a symbol of self-sacrifice rather than a piece of junk jewelry? Or if the Lord's Prayer had been such an integral part of their lives that they could have repeated it at nap time at two?

Grandparenting—biological, adoptive, or surrogate—is a vocation that can open a window to a new view for a child and let the refreshing winds of childhood spiritually blow freely through their lives.

Dear God, thank you that we have gifts to offer. Help us to see your children usually out of our vision and to serve where we are needed.

September 20

Read Psalm 145:13-21.

My friend Polly, now retired, had developed a close relationship with her five grandchildren despite the distance from them. She told me how she had done that. Upon reaching four years of age, each grandchild individually spent a week every summer with her. It took five weeks of her summer, but what treasured weeks! During that time she focused fully on the child. They went to special places, like museums and the zoo. From the time they were small, she also set aside a monthly savings fund for travel and took each grandchild to Europe for two weeks for their thirteenth birthday present.

I thought about Polly as I looked at the family pictures on the refrigerator, feeling the distance between us and longing to be able to do the same thing. I thought of an Italian proverb: "If nothing is going well, call your grandfather or grandmother." The reverse seemed a good idea, so I called Chelsea. My dear daughter-in-love answered the phone and then asked Chelsea: "Grandmom is calling. Do you want to talk to her?"

I heard her little voice in the background: "Sure!"

Sure! What a magic word! Yes! Amen!

I wonder how seriously we take time with God. "The Lord is near to all who call on him" (Ps. 145:18). Do we set aside daily time? Take an annual retreat? Decide to wait until a certain birthday?

God is calling. And God hears our answer: ". . . ."

Dear God, thank you for the joy of a little voice saying, "Sure!" Help us to say that word to you with the way we live out our lives.

September 21

Read Ecclesiastes 3:1-8.

"For everything there is a season, a time for every matter under heaven" (Eccles. 3:1). Advent 1888 was my grandmother's time to be born; today was her time to die.

I remember her watching the first moon landing with us. As Armstrong set his foot on the moon, she walked through her journey on Earth: "I came to Oklahoma in a covered wagon. I witnessed the first silent movie, talkie, radio. The first telephone, TV, color TV. The first car, airplane, jet. And now the first moon landing. What a time to live a life!"

During her 104 years, my grandmother was wed and widowed, gave birth and lost a son, and watched her grandchildren have grandchildren. She wept and laughed, mourned and danced; sought and lost, kept and tossed. Yet, it is her silence that overshadows all of my other images—silently crocheting baby booties and afghans, silently watching TV, silently sitting on the front porch. But when Armstrong's boot touched the moon, it was time to speak!

During her 104 years, her life bridged covered-wagon trains and spacecraft launches. Though it is unlikely that we will span so many seasons, we too are bridges. We span the chasm from the present to the past for our grandchildren. We are connections to medical heredity, family history, spiritual heritage, and to stories of earlier seasons and bygone times.

We have experienced our time to be born; we trust God with our time to die. In gratitude and celebration we proclaim, "What a time to live a life!"

Eternal God, thank you that this is our time to live our lives. Help us to live them as persons of faith.

🍃 September 22

Read 2 Corinthians 5:14-20.

The rising sun slashed the river with its reflection. Its circles of yellow fell across the water like a dam dividing the Mississippi between the old waters and the new waters.

We know that "if anyone is in Christ, there is a new creation: everything old has passed away; see, everything has become new!" (2 Cor. 5:17). Tilden Edwards (*Living with Apocalypse*) says that the "I" that passes away is "an ultimately self-willed, self-centered being" which is "full of possessiveness, fear, greed, anxiety, violence, indolence, untrustworthiness, willfulness, confusion." The new "I" is aware of being "an intimate and unique expression of God's joy and compassion." The waters on both sides of the dam look the same and are cut by the same size barges. What is different is the response we make.

In *Meditations on a Theme*, Anthony Sourozh noted that whether we are "habitually happy and cheerful, or low-spirited and fearful, depends entirely on the quality of [our] mental food. . . . *We are transformed by the renewing of our minds.*"

Among our decisions as grandmothers are the quality of mental food we are going to share with our grandchildren and whether we are going to swim with them in the old waters or the new.

Dear God, thank you for the freedom to choose our attitude in every situation—even when we sail in strange new waters. Help us to nourish our souls with mental food of high quality.

🍒 September 23

Read Jeremiah 31:12-14.

Jeremiah tells us: "Then shall the young women rejoice in the dance, and the young men and the old shall be merry" (Jer. 31:13).

Lunchtime, New Orleans. At a French Quarter patio cafe, a man sings "Hello, Dolly." The jazz band plays it "like it should've been written." A plump older couple take the floor.

She has the beat, does Margarite.

Dancing with her husband with flare and grace, gray hair falling along her face.

Her hand in the air, then on her waist, lifting her foot in a backward kick. Clicking it down on the old red brick.

She wears red slacks and a red-trimmed blouse, neat black loafers that know how to dance. She smiles at her husband, we all smile back, catching their joy in this dance of life. Her three "grands" watch with pride in their eyes, the dance more important than their apple pie.

The music ends and so does she. The loudest applause is from the table of three.

Ah, Jeremiah! We older women rejoice also in the dance of life. Like Margarite, we can show our grandchildren that the celebrative dance of faith goes on . . . and on!

Dear God, thank you for the joy-filled dance of faith. Help us to step lightly and rightly to your beat.

September 24

Read 2 Timothy 4:1-5.

The family sat around the Sunday dinner table at grandmother's house. They talked about Christmas, trying to make plans early, hopeful that all the family could be together. Suddenly little Mike silenced the table by asking, "Grandmom, is there a Santa Claus?"

Wise grandmother, of course, looked at her daughter. Mike's parents went into a lengthy explanation that there is not really a Santa Claus or an Easter bunny or a tooth fairy—that you cannot see them—they are just myths.

Mike listened thoughtfully, then silenced the table again: "I can't see God. Is God a myth too?"

The ever-living, ever-loving God is present in all of creation, in all creatures, and in all sacred human life. But we have difficulty seeing that. We are like the people Marius von Senden described in *Space and Sight* who, blind from birth and suddenly receiving sight through surgery, did not realize that an object in the foreground could hide what is behind it, and that something could be present even though it is not seen. We allow the clutter in the foreground of our lives to hide God's presence. We "turn away from listening to the truth and wander away to myths" (2 Tim. 4:4).

262

The artist Paul Gaugin once said, "I shut my eyes in order to see." Our lives are undergirded not by the clutter but by Presence and Truth, which perhaps can be better seen with our eyes closed.

Dear God, thank you for your patience with our self-imposed blindness. Help us to see you when we open our eyes as well as when we close them.

September 25

Read 2 Corinthians 3:2-5.

My mother read me the most recent letter she had received from a grandchild. She always does. She is very proud of her grandchildren, supportive of them, loving toward them in a strong manner. She has every letter they have ever written to her. As soon as she answers them, she puts them in a box, a box kept within easy reach.

We ourselves are letters. The things we do and say are the contents of that letter, which is read by others. Different portions of our letter are read by different people—family, friends, coworkers, church members, strangers. Our letter is written not on paper "but on the tablets of human hearts." As women of faith "our competence is from God," and instead of writing the letter of our lives with ink that stains others' hearts, we can write it with "the Spirit of the living God."

The little notes, postcards, and birthday messages we send our grandchildren are not nearly so important as the letter of our life. What does the portion they read say? What are we writing on their hearts? A message that speaks to them in the Spirit of the living God is "You are beloved."

Dear God, may we write the letter of our lives in a manner worthy of one of your children. In every portion of that letter experienced by our grandchildren, may they see and hear the word beloved.

Read 1 John 3:14-18.

My friend Shirley, the wife of a pastor in Louisiana, died today. She had beloved grandchildren of her own, but many others also from her large extended family of love. She adopted my granddaughters too, whom she had never seen, but asked for their photographs and prayed for them daily.

Shirley made an exquisite doll as a gift for our first grandchild. The baby doll sleeps. A lace bonnet frames her beautiful china face with its tiny nose and puckered rosy lips. She wears a long white satin dress trimmed in delicate lace and small pink ribbons. Her soft body has a music box inside which, like a prophecy of the mission to come, plays "Lara's Theme" from *Doctor Zhivago*.

One day when Chelsea grows old enough to appreciate Shirley's gift, I will give her the doll and tell her the story of one who loved "not in word or speech, but in truth and action" (1 John 3:18). And one day Chelsea will pass the doll and the story on to her own grandchild. And Shirley's life will continue to touch our family for generations.

I look at the doll now, and I grieve. But even as I grieve, I celebrate her life, a life lived in love, a life that joins with those who can say, "we have passed from death to life because we love one another" (1 John 3:14).

Dear God, thank you for the Shirleys among your children. Help us all to love one another.

Read Psalm 92:1-4, 12-15.

An unforgettable Sacrament of Baptism occurred in Ekaterinburg, Russia just two weeks after the failed coup in 1991. As the choir sang a beautiful anthem, families desiring baptism crowded onto the platform and over-flowed into a long line across the front of the congregation. They stood attentively while the choir finished singing—except for little eighteenth-month-old Seryozha.

He broke loose from the hand of his grandmother and toddled about on the platform. With a smile, the tall bishop scooped him up in his arms. From this new vantage point, little Seryozha could see everything. He and the bishop were good friends by the time the anthem ended, and he was the first child to be baptized.

Little Seryozha and his grandmother were beginners. All of us are beginners when we are baptized. We break loose from bondage and venture forth into a life of commitment to Christ. We see the world around us from the new vantage point of faith. We grow and change and begin again.

As persons of faith, we are always beginners—continually breaking loose from bondage to destructive attitudes and actions, continually getting a new vantage point of prayer and spirituality. Thomas Merton said: "We do not want to be beginners. But . . . we will never be anything else but beginners, all our life!" As we live our lives in an onging process of beginning, we find that "in old age [we] still produce fruit" (Ps. 92:14)—the fruits of the Spirit.

Dear God, thank you that opportunities to grow are always before us. Help us to produce the fruits of the Spirit as long as we live.

September 28

Read Luke 10:1-5.

Cotton time! On one side of the highway the green bushes fluff with white cotton bolls. On the other side the bushes, planted earlier and now brown, are ready for picking. White wisps are strewn along the highway, blown from the cotton trailers on their way to the gin. Long lines of cars caravan slowly behind the cotton trucks on the winding narrow highway.

Cotton time! A group of church members gather together, grandchildren and all. It is time to pick the church's crop and haul it to the gin. It is time to celebrate a job well done in the good Louisiana custom of sharing mealtime as sacred time, with all ages gathered round. It is time to send the money to missions.

Cotton time! This church tradition has held for generations. Grandparents remember their own grandparents gathering at the church at cotton time. Now, they pass the tradition to their grandchildren, sitting around the church tables in the fellowship hall, telling the old stories.

Cotton time! The field is ripe, and in this instance the laborers are many!

Every day of our lives is cotton time if we truly believe the church makes a difference in people's lives. "The harvest is plentiful" (Luke 10:2), and we can be laborers sharing the joy with our grandchildren.

Dear God, thank you for the church. Help us to share the secret that it truly makes a difference in our lives.

September 29

Read Psalm 51:9-12.

At five o'clock one cold summer morning in the mountains, my daughter-in-love Angela and I sat near the fire before the little ones awoke. Separately and silently, Angie and I read our Bibles, each enjoying a personal, private period of meditation, yet sharing together this sacred space of solitude. It is a treasured memory for me.

The fire blazed, then nearly died and had to be rekindled. The words of Heraclitus came to mind:

It ever was, and is, and shall be,
ever-living fire, in measures being
kindled and in measures going out.

Deep within each of us is a yearning for the ever-living fire of the Spirit, for holiness, for wholeness. James Fehnagen (*Invitation to Holiness*) says, "Holiness is that which expands our humanity." During our times of meditation, we close our palms and clutch God's love, not that we may hoard it, but that we may open our hands each day and give it away—expanding our humanity.

Holiness is not a destination but a process, a journey, a quest that lasts all our lives. This quest for wholeness does not require grandchildren; but grand-parenting requires the quest for holiness. Through the fire of the Holy Spirit we learn to speak to our grandchildren a second language, the nonverbal language that proclaims their belovedness. O God, "Do not cast [us] away from your presence, and do not take your holy spirit from [us]" (Ps. 51:11).

Dear God, thank you for the fire of the Holy Spirit. Help us to grow in holiness and in our willingness to expand our humanity.

September 30

Read Colossians 2:1-7.

Toward the end of the movie *Jeremiah Johnson*, an old mountain man reviews Jeremiah's journey through his long one-man war and says, "Tell me, Pilgrim. Were it worth it the trouble?"

Jeremiah Johnson responds, "What trouble?"

To affirm grandmotherhood as a calling is not without difficulties, and sometimes the pilgrimage produces an inner war with the self.

We bite our tongues when our inexperienced children

267

blunder through parenting that first child without asking our advice. (Just as we did.)

We struggle to save money to visit our grandchildren and reconnect during those fast-growing years.

We sacrifice (without pouting) the time-honored tradition of Christmas in our home to be with them in their home.

We commit our summers to individual time with each grandchild—making memories that ripple into the future.

We stretch toward broader love and facilitate healthy inclusive relationships in blended families when our grandchildren's parents divorce and one or both of them remarry.

We give up leisure time to be surrogate grandmothers to strangers' children who need to hear themselves called Beloved.

We carry forward the undergirding joy and overriding disciplines of the faith as our grandchildren watch us live our lives in Christ, "rooted and built up in him and established in the faith, just as [we] were taught, abounding in thanksgiving" (Col. 2:7).

Toward the end of our pilgrimage, a cosmic voice reviews our journey and says: "Tell me, Grandmother, was it worth the trouble?"

What trouble?

Dear God, thank you for the pilgrimage of "grand" parenting. Thank you for the privilege of each sacrifice made to do what is needed for the good of our beloved grandchildren.

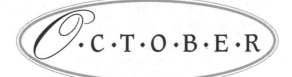

New Beginnings

Nell Mohney

❧

❧ October 1

Read Ecclesiastes 3:1, 2.

Twice a year we have the opportunity for a new beginning. The first, obviously, is on January 1, when the calendar year begins. The second is in the fall when summer vacations are over, children and youths return to school, and our lives take on more structure.

The Greeks have two words for time: *chronos* and *kairos. Chronos,* from which we get the word chronology, is calendar time in which we mark off days and weeks. A prisoner who is counting the days until being released is experiencing *chronos* time. An office worker who dislikes their job and watches the wall clock anticipating 5:00 P.M. is experiencing *chronos* time.

Kairos time is God's time. It is when time seems to stand still. It is full of meaning and eternal significance. Sharing time with someone we love is *kairos* time. So is working at a task that has great meaning for us, or listening to great music, or truly experiencing worship.

October 1981, was full of *kairos* time and new beginnings for me. It was on October 26 of that year when I became a grandmother for the first time. It was like receiving a second chance at life. My life has taken on new dimensions, deeper faith, and a different perspective. Thank God for new beginnings.

Thank you, Lord, for the new beginning of grandparenting. Help me never to treat it as chronos, *ho-hum time but as* kairos *time when I can make an eternal difference in the lives of my grandchildren.*

🍎 October 2

Read Luke 1:26-38; 2 Corinthians 5:17.

When the telephone rang, our son's voice on the other end had a sense of urgency. "Will you and Dad be home around seven this evening so that we can stop by and give you some news?" he asked. "We'll be right here," I replied excitedly. Turning to my husband as I replaced the receiver, I asked, "Do you suppose this is about the job change he has been considering?"

Throughout the day my thoughts returned from time to time to our telephone conversation, and I wondered what a job change would mean to my son's marriage and his professional life. When seven o'clock arrived, I had a zillion questions ready. Our son, Ralph, and his wife, Jackie, looked radiant as they walked into the room.

That fact in itself should have given me a clue, but I was totally stunned when, without any preliminaries, they announced: "You two are going to be grandparents." Both my husband and I gasped in astonishment. After all, Ralph and Jackie had been married for seven years, and though we had laughingly said, "As grandparents we are failures," we knew they would have children when they were ready. But we hadn't thought it was now! After the initial shock, we became ecstatic—squeeling, dancing around, hugging them, and verbally making plans for our grandchild's future. It was one of the most exciting moments of our lives.

Since that day I have often thought of what Mary's excitement, apprehension, and expectation must have been when the angel appeared and announced that she was to have a son. Following the announcement, then and now, the time of waiting must be God's plan to prepare parents and grandparents for the awesome responsibilities and tremendous joys of helping to mold a new life into the likeness of Christ.

O God, as Mary responded to the angel's announcement, let me be filled with honor and joy and anticipation of my new role as grandmother.

October 3

Read John 3:1-16.

I was entertaining speakers for a Christian Worker's School in our home when the telephone rang at about 10:00 P.M. It was our son's voice again—this time with an even greater level of excitement: "We have just checked into the hospital. You should have a grandchild by morning." Since we had moved two hundred miles away and knew our daughter-in-law's parents would be with them, we replied, "We'll leave early in the morning."

It was only a little past midnight when she was born—a beautiful, healthy, perfectly formed, seven-and-a-half-pound baby. When I held her in my arms for the first time, it was awesome. I knew that God had allowed our son and daughter-in-law to become cocreators with him to bring this new life into the world. As I examined the perfectly formed body, from tiny ears and nose to fingers and toes, I realized anew the miracle that occurs in physical birth.

Then I thought of the miracle of spiritual birth. With the acceptance of God's love for us through belief in Jesus Christ, in a moment of time we become a "new creation."

We begin to live with new values, new insights, and new dreams. Spiritual birth, like physical birth, is truly a miracle, but it's only a beginning. We must grow in grace and in the knowledge of our Lord and Savior Jesus Christ. That growth must continue as long as we live.

Thank you, Lord, for the miracles of physical and spiritual birth. Help me to live my life as a "new creation" in Jesus Christ.

❦ October 4

Read Philippians 2:8-11; Ephesians 3:14-21.

In his epochal book *Roots,* Alex Hailey describes a memorable scene. The son of Binta and Omoro has just been born in Gambia, West Africa. According to tribal custom, Omoro takes the newborn outside, holds him high toward the heavens, and declares: "You are unique. You are special. You are created in the image of God. Your name is Kunte Kinte."

Psychologists tell us there is no more beautiful sound to a person than that of his or her own name, which, of course, is why we should remember people's names. As grandmothers, we have a special opportunity to speak the name of a grandchild with respect and honor—never in derision.

One of the fun projects at our house is to keep a continuing "This Is Your Life" book for each grandchild, including facts about where the child was born, how much the child weighed, names of friends and schools, awards received, and so forth. There is always one page called "This Is Your Name" where we tell about the person for whom the child was named.

Helping our grandchildren have a sense of the extended family provides security, a feeling of acceptance, and adds to their self-esteem. In a broader perspective, we need to help children feel they are loved and accepted by God and are a part of the Christian family. This knowledge holds them steady when circumstances change and the storms of life appear.

Eternal God, thank you for loving us all of our lives—when we are not aware of it and certainly when we don't deserve it. Let us be instruments through which your love flows into the lives of our grandchildren.

🍃 October 5

Read Luke 2:52.

Our ten-month-old granddaughter, Ellen, and her parents had been up for a late summer visit. She was pulling up at every table and small chest in the house. Holding on, she walked completely around the coffee table in the living room. In fact, if we held her hands she could walk across the room squealing with delight.

Yet we couldn't entice her to turn loose and "solo." It was only two days after they returned home that we got the news from her excited parents: "Ellen took her first steps alone today." "Did she fall?" I asked somewhat apprehensively. "Yes," they replied, "but she got right up and started again." By the time we saw her a month later, she was walking nonstop throughout the house.

As I thought of this important episode in Ellen's development, I wondered how often I must look like a baby Christian to God. I hold on to old, familiar ways when he is calling me to turn loose, take risks, and take new steps for his purposes. He is calling me not only to trust him but also to trust my own God-given abilities. Even when I fall or fail, I, like Ellen, need to get up and try again, knowing that one day I will be running in God's race as a more mature Christian.

Eternal God, help me to "grow in grace and in the knowledge of our Lord and Savior Jesus Christ." When I fall, help me to remember that underneath are the everlasting arms.

October 6

Read Matthew 25:40.

Last night I saw a TV newscast showing pictures of starving children in Africa. There was a six-year-old who looked as if he might be two and a half or three years old. He was not developing normally simply because his body was undernourished. I realized anew that we have the power to enable all God's children to have a chance at life. A dollar a day given to an overseas relief program will feed and educate such a child. Let us remember Jesus' words: "Just as you did it unto one of the least of these, you did it unto me."

Then I thought of my friend whose only grandchild was born with Down Syndrome. She loves that grandchild as much as I love mine. Yet, she will not see the child achieve normal mental development. Her grandchild will never lack food or physical care, but the child, the parents, and the grandparents will need friends who are sensitive to their needs.

I know of one church that demonstrates this kind of sensitivity by teaching young people to care for mentally challenged children. One evening a month these youths gather with the children in the Sunday school rooms where the children come on Sunday morning. The parents get an evening out while the church provides care for their special children.

We are called to help meet the needs of all God's children—those in our own families as well as those around the world. Let us remember Jesus' words: "Just as you did it to one of the least of these who are members of my family, you did it to me" (Matt. 25:40).

Help us to remember, Lord, how Jesus portrayed himself as the Good Shepherd, caring tenderly for each of the lambs. Enable us to see the children of the world as precious in your sight.

🍂 October 7

Read John 4:7-15.

It had been one of those days! My husband, Ralph, had left early in the morning to attend a church conference. Our two-and-a-half-year-old granddaughter, Ellen, was visiting us for a week. In order to accomplish some necessary errands, I had taken Ellen by our church's preschool program for the morning and for lunch.

After her afternoon nap, we went to the swimming pool, to the playground, to a restaurant to eat, and finally to the grocery store. It had been a long day—especially for a two-year-old. As her plump little legs walked ahead of me when we started upstairs to go to bed, she turned around and said, "Gran, my 'wegs' are tired. Are your 'wegs' tired?"

"Yes, Ellen, my 'wegs' are tired, but my heart is happy because you have come to visit us," I replied.

Being a parent and grandparent is physically tiring, but it is an important investment in helping develop whole Christian personalities. The fatigue also reminds us of the sacrifices God made through Christ that we might be whole.

As grandparents, we must handle our fatigue by pacing ourselves, eating nutritious food, exercising, and getting adequate rest. The temptation as we get older is to give in to fatigue, to use it as an excuse for not engaging in our grandchildren's lives. No investment we make will be more important than the investment of time, energy, thought, and prayer we make on behalf of our grandchildren.

Eternal God, when we are weary and our spirits seem parched, let us remember the living water you offer.

🍂 October 8

Read Psalm 141:1.

The day began with the usual warmth and love I feel when I visit in our son and daughter-in-law's home. Having been invited to present a seminar in their city, I had arrived the night before. Following a leisurely dinner, I had a delightful playtime with three-year-old Ellen before her bedtime.

Early the next morning she was in my room, bouncing on my bed and telling me of her plans for the day. She waited patiently while I had a shower and then said excitedly, "Gran, let's make a mess." That was our secret phrase for getting all my makeup out on the bathroom counter. While I put on makeup, she experimented with lipstick, blush, eye shadow, and all the things little girls like to use while pretending they are grown-up.

When I started to put on my dress for the seminar, I realized that it needed pressing. Ellen went with me to the ironing board in the basement. While the iron was heating, my daughter-in-law called down to me, "Nell, the coffee is ready. Would you like a cup?" Wearing a robe and house shoes, I left Ellen in the basement and went up for the coffee. I in no way envisioned the trauma that awaited us. . . .

Eternal God, help us to remember that you are always with us and that we may call upon you when life's traumas come.

🍂 October 9

Read Ephesians 4:4.

On my way back to the basement, my coffee cup flew out of my hand. Ellen was coming up the stairs to meet me, so I screamed: "Turn around, Ellen! Go back!" She did turn around, but she sat down on the steps. Some of the hot coffee landed on her right shoulder and burned her skin off immediately. In terrible pain she began to scream. All of us ran to her. Our son put ice on her shoulder while Jackie called the pediatrician. They were told to bring her to the hospital immediately. As they were leaving, my beautiful daughter-in-law turned to where I sat dissolved in tears. She put her arms around me and said, "It's going to be all right, Nell. We love you."

That loving gesture, plus my granddaughter's instant resuming of our warm relationship, have taught me so much about God's forgiveness. Though even today there is a scar on Ellen's shoulder, I have never felt anger or recrimination from any of the three of them. I was unworthy of their forgiveness, but they gave it instantly and lovingly. How symbolic of God's forgiveness!

Eternal God, help us to receive forgiveness from you and others, and let us pass it on to those who hurt us.

🐛 October 10

Read Matthew 26:69-75.

It was the day before our second grandchild was scheduled to be born. (Incidentally, I've found, as perhaps you have, that a second grandchild's birth is just as exciting as a first grandchild's birth!) My husband and I were returning from Puerto Rico, and we telephoned our son's home when we arrived in the Atlanta airport. Our four-year-old granddaughter, Ellen, answered the phone and said excitedly, "Mommy and Daddy have gone to the hospital to get our new baby."

After changing our flight plans, we flew directly to Chattanooga. When we arrived at the hospital, our son, Ralph, took us to the nursery window for our first look at our plump, bright-eyed grandson. Then, quietly, Ralph said, "His name is Richard Bentley Mohney. We named him for Rick."

It was a moment of great emotion for me. Our son, Rick, had died following an accident when he was a student at the university. Though God had comforted us through his Holy Spirit and had led us through the valley of terrible grief, I had never lost the sense of sadness that Rick could never fully live out his earthly life. He would never have a vocation that would call forth the best in him; he would never know the love of a woman in marriage and the joy of having his own children. There was a permeating sadness in my spirit when I thought of it. Now, suddenly, God was giving me another chance to love a little boy named Richard, to watch him grow and realize his God-given dreams, and to help him know the God who so graciously gives each of us a second chance.

In the scripture for today we have the story of Peter, who, acting out of fear and stress, denied that he even knew Jesus. Yet Jesus' prayer on the cross included Peter (Luke 23:34). Peter accepted the second chance and became the outstanding leader of the early church. God is a giver of second chances!

Thank you, Lord, for not giving up on us—for giving us second and third chances to be the people you have created us to be.

❦ October 11

Read John 17:9.

Grandparenting has changed since I was a child! My grandmothers never worked out of the home, so when we visited them, they had plenty of time to sit on the front porch, rock, and talk to us grandchildren. They both lived near us, so we celebrated every holiday with them and often ate Sunday dinner with one or the other.

One morning as I dressed to go to work, I felt a real sadness that my husband and I then lived two hundred miles

278

away from our young grandchildren. Actually, that isn't a great distance in today's world, but because my husband was a busy pastor and I served on the church staff, there were no free weekends and little time in between.

The big question for me was, "How do I communicate my love and God's love to these grandchildren we can't see on a weekly or even monthly basis?" Three things worked well for us. First was the weekly telephone call. Our son and daughter-in-law called us every Sunday afternoon. After we talked with them, we chatted briefly with each grandchild. This way the children knew our voices. We always tried to have a short, interesting anecdote or funny story to tell them—about the stray kitten that appeared on our doorstep, or the dog next door that found his way home. Always we ended the conversation with, "We love you." "Love you," parroted our one-year-old grandson. I never finished that telephone call without feeling connected and loved.

God gives all of us the opportunity to stay connected and experience his love through prayer. It is the way God has planned for us to communicate our thoughts and receive his guidance and love.

Eternal God, forgive me when I get so caught up in daily activities that I fail to stay connected to your power source. Teach me the importance of communicating daily with you so that I can communicate your love to my grandchildren.

🍂 October 12

Read Philippians 1:3.

There's nothing quite like a grandchild's excitement in receiving mail from a grandparent who lives in another city. My friend has grandchildren who live across the country and grandchildren who live in a European country. Her "letters" take the form of audio and videotapes. Whether it is a tape or a letter, children love receiving mail.

When our grandchildren were preschool age, I always printed my letters and kept them short. Usually I enclosed something in the letters—something to color, a small puzzle, a piece of wrapped candy or pictures. All children love pictures of themselves. Ones taken when they visited last remind them of happy times spent at Grandma and Grandpa's house.

Six years ago we were fortunate enough to move to the same city as our grandchildren, but I still write them letters. Sometimes I include a spend-the-night invitation, a let's-go-swimming invitation, or a note of congratulations for their part in the school play, church program, or athletic event. Now that our grandchildren are eight and eleven, we are receiving letters from them—a thank-you note for a gift or a fun experience, or a letter from camp. Not long ago we received a long, chatty letter from eleven-year-old Ellen, who was at camp. It occurred to me how much more this very private granddaughter reveals about herself in letters rather than in face-to-face conversation. I thank God for communication through letters.

My guess is that Paul, that brilliant, pragmatic, and no-nonsense leader of the early church, found it easier to express affection in letters rather than in person to the congregations he established. I never fail to be moved when I read Philippians 1:3: "I thank my God in every remembrance of you."

O Lord, help us to remember the value of expressing affection, encouragement, and love to others—especially to our grandchildren.

October 13

Read Acts 6:4.

Our pastor does something each Sunday that I really like. After the closing hymn and before the benediction, he invites the members to be seated and to pray for the people sitting on their pew.

Some wonderful things have happened as a result of that invitation. For example, seated in front of me one Sunday was a young couple whom I knew to be having marital difficulties. Their body language that morning made it evident that they weren't feeling close to each other. Yet, when the minister invited us to pray, I saw the young man reach over and take his wife's hand. I wondered how often they had prayed about their difficulties. Later, they told me that it was that prayer that broke the log jam in their relationship.

One Sunday our granddaughter, Ellen, was seated beside me. As we drove home after church, I said, "Ellen, when the pastor asked us to pray for the person beside us, I prayed for you and for the man you will marry someday." Quick as a flash, she asked, "What's he like, Gran?" "Well, he will be a strong Christian; he'll like the work he is called to do; and he will love you."

We laughed and talked a little about that, and then we went to lunch with her brother and granddad. In the afternoon, we all went swimming. Once when she swam past me she asked, "Is he rich?" Having forgotten all about the morning conversation, I asked, "Is who rich?" Grinning, she replied, "That man I'm going to marry."

"Well, if he is a Christian, has a job, and has love in his life, he will be rich no matter how much money he has," I replied.

Since that day I have thought how we have the privilege of praying for our grandchildren and all their pivotal decisions.

We ask for your guidance, O Lord, in the lives of our grandchildren. We pray that your will may fully be accomplished in their lives.

October 14

Read Matthew 19:14.

One of the rituals when grandchildren spend the night with us is to have devotions around the breakfast table.

Of all the books we have used, our grandchildren most like the book of devotions for children entitled *This Is the Day,* by Carol Rees and R. Daniel Holloway.

When our grandchildren were very young, we read a devotional to them and then each of us said a prayer. As soon as they could read, they took turns reading. They still like to read from that book, and they know exactly where to find their favorites.

Among their favorites are "A Kitten Named Muffin" (how God makes everything beautiful); "Families" (God's plan for families); "When Brothers and Sisters Fight" (handling anger); "Sharing Problems" (how to help others when they are sad); "Clean Hearts and Hands" (clean hands at mealtimes and clean hearts for living); and "Learning to Say 'I'm Sorry'."

Devotional times give us an opportunity to teach important lessons and help our grandchildren see God in everyday life. Children's devotional books make it an easy and fun time to discuss whatever may be bothering a grandchild. Children also have much to teach *us* about the kingdom of God. I am convinced that the best learning about God takes place in the daily events of life that are common to us all.

Eternal God, help us to teach, not preach, to our grandchildren. Let us help them find God's presence in even the most ordinary daily experiences.

🍂 October 15

Read Acts 20:11.

Six years ago when we returned to Chattanooga, Tennessee, the city where our son and his family live, our grandchildren were then ages six and three. We began the practice of having them spend every Friday night with us when we are in town. It is a wonderful time to experience bonding and to get to know our grandchildren as individuals.

Among other things, we ride bikes, go swimming, go fishing, pop popcorn, watch children's movies, and have long talks. When we sleep, my granddaughter stays downstairs with me and my husband takes our grandson, Wesley, upstairs to a guest room.

Wesley is energetic, inquisitive, imaginative, and very talkative. After becoming accustomed to a quiet, petite, lovable but very private granddaughter, Wesley was a shock to our systems. Yet their differences make us aware of the beauty in diversity in all of God's creation.

One evening after prayers, Ralph and Wesley had gone upstairs to bed. Wesley had bounced on his side of the bed for almost an hour, talking nonstop as he jumped. Suddenly he sat down and said, "Granddad, do you know why I like to come down here?" Without waiting for Ralph's reply, he said, "Because I can talk as much as I want to."

Just as God is "the listener" for us, allowing us to pour out all our thoughts, so also we grandparents can become "the listener" for our grandchildren.

Eternal God, help us to remember to take time to listen to our grandchildren. Let us encourage them to articulate their thoughts, questions, and fears. Give us patience as we listen.

October 16

Read Matthew 8:23.

Jesus and his disciples bonded into a close-knit group not only because of their love for one another and their desire to do the will of God, but also because they did so many things together. They traveled each day together; they ate together; they fished together. They were together when Jesus taught and healed and performed miracles.

Their constant togetherness allows us to see their weaknesses as well as their strengths—Peter's impulsiveness; James's and John's ambition (or at least that of their mother); Thomas's doubt, and Judas's betrayal.

Going places with our grandchildren, such as school events, family reunions, church, plays, the circus, water parks, and so forth, makes for natural conversation. It also allows us to really know one another—to see one another's faults as well as strengths.

During the years we lived away from our grandchildren, they came for weekends and week-long visits. We often had more quality time for communicating and understanding than now—when we live close and see one another more often.

Sometimes it is those grandparents who live near their grandchildren who most need to make time for their grandchildren by attending school and church events and extending spend-the-night or vacation invitations. As we learn from Jesus' example, only by spending time together may we nurture our relationships with our grandchildren.

Thank you, Lord, for the privilege of being with our grandchildren. Let our time together always be constructive and loving, never judgmental and "preachy."

🍒 October 17

Read John 15:12.

Children like trying new things and exploring new places, but they also like rituals. How could I incorporate both of these things in helping my grandchildren know of my love and God's love? I wondered. I chose to use a question that had become a ritual in my birth family and yet would be new for my grandchildren.

My father asked the question of his three children. In a playful manner he would ask, "How much do I love you?" Then he would put his palms together and move them apart about the length of a ruler. "That much?" he would ask. "No, not that much," we would chorus back gleefully. Then he would open his arms about the length of a yardstick and ask, "That much?" "No, not that much," we would reply laughingly. Then, as we knew he would, he would open his arms as wide as he could reach and ask, "That much?" "Yes. You love us that much," we would answer.

Usually he would follow with, "Suppose you have disobeyed and I have to send you to your room. Do I love you just that much [length of a ruler]?" Immediately we would reply, "No, you love us this much [arms opened wide], no matter what," we would reply. It was an object lesson in unconditional love.

Often, he followed this ritual by reminding us that when he was standing up with his arms spread open wide, he represented the cross. He told us that when Jesus died on the cross so that we could be forgiven of our sins, it was God's magnificent way of saying, "I love you that much."

When I am with my grandchildren, this has now become a ritual. We often even close our letters to each other with "I love you this much."

O Lord, keep me ever mindful of your loving gift of salvation. Let me never take it for granted but always live my life in gratitude for your love. Enable me to interpret this gift and pass it on to my grandchildren.

🍂 October 18

Read 1 Corinthians 13:6.

Yesterday I shared a ritual begun by my father and now used with our grandchildren. Ralph and I feel that authority and disciplining of children belong to parents, unless, of course, we are left in charge. Even then, we administer the authority carefully, creatively, and in a lighthearted manner. But when we have the responsibility of child care, we must mean what we say.

Our grandson, Wesley, has tested the limits since he was born. He is bright and lovable, but he doesn't like to be told "no." When he was four, my husband was baby-sitting while our daughter-in-law attended a meeting at church. Wesley arrived with a small football. He and his granddad passed the football outside and even played with it in the den before they began to play with Leggos.

Ralph's rule was that Wesley could play with the football in the den but couldn't throw the ball from upstairs into the entrance hall. Things went well until the Leggo ship building was complete; then there was an overwhelming desire to test the limits. Distraction had usually worked for Wesley, but that day it didn't.

Ralph reminded him of the rule, saying that if he threw the football downstairs, the ball would have to be put away until Wesley's next visit. Well, Wesley threw the ball, and Ralph put it away.

For the first time, a grandchild left our house unhappy, feeling that Granddad was unfair. When the football was returned the next day, the two of them had a long talk about what had occurred. Today Granddad and Grandson are the best of buddies, but Wesley knows that Granddad means what he says. Love is not permissive.

Help us, O God, to love our grandchildren unconditionally, but give us wisdom to differentiate love from permissiveness.

🍂 October 19

Read Matthew 28:20.

Power and self-control come from discipline, and the root word for discipline means to teach, not to punish. The

Latin word for discipline means instruction passed on to students to build character. Hence, *disciple* means someone under instruction from a teacher.

At every opportunity, Jesus taught his disciples about the nature of God, the kingdom of God in the here and now and in the world beyond, and the meaning of abundant living. "I came that they may have life, and have it abundantly" (John 10:10). Jesus taught through everyday situations—a lost coin, a lost sheep, a lost son—and through the use of stories or parables.

One of the privileges of being a grandparent is having a little more time to teach values in creative ways and everyday situations. In talking with many parents of young children, I have discovered that the values most parents want to instill in their children correspond with the values of my generation, but in a little different order. These values include self-esteem, love, faith, creativity, responsibility, honesty, patriotism, poise, leadership, communication skills, and cheerfulness.

Though we find interesting and varied ways of teaching these values, none is more important than example. The medium is truly the message, as Marshall McLuhan said in his book by the same name.

Eternal God, help us to incorporate your values into our own lives so that we may pass them on more authentically to our grandchildren.

October 20

Read Daniel 1:20.

I was busily icing a chocolate cake for our evening meal when our five-year-old son, Rick, rushed into the kitchen telling me about a magic show he had just seen on television. With wide-eyed amazement he said, "A man said some magic words and a rabbit disappeared." Then looking somewhat pensive, he added, "But I don't believe in magic words, do you?"

Seeing an opportunity to teach an object lesson about courtesy and politeness, I said, "Yes, I do." Eagerly he asked, "What are they?"

"I know two words that are magic. They are *please* and *thank you,*" I replied.

With obvious disappointment he said, "Those aren't magic words."

"Well, let's try them. You like this chocolate cake I'm icing, don't you?" I asked.

As he danced all around the table, he replied, "It's yummy!"

"Just remember," I said, "that you are much more likely to get a piece if you say please first and thank you afterwards."

That little boy didn't miss many tricks. Realizing that this was a strategic moment, he asked, "Please may I have a piece of cake right now?"

Laughingly I ruffled his hair and said, "Yes, you may have a piece of cake right after lunch."

That episode came back to my mind last Saturday evening when Ralph and I had our extended family over for dinner. When we had finished dinner, each of the grandchildren thanked me and asked to be excused. As I excused them, I thought how words of kindness, courtesy, and politeness are still magic.

Eternal God, help us incorporate your wisdom and loving-kindness into our lives so that we can relate to others in courtesy and love.

October 21

Read Ecclesiastes 3:1.

It had been a long afternoon and evening at the amusement park. Actually, we had taken our grandchildren, then ages four and seven, for what we expected to be a couple of hours on amusement rides and a quick exit for their favorite place for dinner. Imagine our surprise upon entering the grounds to learn that on that special anniversary day, you simply had your hand stamped and could go on as many rides as you liked as often as you liked.

Needless to say, we ate fast food on the grounds and stayed until the park closed at 10:00 P.M. All four of us were exhausted as we walked the long distance to our car. Once in the car, however, I was trying to keep the children awake until we got home and they could have a quick bath and get to bed. So I asked, "What did you like best about our trip to the amusement park?" Ellen, the seven-year-old, answered first. "I liked the Tilt-A-Whirl." Wesley, age four, said, "I liked the giant slide." Looking over at my fatigued husband I asked, "What did *you* like best?" Without hesitation he replied, "Going home."

Later as I laughed about my husband's honest reply, I gave thanks that young adults have the children. That season has passed for us, and now we are in the wonderful season of grandparenting. It is our privilege to encourage, to love, to provide warmth and guidance as needed, to seek to be examples of Christian living, but not to have the day-to-day responsibility and care. Knowing my season enables me to enjoy my grandchildren and happily send them home to their parents.

Lord, thank you for your plan for families. Thank you for young parents who are struggling to rear whole Christian persons in this secular world. Let us be willing to be strong support for these families.

October 22

Read John 15:11; Proverbs 15:13-15.

We have only to read the newspapers or watch a TV newscast to realize that many children have little joy in their lives. Abuse, neglect, divorce, violence in the streets and in the home—these are all prevalent in our society. As a result, many children miss the joy of childhood. Grandparents have the privilege of making happy memories for these grandchildren.

Though Jesus was acquainted with grief and intense in his pursuit of the purposes of God, he nevertheless spoke often about joy: "Be of good cheer"; "Let not your heart be troubled." In today's scripture from the Gospel of John, Jesus is preparing his disciples for his death by bequeathing them his joy. He says, "I have said these things to you so that my joy may be in you, and that your joy may be complete" (15:11).

Far more important than silver, china, furniture, or money that we can leave grandchildren are ideas, ideals, and happy memories. When grandchildren are with us, our major task is not correcting grammar and insisting on clean rooms, though we can find creative ways to encourage these things. Our major task is to provide happy memories that will also encourage good self-esteem, consideration for others, and faith in God.

Eternal God, help us to receive your joy and to pass it on to our grandchildren.

❤ October 23

Read Psalm 139:14.

Wesley was soon to be eight years old, and his parents felt that he wasn't feeling as good about himself as he should. For one thing, his eleven-year-old sister excelled in sports as well as academics. Wesley was doing well in school, but his motor skills hadn't developed well enough to be as good in sports as she.

For another thing, he wasn't as tall as he wanted to be. Though his parents had been assured by his pediatrician that he would be average height or above, Wesley wanted to be as tall as his friend Alex.

Wesley's birthday seemed to be the perfect time to help him feel special. Because I believe that birthdays are a time to celebrate our uniqueness, I always host a family dinner with special themes and decorations and the food most liked by the honoree.

For Wesley's past birthdays, I have used themes such as Sesame Street, Walt Disney characters, and dinosaurs. Since his birthday is February 1, this year I decided to have an "important persons evening." I used VIP invitations and place cards. We all wore red, white, and blue, and pictures of other important persons born in February were on display. A framed poster on the mantel had pictures of George Washington and Abraham Lincoln, with a picture of Wesley in the middle.

In addition to the usual games, there was a quiz concerning important people in government, the world, and the church; and there was a special group of questions about Wesley. The activity that seemed to please him most happened just before he opened his gifts. Each person said what he or she likes most about him. Hearing these accolades seemed to give him a shot of self-confidence. In fact, it was so special that we have done this at everyone's birthday since.

As grandmothers, we have many opportunities to celebrate the uniqueness of our grandchildren and help them grow in confidence and love.

Help us, Lord, to see the uniqueness of each of our grandchildren and to celebrate their God-given talents.

October 24

Read Romans 12:10.

In a small social gathering in our neighborhood one evening, a particular couple monopolized the conversation by talking all evening about their grandchildren. Several of us, including the hostess, tried valiantly to steer the conversation in other directions but to no avail. We always came back to hearing about the superior performances of Sally, Jim, and Sissy. I couldn't believe the intensity of my discontent.

On the way home I tried to rationalize my feelings by saying to my husband that the couple were just poor conversationalists and very boring. Laughingly he asked, "Are you sure that your feeling is not resentment at their not allowing us to talk about our grandchildren?" I didn't have to probe very deep to know that was exactly what I was feeling. I resented the fact that they hadn't asked any of us present if we even had grandchildren.

Strangely enough, I never felt that way as a parent. Maybe it was because all of us were so busy with our responsibilities and so unsure about how well we were doing as parents that we didn't dare brag about our offspring. Suddenly, I saw some of the hidden dangers in this grand new experience of grandparenting.

As wonderful a gift as grandchildren are, they can't be the center of the universe. In the first place, it wouldn't be good for the grandchildren; and second, it would make us insensitive to the needs of others—especially those who want to be grandparents and aren't and those whose relationships with their children and grandchildren are strained because of divorce or conflict. We grandmothers need to keep our focus on Christ in order to keep our perspective.

Help us, Lord, to keep you at the center of our lives, so that your purposes can be fulfilled in all those with whom we come into contact.

❦ October 25

Read Psalm 17:6.

Millie was a junior in college—competent, attractive, well liked by her peers as well as her elders. Yet when she came that day to see my friend Martha, who was her grandmother, she was like an inconsolable child. She was hardly in the door before she burst into uncontrollable sobs.

Her wise grandmother, suspecting the reason for the tears, held her close until the sobs subsided. Then Martha led her granddaughter to the sofa and held her hand as she listened intently while the beautiful young woman poured out her pain. The girl's parents had just told Millie of their plans for divorce, and she was devastated.

Through the years she had seen evidence of problems, but she loved both of her parents. The thought of the dissolution of her home seemed unthinkable. Her grandmother was a person to whom she had gone for understanding and comfort.

Martha knew better than to offer clichés such as, "This too will pass," or "You'll feel better about this in a few months." She knew, also, that now was not the time to help her granddaughter see her parents' point of view. Right now Millie needed a safe place to express her deep feelings. There could be no disallowance of feelings. She needed someone to listen and to love. After all, to listen is to love.

O Christ, who identified so easily and beautifully with the pain of others, help us to remember that to listen is to love.

❦ **October 26**

Read Luke 10:27.

In his book *Future Shock,* Alvin Toffler speaks of the need for "stability zones" in a world of chaotic change. It seems to me that Christian grandparents can provide just such a stability zone. Obviously this kind of relationship doesn't just suddenly happen when a grandchild is in high school or college. It requires a bonding that is developed and cultivated through the years. The bonding occurs through love, respect, thoughtfulness, nonjudgmentalism, and happy memories.

Yesterday I spoke of my friend Martha and her grand-daughter. Millie never would have sought out her grand-mother for comfort if through the years she had not felt safe and loved and respected. In this kind of setting, Martha was able to help her granddaughter work through her feelings rather than bog down in bitterness. Only then could Millie see her parent's needs or understand some-thing of the problems with which they were dealing. Only then could she see some options for her own life.

Jesus provided this climate of respect and caring for all with whom he came into contact—children, lepers, blind persons, people who were lame, sinners, and publicans. He asks us to do the same.

O Christ, help us to be the "stability zones" for our grand-children in a world of chaotic change.

🍎 October 27

Read Proverbs 3:5-6.

Jimmy, age eighteen, was a high school football and basket-ball player. He was six feet three inches tall, weighed 180 pounds, and moved with the grace of a natural athlete. Through the years his academic achievements had equalled those on the athletic field. From time to time he had evidenced the normal periods of self-absorption, though by and large he was thoughtful and sensitive to the feelings of others.

Lately, however, his mother, a single parent rearing three children, had been concerned that Jimmy's grades were slip-ping and that he had grown secretive and introspective. Always active in his church's youth program, recently he seemed to lose interest—even refusing to attend at times. Though she had not seen evidence of it, Jimmy's mother wondered about drugs or sexual promiscuity.

Jimmy's grandmother, Nadine, knew that prayer is one of the most powerful weapons we possess. She set aside each day a specific time in which she prayed for Jimmy. She prayed that God's best would be accomplished in his life and that she and her husband could be used as God's instruments.

Gradually opportunities presented themselves to do more. For example, a magazine ran a wonderful story about one of Jimmy's athletic heroes. Nadine clipped it and mailed it with a simple note: "Dear Jimmy, thought you would be interested in reading this. Love, Nana."

Another time she wrote on Friday, "Am baking cookies for the church. I'm making your favorite chocolate chip cookies. If you have time, stop by for a 'care package'." He did, and gradually he began to stop by more and more often. There was no prying on her part, but she began to believe that his problem was depression.

Providentially, a Christian counselor joined the staff of the church Jimmy attended, and he and Jimmy seemed to have instant rapport. The counselor was able to help Jimmy give up his long-held anger about his father's death. Today, Jimmy is a happy, well-adjusted college senior.

Through her persistency in prayer and, subsequently, her loving actions, Nadine played an important role in Jimmy's "turnaround." When we trust in the Lord, he *will* direct our path.

Eternal God, grant us willingness to be persistent in prayer so that we may be open to your leadership concerning the lives of our grandchildren.

❧ October 28

Read Psalm 89:33.

Most of the grandchildren I have mentioned have had happy resolutions to their problems. What if your grandchild has a drug problem, or is in trouble with the law, or is sexually promiscuous? Annagene had such a grandchild. She was at a spiritual life retreat I was leading in a distant city. I could sense the heaviness of her spirit long before we talked. She was so cast down that she was creating a climate of despondency and gloom. Her grandson, Sam, was only sixteen. He had been using drugs since he was thirteen. He was openly rebellious with his parents, alternating between volatility and withdrawal. He often skipped school and consistently kept his household in an uproar.

From Annagene's observation, her son, Sam's father, was too harsh a disciplinarian, showing little respect or feeling for Sam. Her daughter-in-law, on the other hand, was much too permissive. She seemed unable to refuse her son's requests for money, though she knew he would use it to buy drugs. As a result of their not being unified in their approach to Sam's problem, there was great strain on the marriage.

Annagene's suggestion about counseling and a drug rehabilitation program had been ignored. In the meantime, what was she to do? I suggested that she continue to pray daily for Sam, envisioning him as well and whole; that she pray for her son and daughter-in-law; that instead of offering advice, she should be sensitive to ways she could show love. And, for her own peace of mind, I recommended that she affirm daily God's promise in Psalm 89:33: "But I will not remove from him my steadfast love [whatever happens]." This is a promise of God that each of us should affirm every day.

Eternal God, thank you that in the midst of our pain and sorrow we can count on your faithfulness.

❦ October 29

Read Matthew 7:11.

"What did you bring me, Grandma?" is a question that had come to disturb my friend Kate. She has a four-and-a-half-year-old grandson who lives in the same town as she. She never stops by their home or has them stop by hers without Tom's inevitable question: "What did you bring me, Grandma?" She realizes that she is responsible since she always has a surprise when he comes to visit and takes a small gift when she stops by their house, no matter how often.

One day while reading Matthew 7:11, she suddenly realized that she was not giving "good gifts." Her intentions were good. She loved her grandson and wanted to see him happy. Yet she had turned grandmothering into "grand gifting." She had not shared her talents and time as effectively as her gifts. Changing his perception took time, much conversation, and a little disappointment, but now they are relating as people.

Giving gifts at birthdays, Christmas, special events, or even an occasional "non-occasion" gift is a wonderful privilege, but far more important is the gift of our time, joy, creativity, and faith.

In like manner, God not only gives us the obvious gifts of life, family, talents, and nature, but more importantly, the gift of himself to be with us always. The gift he most desires of us is not just token gifts of service or time, but the unconditional gift of ourselves.

Eternal God, help us as grandmothers to know how to give truly good gifts to our grandchildren, and to give ourselves to you.

🌱 October 30

Read Matthew 18:14.

I felt chilled to the bone as I folded the newspaper. In that one issue, I had read that a thirteen-year-old boy had shot and killed his mother because she refused to buy him some new stereo equipment; birth to unmarried teens has tripled since 1950; 150,000 students carry weapons to school in America each day; the leading killer of youth, ages fifteen to nineteen, is motor vehicle accidents (82 percent of which are caused by intoxication or drugs). Suicide is second and homicide is third in leading causes of death for young people. The latter two are drug related in many cases. In our country the number of children affected by divorce last year alone was 1.1 million. The family in America today is at great risk!

What can grandparents do? First, we need to be aware of what is happening. We need, for example, to educate ourselves about drugs, not only so that we can recognize the symptoms but also so that we can converse knowledgeably with our grandchildren. When we are with our grandchildren, we can speak about our values in a non-threatening, matter-of-fact, "non-preachy" manner. We can make our family gatherings fun and allow them to project the values of extended family and long-term relationships.

On a broader scale, we can support legislation concerning family values; we can work in some phase of youth work—Cub Scouts, Girl Scouts, Big Brothers/Big Sisters, church programs, and so forth. If we are able to do so, we might consider becoming foster parents. The most important thing to remember is that our families need some good role models. We can be grandmothers who radiate love, laughter, hope, and deep faith.

Eternal God, let us do the best things in what seems to be the worst of times for the family. Let us be your instruments in the world.

October 31

Read Isaiah 43:19.

I wish there were some wonderful place
Called the land of beginning again.
Where all our mistakes and all our heartaches

And all our poor sordid grief
Could be dropped like a shabby old coat at the door
And never put on again.

Those wistful words of poet Louisa Fletcher Tarkington have surely been echoed in each of our hearts at some point. How many times, for example, have we wished that we could go back and do some things differently with our own children? We all have 20/20 hindsight.

The glorious truth is that there is a land of beginning again in the experience of grandparenting. If we wish that we had been more patient with our children, we can be more patient now with our grandchildren; if we wish we had given more of our time, we can do it now; if we wish we had exemplified the faith more effectively—spoken of it more convincingly—we can do it now.

But new beginnings mean leaving behind some excess baggage—old ideas that make us rigid in our thinking; old habits that are destructive and enslaving; old fears and anxieties that keep us from taking bold, new steps for God; old grudges that make us weary and old in spirit. Like barnacles covering a ship, these old things make us unworthy vessels on the sea of life.

Lord, help us to recognize the new beginnings you offer us in the role of grandparenting. Let us seize the opportunity and make it eternally significant.

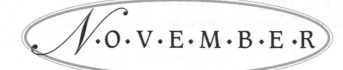

N·O·V·E·M·B·E·R

Thanks-Living

Nell Mohney

November 1

Read Psalm 147:7.

During November, the month of Thanksgiving, we will be looking at the spiritual significance of developing the attitude of gratitude. The psalmist reminds us that we are to "sing to the Lord with thanksgiving." According to Cicero, the Roman orator, statesman, and man of letters, gratitude is the basic virtue from which all other virtues stem. Gratitude opens our hearts to life, to others, to God. Ingratitude snaps them shut, causing us to live in self-imposed prisons.

Grateful people never take life for granted. They see life as a privilege, not as a right. Grateful people translate thanksgiving into thanks-living. Think of Albert Schweitzer who lived out his thanksgiving in a ministry to the sick in Lamborene, Africa. Think of Mother Teresa serving the poor and the outcast of India.

Let us focus this month on the importance of incorporating gratitude into our own lives and passing it on to our children and grandchildren. After all, gratitude is more caught than taught. Let's remember again the words of Ralph Waldo Emerson: "What you are shouts in my ear so loudly, I cannot hear what you are saying." Let us translate Thanksgiving into thanks-living!

Eternal God, help us to remember that all that we are and have comes from you. Let us live our lives in joyful gratitude.

November 2

Read Psalm 92:1.

It was Albert Schweitzer who said: "In gratitude for your own good fortune, you must render in return some sacrifice of your own life for other lives." Schweitzer not only said that but lived that as well. His entire life was one of thanks-living. We may not be able to make the contributions that Albert Schweitzer did, but we can adopt the posture of thanks-living in our daily routines.

I shall never forget an illustration Dr. Norman Vincent Peale used one Sunday when I heard him preach at the Marble Collegiate Church in New York City. He told of the renowned singer Ethel Waters, who was seated beside a drunk man on an airplane. Some people would have asked him to move, or at the very least would have ignored the obnoxious man. Instead she encouraged him to eat his food so that it would soak up the liquor he had been drinking. Then, noting his unhappy look, she said: "Tell me what's on your mind that's troubling you."

The man said that his beautiful young granddaughter was a very talented musician. She had called him on the telephone the week before and asked him to attend her concert. He had chosen to stay home and play golf instead. "And now my granddaughter is dead," said the man. "I'm on my way to her funeral."

"Child," she replied to the middle-aged man, "drinking won't help you in this situation; but there is someone who loves you, and he's going to help you."

The message seemed to get through to the man's alcohol-soaked brain. He put his head back and slept for the two-hour flight. As they were landing, Waters asked the flight attendant to bring a cold washcloth. She then handed it to the man, and he wiped his face as he soberly looked at her and said: "I do want to thank you very much." She replied, "Honey, you thank the Lord; he knew what you needed. He is with you now and will take care of you."

Ethel Waters gave a lesson in thanks-living that day. We have the same opportunity to teach our grandchildren "to give thanks unto the Lord."

Eternal God, help us to accept our talents as obligations to be invested in the common good. Let us translate our thanksgiving into thanks-living.

❦ November 3

Read Ephesians 5:4.

A miserable scene of ingratitude is graphically etched on my mind. It happened during the noon hour in a large department store in the late spring of the year. On the second floor in ladies' ready to wear, there were many customers. Suddenly a woman who looked to be in her late fifties rushed into the dress area. Later I learned that she was the grandmother and widowed guardian of three grandchildren whose divorced mother had left town with a traveling salesman.

When she arrived, her granddaughter modeled a beautiful white prom dress for her, declaring as she swished around, "I've decided on this one." The grandmother, after looking at the price tag, said: "It is beautiful, but I'm not sure we can afford it." There was much pleading and begging, and the grandmother smiled wanly as she said, "All right. We'll manage somehow."

Instead of thanking her grandmother, the teenager rushed to the back and brought out an expensive pair of shoes, an evening purse, and several other items she had chosen. When the grandmother said, "We'll have to talk about that later," the girl exploded in anger. The tearful grandmother left the store in humiliation; an expression of gratitude and a hug could have sent her out rejoicing.

As grandmothers, we not only can take advantage of every opportunity to teach our grandchildren to have a spirit of gratitude, but we also can demonstrate how a spirit of ingratitude hurts others while marring our own souls.

Eternal God, help us to model a spirit of gratitude for our grandchildren.

🐛 November 4

Read 1 Corinthians 13:13.

Recently I was fascinated by an octagonal shaped paperweight in a gift shop. It was made of fine crystal. As I turned it from side to side, I saw the many different dimensions of its shape and the prismatic beauty of the light it reflected.

As I left the store, I thought how that object of beauty symbolizes the Christian woman. Each of our roles represents another dimension of our faith: child of our parents, wife, mother, career woman, church and community leader, friend, sister, grandmother. If we stay close to Christ, our power source, our lives can reflect his presence in prismatic beauty in each of these roles.

Perhaps no dimension can reflect Christ's presence more clearly than that of being a grandmother. By this season of our lives, most of us are comfortable with who we are. This doesn't mean that we have stopped growing; rather, we have accepted our limitations, focused on our possibilities, and come to like the persons we are. The pressures of day-by-day child rearing, car pooling, and attending PTO meetings are over. We no longer have the pressure of getting everybody out of the house on time each day or of baking cookies weekly for Cub Scouts or school activities.

With this gift of less-pressured time, we can see God's purposes more clearly and discern the truly important values from those which are simply urgent or trivial. Faith, hope, love—these are the values we have the privilege and time to pass on to our grandchildren and others.

Eternal God, thank you for the seasons of life, especially the season of grandparenting. Help us to radiate your love in all of its prismatic beauty to our grandchildren.

November 5

Read Proverbs 31:10.

Last year, a friend handed me a copy of the report of a third-grade teacher who asked her students to write their description of a grandmother. One child wrote the following:

> A grandma is a lady with no children of her own so she likes other people's little girls. And a grandpa is a man grandma. He goes to walk with boys and talks about fishing and stuff. Grandmas don't have anything to do but "be there." Grandmas drive you to the supermarket where the pretend horses are and she has lots of quarters ready—or they take you for walks and they slow down past pretty leaves, and they stop for caterpillars. Grandmas never say "hurry up."
>
> Sometimes grandmas are fat, but not too fat to tie kid's shoes. Grandmas wear funny glasses and real funny underwear. They can take their teeth and gums off and they answer questions like "Why do dogs hate cats?" and "How come God isn't married?" When grandmas read to us, they don't skip words and they don't mind if it is the same story over again.
>
> Everyone should try to have a grandma, especially if you don't have a TV, because grandmas are the only grownups who have got time.

Though I laughed heartily when I read this, I became aware that this third grader expressed the deeply felt needs of other children. Basically, they need our love and our time.

Eternal God, help us to remember the privilege that is ours of being a connecting link of faith and love in the lives of our grandchildren. Help us to be virtuous grandmothers.

🍇 November 6

Read Matthew 19:14.

It was an unusual experience. We had three house guests for four days. One of them was a beautiful and charming young lady, who seemed to expect members of our household to be committed to meeting her every need, even her slightest wish.

Most of our house guests make their beds and keep their rooms somewhat orderly. Not this lady! She never offered to make her bed and her belongings were strewn all over the house. One day we took her to a lovely restaurant for lunch. She seemed unimpressed by the excellent food and service. She hardly touched her food and was noisier than anyone at the surrounding tables. At the close of her visit, she left without as much as a "thank you."

You are probably thinking that we will never invite her to our home again. You are wrong! That guest was our nine-month-old granddaughter whom we would like to have visit us every week.

It is true that she didn't say "thank you" for all our efforts but she hadn't learned those words yet. Our thanks came every morning when we walked into her bedroom. The moment she saw us, a smile enveloped her face with the glory of a sunrise at the Grand Canyon. When she reached her arms for us, it was all the thanks that grandparents could ever hope for!

Eternal God, my heart is filled to overflowing when I think of the gift of grandchildren. Help me always to be worthy of their trust.

Read Psalm 103:2.

The year was 1965; it was a cold and windy day in mid-October. The city was Zurich, Switzerland. The towering Alps surrounding that picturesque city were already covered with snow. While my husband, Ralph, was in a meeting, I decided to shop near our hotel. As I was browsing, I noticed a highly polished stick—much like a walking stick. On one side were three carefully carved notches, but the other side of the stick was filled with notches. The manager walked by and said curtly, "That's not for sale."

"All right," I said as I placed it back in its stand, "but won't you tell me what it is?" He looked at me as if he were trying to decide whether to trust me with his story. Then he smiled and said, "It's my gratitude stick. Once when my business had failed, I became depressed. Concerned about my apathy, my wife said: 'John, you are only focused on the bad things that have happened to us. Why don't you make a list of the good and the bad things which have happened and see which list is longer.'"

He continued: "On Thanksgiving Day six years ago, I did just that. I was overwhelmed by our blessings. Later, I bought this stick and carved notches on the left side for the three bad events and on the right side, the multiple notches representing the good things I have to be grateful for. On days when I feel down or a little sorry for myself, I pick up my gratitude stick. I rub the right side and give thanks."

All of us can have an imaginary gratitude stick, and we can mentally rub it and remember our blessings. Near the top of that stick should be a notch for the privilege of being a grandmother.

Eternal God, keep us focused on our blessings and your lovingkindness.

November 8

Read Proverbs 17:22.

Several years ago, I walked past a bookstore and was captivated by the title of a book in the window. I bought and read the delightful, tongue-in-cheek book entitled *I Want a Home with No Problems.*

We have only to be married and have children of our own to discover that there is no such thing as family life without problems. Though we can guide children and give them options, they are born with their own wills and temperaments.

I love the story of the young mother who was trying to give her small daughter a teaspoonful of prescribed medicine. Already fatigued from the battles of the day and experiencing now the obstinacy of the "terrible twos," the mother burst into tears, ran out of the room in frustration, and threw herself on the bed in an adjacent room.

In a few minutes, she heard gales of laughter coming from the kitchen. Going to the door, she saw the child's grandmother, who was visiting for the Thanksgiving holidays and was familiar with the medicine routine, shooting the medicine through a water gun into the mouth of the delighted youngster.

If we are going to survive happily as parents and grandparents, we need to learn some skills of persuasion, distraction, and guidance, rather than anger or force.

Eternal God, thank you for grandparents who make the problems of everyday living seem less formidable through humor and creativity.

November 9

Read Matthew 18:5.

What makes grandparents act so strangely exuberant? From the moment I learned of our first grandchild's birth, a strange transformation took place in my life. Through the years, I have watched in amusement as otherwise intelligent and productive people become maudlin, talkative, even a little crazy when they become grandparents.

In the past, I have been guilty of going in the opposite direction when someone started toward me with a grandmother's book of pictures. Now, I not only understand their actions, I have joyfully joined their ranks! A part of the reason for this strange behavior is that from the perspective of years, we recognize how great a miracle human birth really is. I know an obstetrician who once said: "I know that you believe that spiritual birth is a miracle, and so do I; but I never witness a physical birth without feeling that I am in the presence of the miraculous power of God."

When my husband and I held our grandchild for the first time, we remembered anew the feeling we experienced when we held our firstborn. It is the sure knowledge that parents are really cocreators with God. It's awesome and wonderful to realize that children are gifts to be cherished, not possessions to be owned.

Eternal God, help us to show your gracious hospitality to the grandchildren who are born into our families. Let us value, respect, and love them.

November 10

Read Jeremiah 18:6.

In his popular book *The Prophet,* Kahlil Gibran writes, "Our children come through us but they do not belong to us. They belong to life and to God."

As grandparents, we know how quickly the years pass. It is almost as if children are loaned to us for a few short, if somewhat hectic, years. Parents and grandparents are responsible for helping to build a strong foundation in those early years when behavior patterns are being formed and self-images are being developed.

These words attributed to a public school teacher have haunted me through the years:

> I took a piece of plastic clay,
> And idly fashioned it one day.
> And my fingers pressed it still,
> It moved and yielded to my will.
>
> I came again when days were past—
> That bit of clay was hard at last;
> The form I gave it, it still bore,
> But I could change that form no more.
>
> I took a piece of living clay,
> And gently formed it day by day.
> And molded with my power and art,
> A young child's soft and yielding heart.
>
> I came again when years were gone—
> It was a man I looked upon;
> He still that early impress wore,
> And I could change him nevermore.

Obviously, a big part of the joy of grandparents is the awareness that we have a second chance at life. It is the privilege of building into the foundation of a new life some of our most treasured values—truth, honor, love, and deep Christian faith.

Eternal God, help us to see ourselves as your potters working with human clay. Let us be willing to be clay in your hands.

❦ November 11

Read 1 Thessalonians 5:18.

This month we are remembering anew the tremendous power of praise. The psalmist was fully aware of this

309

power. The psalms are filled with thanksgiving and gratitude. Gratitude not only opens our hearts to God and to life, but it also warms human hearts.

When I was in the fifth grade, a local bank sponsored an essay contest. Not too many people entered that year, and I was lucky enough to win $5.00. The award was presented at school, and I expressed appreciation for it. At home, my father suggested that I write a letter of appreciation to the president of the bank. That didn't seem necessary to me but I did it. To my amazement, I received a letter from the bank president saying that they had sponsored the contest for a number of years and that I was the only award recipient who had written a note of thanks. That day, I learned that even a small amount of gratitude warms hearts.

In a much deeper way I learned that praise can lift you out of deep depression. One bleak November day in 1969, following the death of our son, I was reading 1 Thessalonians and trying to assuage the overwhelming feeling of loss. I read verse 5:18: " Give thanks in all circumstances."

I put down my Bible and asked the question, "In *all* things?" Suddenly I realized that doesn't mean we should give thanks for traumas, such as the death of a child; rather, in the midst of our tragedies, we should give thanks. When I could change my focus from what I had lost and praise God for what I had left, I experienced a strange easing of the pain.

Although most of us do not have primary responsibility for our grandchildren and are somewhat "buffered" from the disappointments and sorrows that accompany parenting, we experience sorrow and grief just as deeply as any parent when misfortune or tragedy touches the life of our grandchildren. At those times we may find release by remembering "to give thanks in all circumstances."

Eternal God, help us to remember that genuine appreciation warms hearts and overcomes grief and depression.

Read Philippians 1:3.

During this month of giving thanks let us remember that encouragement and affirmation are excellent ways of expressing gratitude. Think of the people who have encouraged you through the years and give thanks.

I once heard a speaker tell of an elderly nurse who worked in a mental institution at the turn of the century. The nurse believed there was hope for all God's creatures. Each day she would take her lunch to the dungeon outside the cage of "Little Annie," who had been declared hopelessly insane. In many ways, "Little Annie" was like an animal. On occasion, she would violently attack the visitor who came to her cage. At other times she would ignore her.

Each day the elderly nurse talked to "Little Annie," but there was no response. One day the nurse left brownies outside the cage. When she returned they had been eaten. Gradually, "Little Annie" began to talk. Later this "hopeless case" moved upstairs. Eventually she was released and declared completely well.

Many years thereafter, Queen Victoria, while pinning England's highest award on Helen Keller, asked, "How do you account for your remarkable accomplishments?" Without a moment's hesitation she replied that if it hadn't been for Ann Sullivan ("Little Annie"), her own name would be unknown.

Let's commit ourselves to being God's instruments of love, encouragement, and affirmation to others—especially to our grandchildren.

Thank you, Lord, for all the people who have believed in us even when we didn't believe in ourselves. Let us be your instruments in the lives of others.

Read Acts 4:36.

Randy was a hyperactive four-year-old who seemed to be consistently in some kind of trouble. His grandmother told me that he was not hostile or malicious. Instead, he was bright, inquisitive, energetic, and mischievous. Even so, his playmates often were in tears when with him, and his older brother and sister complained about their "into everything four-year-old brother." When his mother put him to bed at night, she would sometimes say, "Randy, do you need to ask God to forgive you for anything you did today?"

One day Randy's grandmother was visiting him, and Randy was very well behaved. He shared his toys, played well with his friends, and didn't break a single thing. That night, after his mother had heard his prayers and was on her way downstairs, she heard a plaintive little voice calling out, "Haven't I been a pretty good boy today?"

Suddenly Randy's mother realized that she had always been quick to point out his faults, but she had failed to praise him when he had done well. Being good for twelve hours was quite a feat for a rambunctious child like Randy, and he needed lots of affirmation.

Barnabas is one of my favorite Bible characters. He was an encourager to others—to Paul when the apostles were hesitant to accept him; to young Mark when Paul decided not to take him on a second missionary journey. A big part of grandmothering is being an encourager, a cheerleader. As grandmothers, we need to remember that words of encouragement and praise are as necessary for the greening of the human spirit as breathing is for the physical body.

Eternal God, let our words and actions reflect your patient and everlasting love.

Read Psalm 100:4.

The autumn of 1621 must not have been an easy time to plan a Thanksgiving celebration. Yet we, like the Pilgrims, know that in the midst of our difficulty is the time we most need to give thanks to God for his blessings. Gratitude enables us to appreciate goodness and beauty, to see possibilities for the future. It even lifts the dark clouds of depression and despair.

My husband studied homiletics under the late Dr. William Stidger at Boston University School of Theology. Dr. Stidger told his students of a time when depression invaded his mind and lasted for several months.

Finally, one of his friends suggested that he make a list of some people who had enriched his life. "Then," said the friend, "write a note of appreciation to each of them." Without much enthusiasm, Dr. Stidger wrote to a high school teacher who had encouraged him and given him a love of poetry.

To his surprise, he received an immediate reply. "Dear Willie, I taught school for over fifty years, and this is the first letter of appreciation I have ever received. I will treasure it as long as I live. May God bless you. Miss Annie."

Dr. Stidger reported that he felt so good about her reply that he wrote another and another note. Gradually his depression began to lift. By the time he completed the list, he had moved from despair to optimism.

When we feel discouraged or depressed, let us remember the people who have enriched our lives and let us give thanks. Surely high on that list will be the wonderful gift of grandchildren.

Eternal God, on our dark days, help us to remember all those who have blessed and are blessing our lives. Let us not forget our blessings, which come from you.

Read Isaiah 11:6.

Helen's daughter, Anna, had called to say that she and her husband needed to attend a company dinner and the babysitter could not come. Anna asked if Jason, age eight, might stay with Helen and her husband, Jim, for three hours.

Suddenly Helen heard Jason say in a loud voice, "I don't want to go over there! Nana is always mad!" Apologizing profusely, Anna said, "I don't know what has gotten into that boy lately." Helen replied softly, "Leave him alone, Anna. You and I both know that he is right. This is something which God and I must deal with immediately."

Since she and her husband had lost their jobs in a corporate merger months earlier, Helen's anxiety and fear had hardened into bitterness. She had resented her husband for taking a job at a much reduced salary, and she envied her friends with good jobs and happy circumstances. She became irritable, defensive, argumentative, and demanding.

Just the night before, Jim had remarked, "The sad thing is not that we have lost our jobs, but that our home is being destroyed by bitterness." Those words combined with Jason's honest protest caused Helen to fall to her knees and ask God to forgive her shortsightedness. She began to give thanks for his bountiful blessings. It was the beginning of a new and happy chapter in Helen's life.

Sometimes our grandchildren are the teachers, and we are the students. May we always be willing to learn!

Thank you, Lord, for the honesty of children who help us to face what we fail to see. Make us humble students.

Read Ephesians 6:1-4.

Thanksgiving and families go together like apple pie and ice cream, or a horse and carriage, or love and marriage. Everybody who can, wants to be home for Thanksgiving. Everybody who can't be home will be reminded of home through a song, a conversation, or a TV program.

The unquestionable importance of the family was confirmed for me several years ago when I read the report of a social worker at a home for abused children in New York City. She reported: "Most of these children came to us from homes not worthy of the name. Their homes were characterized by neglect, alcoholism, violence, or abuse. In our institution they received good food, clean sheets, and compassionate care. Yet the bruises on these children were scarcely healed before they were crying to go home again." Home is where the heart is!

When our own children were growing up, we planned our Thanksgiving celebrations around food, fun, family, and faith. I wanted the food to be good and adequate, but I didn't want it to be the focal point of the day. We invited as many members of the extended family as possible, which gave the celebration a special, festive feeling. Between the meal and dessert we had a small service of thanksgiving for which each child was to find a poem, write a litany, or read scripture. All of us mentioned what we were thankful for. The fun part of the day came in games—relays, charades, parlor games, or good children's movies.

As grandmothers, we have a perfect opportunity to think creatively about the celebration of this national holiday so that our grandchildren will have a feeling of security and warmth that comes from an extended family. In this and other ways, we too can help to "bring them up in the discipline and instruction of the Lord" (vs. 4*b*).

Eternal God, help us to use holidays to celebrate families and to glorify your name.

❤ November 17

Read 2 Corinthians 4:7.

In the milieu of today's society—stress, fast-paced living, overwork, economic insecurity, divorce, violence, crime—it is not easy to be responsible, caring, faithful parents. Yet we have no alternative if our children are to be whole.

My own parents were far from perfect, but they gave me the foundation for wholeness. Whether or not I accepted responsibility for building on that foundation was up to me. Let me mention a few of the building blocks which they put into my foundation so that my house of life would stand. These are the building blocks I am trying to pass on to my grandchildren.

First, they gave me unconditional love. They never said by their words or actions: "We love you . . . if you are good . . . if you make good grades . . . if you do what we want." I knew exactly what they expected, but I also knew that whatever happened, they would always love me. That provided the most wonderful security in the world.

Second, they stressed the importance of education. Though my parents married early and limited their own educational opportunities, they seemed to know intuitively the importance of education for their three children. They expected us to work and help pay for our opportunities, but they always encouraged us to take the next step up the ladder.

Third, my parents never compared their children with one another. My sister, brother, and I have very different personalities, interests, and talents. My parents encouraged us to find our own treasures and to respect those of others. It was not until I had children of my own that I realized how difficult that really is. And now, as a grand-mother, I realize how important it is!

Eternal God, thank you for good values given us by our parents. Help us to be loving links between them and our grandchildren.

🍎 November 18

Read Galatians 5:1.

Yesterday I listed some of the building blocks that my own parents used in the foundation of their children's lives. There are two other blocks they used very effectively. You will think of additional ones as you gratefully remember your parents.

I am grateful that my parents and early public school teachers instilled in me the pride of being an American. They enabled me to see that the privileges of living in this great land carry certain responsibilities. They often said, "There are no free lunches," as they were building in me respect for work, discipline, and the importance of a productive life.

Also, there is no wholeness, no integration, without a solid sense of values that serve as an inner gyroscope. In my family, the value system came from the Christian faith. At times in my teen years, I reacted against what I considered the restraints of religion. It was later that I learned that Christ didn't come into the world to make us slaves to God's laws. Instead, he came to show us how much God loves us and to give us the Magna Carta of real freedom, as suggested in Galatians 5:1: the freedom to be all that we were created to be.

I thank God today for all parents who are helping their children to be responsible and patriotic citizens and faithful disciples of Jesus Christ.

Thank you, Lord, for the valuable lessons learned from our parents. Let us joyfully and energetically pass them on to our grandchildren.

🌰 November 19

Read 2 Timothy 1:5.

Perhaps more than any other person, my paternal grandmother, Maria Webb, sowed the seeds of strong faith in my life. I never think of her without recalling a statement that was like a credo for her: "God always answers prayers. Sometimes he says 'yes'; sometimes he says 'no'; sometimes he says 'wait'." My grandmother believed that with every ounce of her five-foot-two-inch petite being. To understand the intensity of her belief, you need to know something of the life and struggles of this godly woman.

Though she was godly, there was not an ounce of pretense or false piety about her. She was full of fun, and I always felt lighthearted after being around her. She was very strict about the observance of the Sabbath. When we visited her, we went to Sunday school and church, no matter what. Yet, even in her insistence on that, she conveyed a great sense of expectancy, not tedious responsibility. When I was very small, she would give me a bath on Saturday night and say with a lilt in her voice, "Tomorrow is Sunday, and we are going to Sunday school and church."

There was no indication of it being a chore. She never implied that we had to go but that it was a marvelous privilege, and we could expect good things to happen.

Eternal God, thank you for grandmothers who understand that faith is more caught than taught. Let us be such grandmothers.

November 20

Read Psalm 24:1.

Yesterday I mentioned the powerful influence of my grandmother in sowing seeds of faith in my own life. For the next few days I will mention lessons I have learned from her godly life.

My Grandmother Webb's faith in God seemed synonymous with a sense of expectancy. At her house we would awaken to the smell of bacon, eggs, and freshly baked bread and to Grandmother saying, "Let's see what God is up to today."

After our chores were done, she would take us children on walks to discover wild flowers or to find a bird's nest or to wade in the creek. Always she spoke of "God's good earth" and how we need to care for it. I never heard the word *environmentalist* used in those days, but that is exactly what my grandmother was. She gave her grandchildren the belief that we are stewards of all God's creation.

One scene is graphically etched in my mind. On a summer day, my grandmother had four of her grandchildren seated with her on a log as we all dangled our feet into the creek. It was such a pleasant, peaceful scene that her words had special impact. "Remember, children, we must all leave the world a better and more beautiful place than when we found it."

Eternal God, help us to teach our grandchildren that "the earth is the Lord's." Allow us to happily instill a great sense of appreciation for the gift of life.

November 21

Read James 5:16b.

One of the things for which I feel most grateful was my grandmother's strong belief in the power of prayer. Ten years following her marriage and soon after the birth of their third child, my grandfather died very suddenly. It was then that my grandmother faced the biggest challenge of her life.

All at once, she had to work through her terrible grief and take full responsibility for running the farm and rearing their three young children alone. Her friends said she managed with grace because of her good humor, laughter, and perseverance.

Her family said that all those attributes helped, but that there was no way to explain her success without understanding her prayer life. Like her heroine, Susanna Wesley, my grandmother had a regular time each day for meditation, Bible reading, and prayer. According to my dad, no one disturbed her at that time unless the house was on fire or someone had died. My Aunt Mary said that her mother came out of her quiet time with a radiant countenance and a certainty about the next step.

I am grateful for a grandmother who was energized by God's presence in her quiet time and guided in her everyday living by her communication with God in prayer.

Help us, Lord, to demonstrate the power of prayer to our grandchildren.

November 22

Read Deuteronomy 6:7.

Recently I was speaking for a women's group in a church of another denomination. Just before the dinner began, an attractive woman whose eyes sparkled with interest and zest introduced herself as my grandson's second-grade teacher for the previous year.

She said all the things a grandmother wants to hear about her grandson—a good student, gets along well with other students, enjoys life. Then she told of an incident that warmed my heart.

The year before I had given the first two copies of my new book to our grandchildren because the book was dedicated to them. They both had thanked me dutifully, but as I expected for their ages of seven and ten, neither seemed to be impressed with the hard work that the book represented.

Yet, according to Mrs. O'Neil, the following day our seven-year-old grandson had brought the book to school and at "show-and-tell time" showed his classmates the book and read the dedication. Except for that teacher, I never would have known about the incident.

As I drove home that evening, I gave thanks for the many men and women who have the awesome task of molding the minds of our children and of helping to build character.

This Thanksgiving season is a wonderful time to write a note of appreciation to our grandchildren's teachers. In the midst of their highly pressured and stressful days, a note of appreciation may be like an oasis in the desert.

Eternal God, we pray for a special measure of your strength and love in the lives of teachers. Thank you for the gracious influence they bring into the lives of our grandchildren.

November 23

Read Psalm 95:2.

Henry David Thoreau was one of America's greatest philosophers. He was a rugged individualist who lived life simply on Walden Pond near Concord, Massachusetts. He made time for contemplation and an understanding of the meaning of life. Every time I read his book *Walden,* I feel that the dry places of my spirit are being watered.

One of the wise things he said was that every human being ought to give thanks at least once a day for the fact that he or she was born. Thoreau said that he himself did that.

Think what we would have missed if we hadn't been born! For one thing, we would have missed the world's beauty. When the leaves turn each year, I think it is my favorite season until the first snow falls or the flowers bloom in the spring. Such beauty!

We also would have missed the joy of friendship and love. We would have missed the thrill of finding a person with whom we want to spend the rest of our life; the joy of seeing children grow and develop; and the unspeakable joy of having grandchildren!

Eternal God, help us to come into your presence with thanksgiving each and every day!

🍎 November 24

Read Matthew 26:26-28.

Some years ago, an incident happened at the grocery store during the week before Thanksgiving that has caused me to think deeply about the importance for all ages—especially for grandchildren—of a "common meal."

I stood in the checkout line behind a woman who was throwing her groceries on the counter with a vengeance. There was hostility in her every move. Suddenly, she turned around and said, "I can't wait for Thanksgiving to be over!" Somewhat taken aback, I asked, "Why do you dread Thanksgiving?" She retorted, "Because all six children and their families will come home—twenty-five in all—and I will work like a slave to prepare a meal that will be eaten in twenty-five minutes. I hate it!"

At first I was amused by her response. Then all kinds of things went through my mind. Almost every woman alive has had something of the forlorn feeling that comes when you see your gourmet masterpiece inhaled in a matter of minutes. Yet most of the time we have been able to focus on the reason for our getting together. Joy and warmth

322

result when people who love one another get together over a common meal.

Jesus understood this when he shared a meal regularly with his disciples. In the early church, communion was not just sharing the bread and wine as symbols of Christ's body and blood, but it included the sharing of an entire meal. I'm convinced that sharing a meal with people we love is always a sacred kind of communion.

O Lord, help us to see you in all of our experiences—especially in the sharing of a meal. Let us be grateful for the privilege.

🍎 November 25

Read John 14:18.

The Thanksgiving Day that is sadly etched in my memory is the one that came only four days after the memorial service for our twenty-year-old son, Rick. Rick had been injured in an accident and had lived for ten days. During those days, our emotions were like a yo-yo, alternating between hope and despair. His untimely death was the first tragedy in our immediate family.

The Thanksgiving holidays had always been special to our family, but we didn't look forward to that one. Though several wonderful families in our church had invited us to share their celebration, we weren't up to anything festive; we didn't want to dampen their family fun. Besides, our younger son would be home from college, and we wanted to spend time alone with him.

We attended the Thanksgiving service at our church at 11:00 A.M. and then made a visit to Rick's grave. We decided to eat our Thanksgiving meal at a restaurant at which we had eaten only once or twice and had never seen anyone we knew. I'm sure the food was good, though none of us ate with enthusiasm or a good appetite.

On our way out we stopped to pay our bill and were told by the cashier that our bill had been taken care of. "By whom?" we asked. "I don't know the man's name," she replied, "but he was from out of town." To this day we do not know the man's name. But he must have responded somehow to our pain. He was our "angel unaware."

This Thanksgiving, may we be sensitive to the pain of those who are close to us—including our grandchildren—as well as those who are strangers.

Thank you, Lord, for coming to us in our sorrow. Help us also to give comfort to others.

🍂 November 26

Read Psalm 103:1, 3.

Of all the memorable Thanksgivings, none has been as glorious as Thanksgiving 1991. On Tuesday of Thanksgiving week, Dr. Charles Portera smiled as he entered my room on his usual rounds at Memorial Hospital. My "second-look" surgery had gone well the preceding week, and the doctor told me that everything looked good. Yet, he cautioned that we couldn't know for sure until we received the pathology report on Tuesday.

On Tuesday morning his smile looked particularly promising. I waited anxiously as he said, "I have great news. All the reports are excellent. There is no evidence of cancer." Then in true professional manner he went on to remind me of the percentage of cases in which ovarian cancer recurs. I had stopped listening. My mind was shouting, "Cancer free! Cancer free!" and my heart was singing the doxology.

My eyes were filled with tears as the doctor turned to leave, and I tried to express my profound thanks to him. It was not until I telephoned Ralph to give him the good news that my tears overflowed. "Thank God," he said.

As we pulled into the driveway of our home on the eve

of Thanksgiving, there was a huge banner across our garage door. It was made by our grandchildren, and it read, "Welcome Home, Gran. We love you." It was my best Thanksgiving ever!

Eternal God, thank you for the gift of physical health and family love. Help us never to take either for granted.

🍂 November 27

Read 2 Corinthians 9:11.

A nostalgic Thanksgiving of days past has been portrayed by Lydia Maria Child in these words:

> Over the river and through the woods
> To grandmother's house we go.
> The horse knows the way to carry the sleigh
> Through the white and drifted snow.

Most children today don't go by horse-drawn sleigh over the river to grandmother's house. Rather, they often go through small towns and city streets to grandmother's highrise condo or town house. Where we celebrate is not important; only the joy and warmth and security of being together as a family.

Though we usually have the traditional Thanksgiving dinner at our house, there are two very different celebrations we like to remember. One celebration was at my brother-in-law's condominium at Pompano Beach, Florida. The weather was great. Some of the adults played golf while the grandchildren swam in the pool and built sand castles on the beach. We ate at home in the evening in a very relaxed setting. There was no "white and drifted snow," but lots of love and the usual giving of thanks.

Another year our family used frequent flyer miles to fly to New York City for sightseeing and the Macy's Thanksgiving Day Parade. In the three days we were there, we did everything from visiting the Empire State Building and going ice skating at Rockefeller Center to seeing the Christmas program at Radio City Music Hall. That year we ate Thanksgiving dinner at the World Trade Center.

Your family has its own memories of special Thanksgivings. Whatever our setting, our gratitude to God can be expressed with joy and love.

Help us, O Lord, to give thanks for your lovingkindness in whatever circumstance we find ourselves.

❦ November 28

Read Ephesians 5:20.

As a young person during World War II, I had the privilege of meeting a national hero, General Dwight D. Eisenhower. While attending a meeting in Chicago, I was staying at the old Blackstone Hotel. One morning as I got off the elevator in the lobby, I was whisked along with the crowd into a cordoned area. General Eisenhower and his entourage were coming. A band was playing a John Philip Sousa march as the general entered.

Standing on the front row of the cordoned area, I took advantage of an unexpected opportunity. When the general paused for a moment in front of me, I extended my hand. He not only shook my hand but also chatted briefly with me. It was very exciting.

Later, when he became president, I read his words about thanksgiving. He told a reporter that when he went to bed at night, he prayed something like this: "Lord, when I thought about you today, I've made good decisions. When I've forgotten you and depended only on Dwight Eisenhower, maybe I didn't do so well. Now, Lord, I am going to sleep. I am tired. You take over and run the country while I am asleep." Then he would say, "Thanks for everything," and peacefully drop off to sleep.

When we feel pressured or overstressed, it may help us to remember how a president of the United States—who also was a grandfather—turned to God in thanksgiving and trust.

Eternal God, we may not have a country to run, but we have been entrusted with the care of ourselves, our families, our friends, and even strangers. May we begin and end each day by turning to you in thanksgiving and trust.

❧ November 29

Read Psalm 27:11.

She looked as if she were in her early thirties. She was average height, average weight, average in every aspect of outward appearance and yet she was totally appealing. Each person seated in the room waiting for the seminar to begin noticed her that day.

There was an aliveness about Kathy. She exuded energy and interest, joy in being alive, and openness to others. Though I had heard we all radiate our character and personality, I had never seen it as vividly as I did that day.

Later, over dinner, I learned that Kathy had not always radiated such wholeness. In fact, she had grown up in a dysfunctional family where she was the victim of verbal abuse by her mother and physical abuse by an alcoholic father. An only child, she grew up feeling lonely and rejected.

It was a compassionate, loving sixth-grade Sunday school teacher named Mrs. Parsons who first enabled Kathy to like herself and to discover her unique talents. Mrs. Parsons saw her students as individuals and wanted to help them become whole persons in Jesus Christ. In Kathy's case, it was Mrs. Parsons who led both mother and daughter to a heartfelt commitment to Christ and hence to a strong friendship with each other. The joyful empowerment I saw in Kathy came through years of personal and spiritual growth that allowed her finally to forgive her father.

It occurs to me that we grandmothers have the skill and wisdom to become the compassionate teachers of today's children.

Thank you Lord, for Sunday school teachers who are able to communicate your power and love to children and youths. Help those of us who are compassionate teachers of our grandchildren find ways to use our gifts to touch the lives of other children as well.

🍂 November 30

Read Matthew 16:18.

On the weekend before Thanksgiving 1983, I had accompanied the leaders of our church's singles' ministry on a planning retreat at Beech Mountain in North Carolina. By the time we reached the foot of the mountain, snow had quietly begun to fall and the wind was whistling through the valley with such intensity that the cars were swaying. In 22 degree temperature the mountain roads had become dangerously icy. One of the cars in our group had to be abandoned midway up the mountain.

When we were safely inside the chalet and eating popcorn before an open fire, we began to talk of Thanksgivings past. Our group remembered Thanksgivings celebrated from Canada and New York to Los Angeles and Vietnam. We listed things we were grateful for—our country, our heritage, the winter wonderland of snow, family, friends. Most of all we spoke of gratitude for the church—and for its special nurturing at this particular time in our lives.

When I retired that evening, my thoughts cascaded one after another in happy memories of my own gratitude for the church. One special memory popped immediately into my mind. It was the love and compassion extended to us by members of our local church following the accident and death of our son. Our younger son, commenting on the church's compassion, said, "I can't get over all the things people are doing for us." My response was, "Honey, you've often seen the church as a place where your dad and I went for committee meetings, but this is what it really is—a caring, sharing, redemptive fellowship, the body of Christ."

Through our example, we can demonstrate for our grandchildren the importance of the church and its redemptive fellowship.

Eternal God, enable us gratefully to become a part of Paul's vision of the church as the body of Christ and to share this with our grandchildren.

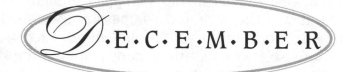

The Gift of Love

Nell Mohney

❧

❧ **December** 1
─────────────────

Read Luke 2:12.

Only God could have thought of it! With consummate skill, he used a new approach and brought us hope for new life in the form of a baby. Though Jesus was the Son of God, he was not born as an elitist in a palace, but in a stable. People, no matter how humble their life-styles, could identify with this child of God.

The universality of Jesus was symbolized by the people who came to worship at the manger. There were shepherds, representing the workers of the world; there were wise men, representing the thinkers, the dreamers, the intellectuals; and there were angels, representing the approval of God and bringing glory to him. This is the world's greatest love story—that God himself, in the person of Jesus, came into the world to identify with us, to show us how to live, and to draw us to him.

In her book *Grandmother Time,* Judy Gattis Smith suggests a number of things we can do to make the Christmas story real to young grandchildren. Rather than just singing "Jingle Bells," she suggests we sing the carols that have to do with shepherds, such as "It Came Upon a Midnight Clear," "O Little Town of Bethlehem," "While Shepherds Watched Their Flocks by Night," and "Silent Night." She also suggests having a shepherd's parade in the house or in the neighborhood and then returning home for hot chocolate and cookies.

What a privilege it is to help our grandchildren experience the wonder of the Christmas story in creative and fun ways!

Eternal God, help us never to forget the tremendous power of your love expressed in the Christmas story. Let us pass this on to our grandchildren in loving and memorable ways.

🍎 December 2

Read Luke 2:1-7.

Yesterday we reflected on the beauty and universality of the Christmas story. Today we need to see its glorious simplicity. Many great writers require huge books to tell their stories, but the Christmas story as told by Luke requires less than one chapter. Those carefully but simply written words are the source of the greatest art humanity has ever created and the most inspiring music the world has ever heard. For all these twenty centuries, the simple story of a baby born in Bethlehem has cast its benign influence over all humankind.

The Christmas season has become a time of frantic activity in many homes. Often we get caught up in the hurry and pressure and become exhausted and "stressed out." As grandmothers, we can make the decision early to keep ourselves calm, emphasizing only the important tasks and relationships. We can make our homes places of quiet beauty where grandchildren can realize the glorious simplicity of God's story. But this will never just happen. It will occur by our conscious choice and courage to follow through on our decisions.

Eternal God, let us experience anew the profound truth, beauty, and simplicity of the Christmas story. Then, let our lives reflect this beauty.

Read Luke 2:10-11.

In a season that has become increasingly commercialized, we have to focus on Jesus as "the reason for the season." The late Dr. Peter Marshall once said, "Your Christmas does not have to be commercialized unless you allow it to be." We can do our errands of love early this year so that we have time to read a story to a preschool grandchild, or bake cookies with an elementary-aged child, or shop leisurely with a teenager. We can keep our decorations and our activities focused on the spiritual meaning of Christmas. Even so, sometimes young children have a hard time "getting the story straight."

A few years ago, some friends whose children are now grown and married told of an incident that happened when Zack was four and his sister, Elizabeth, was two. Zack loved going to Sunday school and hearing the story of Mary and Joseph and the baby Jesus. He was equally captivated by the television show featuring Roy Rogers and his horse, Trigger. Zack got the stories a little confused as his mother discovered the day after Christmas. Elizabeth was happily playing with her new doll when Zack walked by and commanded: "Mary, swaddle that baby and jump on Trigger cause we're heading for Bethlehem!"

As grandmothers, we can help our grandchildren—of every age—"get the story straight" by helping them to focus on the true meaning of the season!

Eternal God, help us always to "get your story straight" as we interpret it to grandchildren through our actions and words.

🍎 **December 4**

Read Luke 2:14.

As we enjoy the beautiful decorations in the stores and the sound of carols being played this Christmas season, our thoughts are led back to the reason for the celebration—the one whose birthday we celebrate.

Last year, I was amused by a reported conversation of two New Yorkers on Christmas Eve. One was complaining about the terrible traffic jam. The other replied: "Well, when you stop to think about it, it's a miracle that a baby born in a stable thousands of miles from New York City could cause a traffic jam on Fifth Avenue twenty centuries later."

It is worth noting that businesses not only benefit from Christmas, but they also are affected by the spirit of Christmas. Businesses are not some impersonal entities; they are made up of people. Some of these people never go to church, but during Christmas they will hear Christmas music in stores—beautiful hymns and many voices singing the old carols that tell the story of the birth of our Lord.

As grandmothers, let us not become complainers about the commercialization of Christmas but people who choose the values we wish to emphasize. Let us make opportunities to help our grandchildren enjoy decorations, drama, music, and festivities, but always with interpretation of their true meaning.

O Lord, for whom all of life was sacred, help us bring the sacred meaning of your life into our daily activities.

🍂 December 5

Read Luke 1:31.

As magnificent as God's plan for the salvation of the world was, he needed human participation. I have often thought how stunned a fourteen-year-old peasant girl in Nazareth must have been to have received the angel's proclamation that she was to bear the Messiah.

It is obvious that she resisted somewhat as she declared her unworthiness. She also must have been thinking about the consequences for her, such as rejection by family and friends. Surely she must have been concerned that Joseph might think she had been unfaithful. If that were the case, he had the options of public renunciation (which could result in stoning), divorce, or proceeding with the marriage.

Mary's submission to God's will was certainly justified. The angel appeared to Joseph, letting him know that the child Mary was carrying was indeed the Son of God. The affirmation for her actions came, but not without some pain and suffering on her part.

It occurs to me that we often want God's purposes to be accomplished, but without effort or pain on our part. Grandparents are to be involved in the fulfillment of God's purpose for families. If our grandchildren are to become faithful disciples, they need grandparents who take the time, the trouble, and the commitment to model a joy-filled faith.

Eternal God, help us to be splendid instruments through which your love, joy, and power are passed on to our grandchildren.

December 6

Read Luke 2:7.

Every year Christmas seems to move me in a special way when I attend the children's pageant at our church. Maybe it is the children's simplicity and their unprofessional performance that makes the story seem authentic. After all, the participants in that first Christmas drama were unsophisticated, unpolished human beings. In a simple manger scene, God's great gift of love was made known to them.

One of my favorite stories of a children's drama has been reported in various publications through the years. Fifth-grade Sunday school students were asked to put on the annual Christmas play. The teacher asked the students to select the characters who would have speaking parts. They chose Wally for the Innkeeper. Wally was a large boy who was friendly, kind, and loved by the other children. He was also mentally challenged, so they gave him a part that had only two sentences: "Go away. There is no room." He was to say the line and then repeat it.

During rehearsal, Wally got along fine. On the night of the performance, he was so impressed with the colorful costumes and the "packed house" that he really got into the part. When Mary and Joseph first appeared, Wally said his lines correctly. But when they turned to leave, Wally, with tears running down his cheeks, called out: "Come back, Joseph; come back, Mary. You can have my room."

That simple story always confronts me with this soul-searching question: Is there room in my life for Christ or am I crowding him out because of trivial pursuits?

Help us, O Christ, to retain room in our lives for your gracious influences and to make those influences known to those around us, especially our grandchildren.

🍂 December 7

Read John 15:2.

Yesterday we asked the question of whether or not there is room in our lives for Christ. I remember an incident that happened several years ago when I was packing my suitcase for a trip to Oberammergau, Germany, to attend the Passion Play. Though I have never been known for traveling light, that suitcase was fuller than usual.

We were to be away for a month, so I thought of every eventuality and packed accordingly—hot weather, cold weather, rainy weather, colds, flu, tummy upsets, even some things I had never had before like toothaches, backaches, and broken legs. I was going to be ready for whatever happened! The trouble is that when I finished packing, I couldn't close the suitcase.

Suddenly I thought, "This suitcase is symbolic of my life—overstuffed." I knew my life was overstuffed with activities that were pleasant but didn't really make a difference for God in the world; overstuffed with material things that took time to maintain and repair; overstuffed with food that didn't contribute to fitness; and overstuffed with habits that were energy depleting and goal defeating.

That day I began to pull things out of my suitcase, but more important, I consciously began to work on a plan to simplify my life. I still have a long way to go, but December is a good time for all of us to test our overstuffed lives. The questions are: Have I cleaned out enough debris so that there is room in my life for the spirit of Christ? Is there room in my life for grandchildren with their needs and dreams? What needs pruning in my life to make me a more worthy instrument?

Eternal God, forgive us for overstuffing our lives with things and habits that bind our spirits. Let us be willing to turn loose the clutter.

December 8

Read Luke 2:49.

For the past two days, we have considered the importance of making room for the spirit of Christ in our lives. Join me in answering the following questions as we prepare for a worthy celebration of the birthday of our Lord.

First, is there room in my life for Christ's clarity of purpose? Even at age 12, Jesus seemed perfectly clear about who he was. He said to his parents, "Did you know that I must be in my father's house?" Without steadfast purpose, it is easy to become fragmented and pulled in all directions.

Second, is there room in my life for Christ's love, or do I crowd him out by resentment or bitterness? Little irritations and worries are like barnacles that cover a ship and make it unseaworthy. If our lives are trivialized by these things, we, too, are not life worthy.

Third, is there room in my life for the worship of the true God, or do I worship at other altars? In Bethlehem, they crowded him out because they didn't know who he was. We know who he was and who he is. The question is, Are our lives so overstuffed that we say with the innkeeper, "No room. No room"?

Fourth, is there room in my relationships for Christ's spirit of acceptance, understanding, and compassionate caring? In our relationships with grandchildren, we have the opportunity to affirm and encourage them and to liberate their unique talents. This happens only as we make room and time for them in our lives.

Eternal God, help us to be able to say, like Jesus, "I must be about my Father's business."

December 9

Read Matthew 28:20.

We heard the story while we were visiting in Florida during the Christmas season a number of years ago. It happened near Fort Lauderdale on the day after Thanksgiving. Bob and Helen Evans decided to show their houseguests from the north "a bird's-eye view of paradise" from their Lear Jet. Bob, an experienced pilot, took the plane up at least twice weekly. Helen had decided to learn to fly and had received two lessons, but she had never soloed.

On that fateful day, the plane had been in the air less than thirty minutes when Bob suffered a massive heart attack and died instantly. His wife and the two other passengers did everything they could to resuscitate him, but it was too late.

Though traumatized by her dead husband's body slumped over the controls, Helen knew it was her responsibility to land the plane. She had enough presence of mind to call the tower and report the situation. Immediately an air controller radioed a pilot who was flying in her area.

The pilot, then, flew alongside Helen giving her instructions about bringing the plane in for a safe landing.

As Helen emerged from the plane, pale and visibly shaken, she told reporters that she never could have made it without the support of the pilot who flew along beside her.

Christmas comes as a reminder that Jesus came not only to bring salvation and eternal life but also, through the Holy Spirit, to walk alongside us for support and guidance. We are not alone. In this day of uncertainty and stress, there is no better message we can pass along to our grandchildren!

Eternal God, help us to remember that we can easily "crash and burn" on our life's journey if we don't turn to you for guidance and support.

❤ December 10

Read John 15:12.

Jimmy, age five, was visiting his grandparents for a week. Jimmy, who lived in a city some four hours away, had spent time at his grandparents' home before, but his parents had always been with him. This time he had come by plane without any other family member.

On the first day of his visit, Jimmy had a marvelous time. He and his grandparents went swimming, fishing, and picnicking. He also rode his favorite pony. He didn't even miss his parents—until he went to bed.

His grandmother read him a story about the runaway bunny and told him that God was like the bunny's mother, who always was there for him. Then his grandmother heard Jimmy's prayers and tucked him in. As she started down the hall, Jimmy asked, "Will you leave the hall light on, please Nana?"

Coming back in and sitting on the side of the bed, his grandmother said, "I will do that, Jimmy, but you don't have to be afraid. God is right here with you."

Jimmy smiled and replied, "I know, but I want someone with skin on."

We can share God's love by being "someone with skin on" for others—especially for our grandchildren.

Eternal God, let us be the "people with skin on" who represent your presence to those who are frightened, lonely, or hurting.

🍀 December 11

Read Luke 2:10-14.

One of the classic films our extended family enjoys watching during the Christmas Season is *Miracle on 34th Street*. The story has endured because it reminds us to look beyond outer circumstances to see eternal truths.

These verses from the Gospel of Luke tell of a wonderful miracle, a precious gift. But in Bethlehem, the skeptics saw only a poor carpenter whose wife gave birth to a baby in a stable. Only those with eyes of faith could understand the significance of God's great gift of love in the form of a baby.

Without eyes of faith, we can miss the miraculous gifts of God that come into our everyday lives. Children often recognize these gifts more easily than we adults. This holy season—and every day of the coming year—may we look at the world through the eyes of a child, through eyes of faith!

O Lord, help us to keep the miracle of Christmas in our hearts throughout the year.

🍀 December 12

Read Isaiah 9:6.

Today I want to share a special story: the story of a friend's grandson.

"Mommy, I saw God and some baby angels with big trumpets." This is one of the few memories that three-year-old Brandon has of a terrifying five days when he hovered between life and death. A victim of H-flu meningitis and septic shock, Brandon was unconscious during the entire ordeal.

After he regained consciousness, his mother, wishing to check the validity of the young child's statement, asked, "Brandon, will you tell me again about seeing the angels?"

"They were baby angels and they had big trumpets, and I saw God," replied Brandon as matter-of-factly as if he were talking about his closest playmate.

"Did you play with the angels?" his mother probed.

"No. God told them to take me back to my mommy," he answered.

Brandon's mother is sure of one thing: The nightmare is over, and she and her husband have their only child back safely on this side of death for the celebration of Christmas. The words of the scripture have special meaning for them: "For a child has been born for us, a son is given to us" (Isa. 9:6).

Eternal God, help us to remember that children come through us but don't belong to us. Let us as parents and grandparents joyfully accept responsibility for being their teachers and guides during their years upon this earth.

🕊 December 13

Read Luke 2:42.

Mary, Joseph, and Jesus made the trip to Jerusalem for the festival of the Passover because it was the custom—the tradition. Tradition has always been an important part of family life. In our fast-paced, changing world, family and faith traditions take on even more importance.

As grandparents, we have a wonderful opportunity to strengthen family ties and faith values as we continue family traditions and develop new ones, particularly during seasons of importance to the Christian faith such as Advent and Christmas.

Some of our family's Christmas traditions are singing traditional carols; rereading classics such as "T'was the Night Before Christmas," "The Other Wise Man," and the Christmas story from the Gospel of Luke; and attending Christmas productions with our grandchildren. One year we took them to see the production of Charles Dickens' *Christmas Carol*. To this day they remember watching Scrooge's bed move across the stage and Ebenezer Scrooge fly in Peter Pan fashion from his bed to an upper platform where he met the ghost of Christmas present.

Your family traditions may include using certain decorations for the home or Christmas tree, helping a needy family, preparing and enjoying family dinners featuring traditional foods, or attending Christmas Eve services together. In all these events and activities, we are building memories that will bless and strengthen the lives of our grandchildren.

Eternal God, help us to nurture our relationships with our grandchildren and teach them of your love as we make family memories together.

❦ December 14

Read 1 Corinthians 10:32.

Dr. Norman Vincent Peale once told of an incident that happened on Christmas Eve when he was very young. He said that he and his father were doing some late Christmas shopping. It was cold, and he was tired of carrying the heavy packages and thinking how nice it would be to get home.

Suddenly a bleary-eyed beggar, who was unshaven and dirty, came up and asked for money. Young Peale instinctively recoiled and brushed him aside. Peale remembers that his father reprimanded him with these words: "Norman, you should never treat anyone that way."

"But Dad, he's nothing but a bum," young Peale replied.

"Maybe he hasn't made the most of himself," said young Peale's father, "but he is a child of God. You must treat each person with respect." Then he gave the young boy a dollar and instructed him what to say.

Young Peale ran to catch up with the old man, clutched his dirty sleeve, and said, "Excuse me, sir. I give you this dollar in the name of Christ."

The old man looked at the boy in absolute surprise. Then, smiling broadly and bowing graciously, he said, "I thank you, young sir, in the name of Christ."

Peale concluded by saying that on that Christmas Eve, his father taught him the importance of offering the gift of respect to all of God's children. It is a lesson he has passed on to his children and grandchildren, and one that we can pass on as well.

Eternal God, help us to offer the gift of respect to others in the name of Christ, who has brought us the gift of salvation. And help us demonstrate to our grandchildren the importance of these gifts.

December 15

Read John 3:16.

It was the most beautiful coat I had ever seen. It was emerald green, and its princess lines and Peter Pan collar were perfect for a short person like me. It was even more appealing because it was tastefully displayed before a backdrop of gold and white.

My sales job during that high school Christmas vacation was in another department store located three blocks from the store that had my dream coat. Each day during my lunch hour, I would look longingly and wistfully at "my coat." I could see myself wearing that coat on Christmas Day and walking through the snow to the services at our church.

Of course, there was no way our family could have afforded a large expenditure that year. We were in the middle of financial reverses and had agreed that each of us would receive only one small gift. Even so, I continued to dream about my coat. Naturally, I was disappointed when it disappeared from the window two days before Christmas. Hurriedly entering the store, I asked what had happened to the green coat. "It was sold," came the curt reply.

On Christmas morning there wasn't much jubilation at our home as we each opened our small gifts. Then my mother reached behind the tree and pulled out a large white package tied with a green bow. "Could it be?" I wondered. It was! The beautiful emerald green coat was mine! As I whirled around in it I asked, "But how could we afford it?" Calmly my mother replied, "I found some extra money." It was years later that I learned that I received my wonderful coat because my mother had sold her treasured watch.

We all make sacrifices for our children and grandchildren. These acts of sacrificial love are symbolic of God's gift to us at Christmas. The gift of himself in Jesus is incomparable. Even if we have accepted it, it may be years before we fully realize the greatness of the gift or the redemptive love that prompted it.

Eternal God, help us live our lives in gratitude for your great gift of love.

🍂 *December 16*

Read Isaiah 7:14.

A number of years ago a group of friends were sharing their most memorable Christmas experiences. Most of us had told of happy experiences—surprises, gifts, an unusual trip, a special homecoming, a Christmas wedding. One young minister told of lessons he learned during his most painful Christmas.

His parents were divorced, and he and his mother were living with his grandparents. He said, "We were as poor as the proverbial church mouse, but I was only six and still thought Santa Claus brought the gifts we wanted." Even though a red bike wasn't under the tree on Christmas morning, he kept thinking that Santa would return during the day and bring it. He told us, "I learned the hard lesson that we don't always get what we want."

Later that Christmas week when his golden retriever died, he learned that "we can't always keep the things or people we love." He reminded us that many people are depressed and unhappy during the holiday season. Psychiatrists tell us that suicide rates are higher during this season. Their explanation for this phenomenon is that in the midst of seasonal joy, the hard lesson seems harder and the loneliness more intense.

Then he told us that the third lesson he learned through the years and that propelled him toward the Christian ministry is that the one whose birthday we celebrate will be with us in the difficult places to bring comfort and joy.

"Look, the young woman is with child and shall bear a son, and shall name him Immanuel" (Isa. 7:14). *Immanuel:* God with us. In the midst of our seasonal joy, let us be sensitive to the pain of others, always helping them to know that the message of Christmas is that God is with us.

Eternal God, as we learn the hard lessons of life, let us stay close to the One who can show us "the way, the truth and the life."

December 17

Read Matthew 25:40.

Christianity began in an era of cruelty, evil, force, and discrimination. It came into the world when there were no abiding principles of concern for individuals. Many people

344

were like chattel. The quiet principle of love was injected into the human family on that first Christmas night by the God who knew the duality of good and evil, but was determined that the good would dominate.

Reaching out to care for others should be second nature for Christians. Through church and civic groups as well as television appeals, we have the opportunity to help those less fortunate than we. We do it because of the principle of love that came into the world through Christ.

A friend of mine has a wonderful plan for involving her grandchildren in giving rather than receiving. During the summer, she "applies" through the human service department for two needy families with children whose ages are near to those of her grandchildren. They learn the names of the children and what their needs are in clothing as well as one toy each would like to receive.

Throughout the fall the children save their money for the purchases. In early December my friend chooses a Saturday for shopping for their friends. Not only is that shopping day a fun experience for a grandmother and her grandchildren, but it also is a teaching experience of sensitivity and Christian compassion.

Eternal God, enable us to allow the love that came down at Christmas to flow through us to others, and help us to encourage our grandchildren to give the gift of love.

December 18

Read Luke 11:13.

On my maternal grandmother's side I had dozens of cousins, and on Christmas Day we all got together at Grandmother's for dinner and the exchanging of gifts. Before we "wised up" and realized that we should draw names for gift giving, we each gave every other member of the large family a gift.

Obviously the gifts had to be small and inexpensive. It

was a chore to buy them, and nobody looked forward to receiving them. In fact, I often put away the gifts I received to give to other friends next year. One year I ran out of money before I bought a present for Kathleen, my negative, unhappy, eleven-year-old cousin.

Deciding to choose a gift from my stock in the closet, I chose a purple ceramic cat. Unfortunately, I had completely forgotten that Kathleen had given me that cat three years earlier. She had not forgotten and was furious. The incident precipitated a family crisis. That may have been the year when we decided to draw names. Since that time so long ago, I've learned the importance of knowing and caring about the person to whom we give a gift. We should give something of ourselves in each gift.

This is an important lesson for our grandchildren, particularly in a day when personal gain and pleasure are "the name of the game." We can help shift the focus of gift-giving, and we can begin with ourselves.

As we think of our gifts to Christ, we should also know him—who he is and what he has done for the world—and we should give something of ourselves. Remember the words of Christina Rossetti: "What can I give him, poor as I am? If I were a shepherd, I would bring a lamb; If I were a Wise Man, I would do my part; what can I give him; Give my heart."

Forgive us when we have offered our gifts in arrogance or unconcern. Let us give something of ourselves in each gift—and always from our hearts.

December 19

Read John 10:10.

As we move closer to Christmas Day, a kind of magic seems to fill the air. It is evidenced in the livelier way we walk, in our smiles, and in our generosity. It's enhanced by the dancing eyes of little children, by candlelit homes and churches, by the smell of fruitcake cooking, by the sound of Christmas carols, and by snow quietly falling.

People who complain about commercialization of the season have overlooked the benign influence of Christmas in the life of the world. It is one season when the Christian gospel escapes the structure of the church and flows into the world. Many nonbelievers hear the good news of God's love as we celebrate the birthday of Jesus—not the birthday of Buddha or Muhammad, but Jesus.

A grandmother told the story of Bobby at a December gathering. I'd heard the story before, but when she told it I became more acutely aware of what our world would look like if Christmas had not come.

In a dream, Bobby, age seven, descended the stairs to find no Christmas tree, no presents, and no decorations. His parents were irritable on their way to work; there were no churches, no hospitals; and only a few children of the elite families could go to school. Most worked in factories or shops. Bobby's dream ended happily when his mother called him, saying: "Wake up, Bobby. It's Christmas morning!" Bobby jumped out of bed, hugged his mother, and said, "Mom, I'm glad Jesus came into the world." His mother replied, "Yes, Bobby, and so am I."

Most children probably do not dream about what our world would be like if Jesus had not come. Take a few moments this season to "dream aloud" with your grandchildren. Then give thanks together for Jesus' gift of abundant life!

Thank you, Lord, for coming to save the world and the people therein. Let us celebrate your coming.

December 20

Read 2 Peter 1:12; Luke 2:19.

Christmas is a time when our memories are stirred at a very deep level. We seem to want to go back to our roots, to recall our childhood and the special events of Christmases past. The song "There's No Place Like Home for the Holidays" strikes a responsive chord in most people. Even when there has been tension or conflict, most people want to return home for Christmas.

Christmas is indeed a time for remembering. In your quiet time today, think of your most memorable Christmas. It may be a time when you received a longed-for gift—a doll, or bike, or watch.

I heard of a nine-year-old boy named Allen who wanted a watch desperately. In fact, he talked about it constantly for two months before Christmas. Two weeks before Christmas, the little boy was accelerating the pace of talking about a watch. In frustration, his father said, "If you mention 'watch' one more time, you won't receive it."

With great restraint Allen resisted the impulse, but a few days before Christmas he wondered if they had forgotten. Then he thought of a plan. This family had morning devotions around the breakfast table with each person saying a Bible verse. Allen looked through the Bible until he found the perfect verse. On Christmas Eve when it was his turn, he opened the Bible to Mark 13:37 and read: "And what I say to you I say to all: Watch" (RSV). Allen got his watch!

This holiday season, pass on your happy memories to your grandchildren so that each of them has an even warmer feeling about being home for the holidays.

Eternal God, during this season, let us take time to recall happy memories that have blessed our lives. Let us especially remember what you have done for us through Christ.

🐞 December 21

Read Mark 10:15-16.

Children love hands-on experiences—whether they be making cookies, trimming the tree, putting out old familiar decorations, making new decorations, going caroling, or being in a school or church play. Children of all ages like to be involved at some level. As we draw ever closer to Christmas Day, let us continue to think of special "gifts" we may give our grandchildren—gifts such as simple songs to be sung, action stories to tell, fun games to play, and things to make. These are much better than ribbon-tied gifts!

This year, let us grandmothers find the time and the creativity to make God's story of Christmas come alive for our grandchildren.

Eternal God, help us not to give in to the temptation just to buy things for our grandchildren, but to involve them in reliving your story.

🍂 December 22

Read John 1:11.

Most of us grew up in a left-brained society and school system where we were taught to look for the rationale in each situation. We ask on what principles an event is based.

The rationale for God's gift of himself in Christ seems to be that he tried through the centuries to reach humankind and reconcile them to himself—to enable them to know his purposes, his redemptive love—by using patriarchs, kings, and prophets; but people still chose their selfish, self-centered ways.

Christmas was God's gift of himself to live among us, to identify with our needs, to show us how to live. Many people still rejected him. "He came to what was his own, and his own people did not accept him" (John 1:11). It finally took Calvary, where he bore all our iniquities to enable us fully to see his redemptive love.

Many people today see Jesus as just a man, an example. He was a good man; there is no doubt about that. The agnostic historian Lecky said: "Jesus was the loveliest character who ever walked the planet earth. The simple record of three short years of active life has done more to regenerate and soften mankind than all the lectures of philosophers or the exhortations of moralists." But if we simply try to imitate Jesus, we will fail. Jesus opened his life totally to God, and God lived in him.

Christmas challenges us to do the same in order to be more effective wives, daughters, friends, mothers, and grandmothers.

Eternal God, enable us to see the immensity of your gift and purposes. Let us allow your spirit to dwell in our lives totally.

🍂 December 23

Read Matthew 16:13, 16.

Jesus is the Son of the living God, but he also is the Son of Man. Jesus drew upon his humanity in order to reach the people with his message. His teachings are perhaps reflections of his own boyhood experiences and observations: sweeping the floor to find a coin, the cost of sparrows in the marketplace, sewing patches on old garments, the working of leaven in the dough, hens gathering chickens under their wings.

In Jesus' spiritual life, we see the humanness of Jesus as well. He prayed not as if he were God but as if he were man. Sometimes he prayed in triumph—as at the transfiguration. Sometimes he prayed in grief—as at Gethsemane. He faced his temptations in simple, childlike dependence on God.

Christian educators tell us that young children need to see Jesus as a friend; younger elementary children need to see Jesus as an example; older elementary children need to be challenged to follow Jesus—to commit their lives to him; and youths need to make Jesus Lord of their lives. Adults, of course, need to do all of the above!

As grandmothers, we can help to make Jesus "real" for our grandchildren—of any age. We can do this by helping them to remember that Jesus was human as well as divine.

Eternal God, help us as grandmothers to remember the humanity of Jesus so that we may make him "real" to our grandchildren.

December 24

Read Luke 1:35.

Yesterday we considered the humanity of Jesus and how he could identify with our frailties and our struggles because of it. Today, on the eve of our celebration of his birth, we consider the other dimension of his life—his divinity.

If your grandchildren have difficulty with the idea of God coming down to earth, tell them this popular story. There was a family—mother, father, and two elementary-aged children. The father was not a believer and never went to church. On Christmas Eve, his wife and children invited him to join them for the midnight service. He declined, saying that he didn't believe that God came to earth in human form to show us how to live.

As the mother and children left, snow began to fall. The man, sitting in front of an open fire, began to hear something that sounded like pebbles hitting the picture window. Upon investigating, he discovered that the noise was caused by birds trying to escape the extreme cold. Going outside, he tried to get them into the barn where they would be warm, but he couldn't communicate with them. They were frightened by his presence. Then he brought bird seed and made a path leading to the barn. They nibbled at the bird seed but wouldn't go into the barn. "If only I were a bird, I could show them what to do," he thought.

At that moment, the church bell began to ring, and the man said aloud, "Lord, I understand why you came to earth to show us how to live." He put on a topcoat and left to join his family at church.

Eternal God, thank you for loving us enough to come to earth in human form to save us from ourselves. Let us celebrate this fact with gladness.

❦ *December 25*

Read Luke 2:11.

Perhaps no worship service has ever depicted the glory of Christmas more graphically than the Christmas show I saw at Radio City Music Hall. Because they were celebrating their sixtieth anniversary, the show was more spectacular than usual. In addition, the evening had special meaning for me because I was surrounded by my family—husband, son, daughter-in-law, and grandchildren.

Hundreds of hurried, hassled, jaded Americans sat spellbound as the images of the first Christmas came to life with kings, wise men, shepherds, and a crèche housing Mary, Joseph, and the baby Jesus. In a pluralistic, secular society where many people never enter a church or synagogue, this amazing story of God's redemptive love through Jesus Christ was presented without apology. It also was presented with such sensitive beauty that I wept throughout the entire scene.

The finale featured the words of the famous tribute to Christ entitled "One Solitary Life." Flashed on a giant screen, the words were read by a deeply resonant masculine voice: "All the armies that ever marched, and all the navies that ever sailed, and all the parliaments that ever sat, and all the kings that ever reigned, put together have not affected the life of man upon this earth as powerfully as this one solitary life."

O come let us adore him!

Thank you, Lord, for the wondrous gift of your saving love for each of us. Let us accept it with humility and gratitude.

❦ *December 26*

Read Luke 10:38-42.

I overheard someone on an elevator say once, "There is nothing so 'over' as Christmas." It is true that on the day after Christmas, the air of festivity is gone. We are tired from overeating and too much pressure; the house is full of clutter; and the children are noisy. Yet this is a time for enjoyment.

We no longer have to rush to clean house or prepare food. If grandchildren are visiting, take time to play a game or read a story with them. Even if grandchildren or other house guests are not with you, don't start writing thank-you notes or cleaning. Take time to enjoy the beauty of your lighted Christmas tree while listening to Christmas music. Take time to reread your Christmas cards and the Christmas story from Luke. Let its significance permeate your spirit.

Perhaps this is the day when women need to read again the story of Mary and Martha. For weeks before Christmas we have been like Martha—busy preparing food and cleaning the house. Jesus did not put Martha down for that. Her irritation and anger indicated, however, that she had become consumed by her busyness. I think Jesus was telling her to be still for a while and let her spirit catch up with her body. He was asking her to be still and appreciate the significance of the moment.

Though this balance should be a part of our daily living, it is especially important to find it on the day after Christmas.

Eternal God, forgive us for our emphasis upon doing rather than being. Let us make time to allow your love to permeate our spirits.

❧ December 27

Read Romans 15:13.

Yesterday we looked at the story of Mary and Martha and the importance of choosing the better part of allowing Christ to water the dry places of our spirits. Well-known author Taylor Caldwell tells how she renews her spirit each year by remembering her Christmas miracle.

The miracle came at the lowest point in her life. She was in her twenties and separated from her husband. She had been able to find only temporary employment at a very small salary. In six months she had been able to save only eight dollars for her little girl's Christmas. Her last job ended the day before Christmas; her $30 rent was due soon; and she had only $15, which she and Peggy would need for food. She felt abandoned, and she began for the first time in her life to doubt the existence of God.

After she and Peggy had eaten their meager meal on Christmas Eve, the doorbell rang. There stood a man with his arms filled with packages. "There must be a mistake," she said. When he read the names, the packages were for her and Peggy—a large doll, a beautiful purse, candy, and gloves. These were from a school teacher whose beautiful umbrella Taylor had found and returned six months earlier. Hope began to rise in her heart.

After Peggy was in bed, Taylor sat down to open her bills. Among them were two white envelopes. One contained a $30 check from a company where she had been a temporary employee in the summer. The check said: "Your Christmas bonus." It was the exact amount needed for the rent. The other envelope contained an offer for a permanent position with the government—to begin two days after Christmas.

The church bells began to ring for the midnight service. People were hurrying to the church to celebrate the birth of the Savior. As they walked, they were singing, "O Come All Ye Faithful."

"I am not alone," she thought. "I was never alone."

As we end one year and prepare to enter a new one, let us, like Taylor Caldwell, remember the hope given us through the presence of our Lord. With hopeful hearts we are better prepared for the tasks of grandmothering ahead.

Eternal God, as we prepare for the years of grandmothering ahead, let us take time to allow your presence to renew our lives.

🍂 December 28

Read Matthew 1:23.

Our God is a loving God who hears our pain and answers our prayers. The evidence comes in a myriad of ways, even some that seem miraculous. Spend some time today recalling some of the evidences of God's presence in your own life.

One of those evidences for me happened on the Christmas Eve that came only four weeks after the death of our twenty-year-old son, Rick. Christmas has always been special in our family, and I dreaded the thought of it without Rick. Yet, in an attempt to keep things as normal as possible, I had prepared our usual turkey dinner and had invited some close friends to join my husband, our college-age son, and me for dinner.

About an hour before the guests were to arrive, the doorbell rang. A woman I had never seen before handed me the most beautiful wooden purse which had been hand painted. She simply said, "Your son ordered this for your Christmas." At first I thought she meant our son who was home for the holidays. When I opened the lid, however, there burned in the wood were the words: "To Mother with love, from Rick." He had ordered the purse three days before his accident.

In a beautiful way, God had allowed Rick to be with us for Christmas and had sent a special assurance that life does not end in death!

As we approach the new year, may we remember that God goes with us.

Eternal God, help us to remember all the gracious evidences of your presence in our lives.

🍂 December 29

Read Matthew 7:7.

The week before the beginning of a new year is a good time to renew our spirits and prepare ourselves for whatever lies ahead. The role of grandmother requires more than just doing. This week can be a wonderful time for remembering and reflecting on the significance of the Christmas story for our family and our world family.

One of my happiest memories is seeing the top of the Matterhorn mountain in Switzerland. We were staying in the charming Swiss village of Zermatt, which you can reach only by cog railway. It is also a place where there is snow on the mountain even during the summer.

Each day during our stay we would sit on the small bridge hoping for a glimpse of the top of the Matterhorn, but the clouds shrouded it. Early in the morning of our last day in Zermatt, we were walking toward the dining room. As we looked up, we saw the mighty Matterhorn standing clear and majestic just ahead of us. It was breathtakingly beautiful.

It occurred to me that even after 2,000 years, Jesus stands like the majestic Matterhorn over our civilization. An Athenian philosopher once said, "The Galilean is too great for our hearts." Napoleon is reported to have said, "Caesar, Charlemagne, and I have built great empires on force, but they have collapsed. Jesus built His empire on love and centuries later, one third of the world's people follow Him."

If we truly seek him, we will find him.

Eternal God, let us seek and find you and allow your spirit to live in our lives.

🍂 December 30

Read Proverbs 23:7; Mark 9:23.

You may have heard of the San Francisco Bay experiment. Two teachers, who believed they had been given very gifted students, found that the students performed at phenomenal levels with very high achievements. At the end of the year they were told that the students in their classes were not gifted but rather were chosen at random. The students' high achievements could only be attributed to the high expectations of the teachers.

Low expectations are even more powerful. One of the most unforgettable films I have seen is "A Cipher in the Snow." It is the story of a shy, sensitive boy whose verbally abusive stepfather criticized and ridiculed the boy's every expressed thought and action. The boy's passive, victimized mother had no ego strength left for affirming her son. At school he had no friends. One day as he got off the school bus, he fell in the snow and died. At the funeral, a teacher said, "That boy died of a broken heart. He was a cipher in the snow."

Jesus understood this principle well. Throughout his life he affirmed the best in others—Peter as a rock, Zacchaeus as an honest man, Mary Magdalene as a woman of virtue.

Jesus is calling us to expect and affirm some good things in the people around us. What an opportunity we have to make a difference in the lives of our grandchildren by great expectations and positive affirmations!

Eternal God, thank you for the privilege of having great expectations for those around us and for the opportunity to offer positive affirmations. As we affirm others, let us always remember how you have affirmed us.

December 31

Read Deuteronomy 3:28; Philippians 1:20.

As we prepare to walk into a brand new year, let us remember that so much of what happens will be determined by expectations.

Several years ago I read about a group of people who had experimented with expectations. There were six couples who were having dinner together on New Year's Eve.

One man asked the group to experiment with the theory that our deep expectations help to determine what happens in our lives.

When they agreed, he asked each person to write on a three-by-five card what they deeply expected to have happen in their lives during the coming year. They placed the cards in envelopes, sealed them, and put them aside until the next New Year's Eve. The following year there was a strong coincidence between what they had expected and what had actually happened.

After reading this, I began to ask myself if I were missing something that God had planned. As I thought and prayed about the experiment, I realized that God gave us the ability to imagine, to envision, and to dream his dreams. So, on one New Year's Eve about twenty years ago, I wrote my first list of "great expectations"; and I continue to do that each year. Not all my expectations have become realities, but so many have that it has confirmed for me the power of expectations.

As grandmothers, one of the most precious lessons we can teach our grandchildren is the power of expectation. What better time to begin than at the beginning of a new year!

Eternal God, go with us into the new year and give us the power of expectation.